THE DECLINE OF
AMERICAN LIBERALISM

THE DECLINE OF
AMERICAN LIBERALISM

BY

ARTHUR A. EKIRCH, Jʀ.

PROFESSOR OF HISTORY, AMERICAN UNIVERSITY

LONGMANS, GREEN AND COMPANY

NEW YORK · LONDON · TORONTO

1955

LONGMANS, GREEN AND CO., INC.
55 FIFTH AVENUE, NEW YORK 3

LONGMANS, GREEN AND CO., LTD.
6 & 7 CLIFFORD STREET, LONDON W 1

LONGMANS, GREEN AND CO.
20 CRANFIELD ROAD, TORONTO 16

THE DECLINE OF AMERICAN LIBERALISM

FIRST EDITION

LIBRARY OF CONGRESS CATALOG CARD NUMBER 55-11447

Printed in the United States of America

To My Wife
Dorothy Gustafson Ekirch

Foreword

To MANY readers the idea of the decline of American liberalism may seem a paradox. American optimism, faith in progress, and confidence in progressive democracy are all at odds with the notion of decline. Yet it is hardly a secret that liberals in recent years have been beset by various pressures and seem in our time to be on the defensive. Nor is it in any way unusual today for thoughtful people to reflect with Arnold Toynbee, and other cyclical interpreters of history, upon the causes of the decline and fall of ancient civilizations. What seems radical or paradoxical in the idea of decline, therefore, is merely the peculiar juxtaposition of terms that links such a decline with the conditions and prospects of American liberalism.

For most of us speculation over the downward course of past civilizations is more entertaining than contemplation of the likelihood of the decay of liberalism in our own civilization. This unpleasant possibility we disguise by talking of the transformation in liberalism, or by referring to the current crisis in liberalism as a temporary phenomenon. In other words, some modern liberals would have us believe that what appears as a decline of liberalism is largely a product of hysteria or semantic confusion. The obvious descent from the tenets of classical liberalism they interpret as a move in the direction of a more realistic, or tough-minded, program. Against this view, the following pages offer the thesis that the decline of liberalism, though sometimes hardly perceptible, often uneven, and occasionally reversed, is nevertheless a real descent.

Despite the pessimism implied in such a stand, I wish to disclaim any intent to essay the role of a Jeremiah or a Cassandra. My purpose is rather that of an historian and social scientist. I desire to examine the history of liberalism because I think that evidence of a decline would tell of an important facet of our history, deserving more consideration than it has hitherto received. Parallel with any decline of the liberal tradition may be, of course, the rise or growth of other philosophies and values. The historian, whatever his own feelings, cannot be positive that losses in one direction are not matched by gains in another. Thus the decline of liberalism need not necessarily mean the decline and fall of Western civilization, including that of the United States. (But I believe the weakening of the liberal tradition should be of sufficient concern to cause us to reassess that easy assumption of continual progress which has so frequently characterized American historical writing.)

Surely, in the light of two world wars and an intervening world-wide depression, the almost universal interpretation of American history in terms of a "rise" or "growth" is open to question. And though few contemporary observers would deny that liberalism at the present time is in retreat, no historian, with the possible exception of Vernon L. Parrington in his *Main Currents in American Thought,* has ventured to apply such an interpretation to any extended period of United States history.[1] In other words, our historians have argued that such periods of illiberal reaction as we are experiencing today are atypical interludes in the mainstream of national progress—minor cataclysms which do not fit into the grand evolutionary pattern of our history.

In contrast to this view, (I would suggest that our present-day conservatism is only the most recent and glaring example of a decline in liberalism that goes back to the very beginnings of our national history.) The decline of American liberalism is a product of no single cause or event; it has been gradual and cumulative. (Since the time of the American Revolution, the major trend in our history has been in the direction of an ever-greater centralization and concentration of control—politically, economically, and socially. As a part of this drift toward "state capitalism" or "socialism," the liberal values associated with the eighteenth-century Enlightenment—and especially that of individual freedom— have slowly lost their primary importance in American life and thought.)This has, of course, been true of other civilizations, including that of modern Europe; and it is possible to draw a close parallel between the experiences of the Old World and the New. I realize too that, in all this, I am construing liberalism in rather precise and rigid terms. On the other hand, what frequently passes for liberalism today is too often an opportunistic philosophy which, by its extreme relativist definition of terms, effectively conceals the disintegration of the liberal tradition.

Historically, liberalism is not easy to define, but even this difficulty pales into insignificance in comparison with the extraordinary contemporary confusion over the term. In the United States many of those who consider themselves liberals have been enthusiastic disciples of what might be called the progressive tradition, stretching from the Square Deal of Theodore Roosevelt, through Wilson's New Freedom and Franklin Roosevelt's New Deal, to the Fair Deal of the post-World War II era. These progressive liberals have accepted the linkage made in John Dewey's book *Liberalism and Social Action*. They regard the growth of some sort of collectivism as inevitable, and stress the need of government regulation to preserve ancient liberties and to meet the problems of modern industrial development. On the other hand, conservatives and libertarians, who also include themselves within the ideological confines of liberalism, complain that

this modern liberalism has sacrificed many of the traditional liberal values associated with the free individual.
"Maybe among the blessings of the year 1953," a conservative columnist wrote, "will come a new understanding of
'liberalism' and a rescue of the word from those who in the
recent past have monopolized it while at the same time imposing further and further restriction on the liberty of
thought of the individual." [2]

Under attack from the right and the left, traditional liberalism has yielded its rich heritage of values to both of these
two extremes. At the same time, the few individuals who adhere closely to classic liberal postulates run the risk of being
labeled "doctrinaires." Replying to some of its present-day
critics, a defender of liberalism in its historical form has well
pointed out:

When the modern liberal has challenged the reasonableness
or justice of particular orders made by official spokesmen for a
ruling group, he has sometimes been rebuked as an advocate of
disorder or of disunity; or if he has appealed for the restoration
of earlier freedoms, he has been rebuffed as one vainly trying
to revive outmoded ideas. When, in a community with a democratic form of government, he challenges the justice or practical-
ity of a particular decision of the official political majority, he
is represented as rejecting the principle of majority rule; and
when his reasoning in behalf of freedom runs counter to the
reasoning of spokesmen for a particular religion, he is sometimes charged with exalting reason above faith. [3]

Probably it would be fairer if modern liberals would
agree to being called progressives, socialists, nationalists, etc.,
although, of course, the problem goes deeper than a mere
exercise in semantics. In any case, I would suggest that our
history cannot be fully understood unless, remembering the
dictum of Tocqueville and others, we keep clear the dif-

ference in meaning between liberalism and the often confused values of democracy, nationalism, *et al.* For example,
it may be possible that in the United States the conquest of a
continent, civilization of the wilderness, extension of political democracy, and widening of economic opportunity
have all taken place at the expense of liberal values. Thus the
very things over which we are accustomed to pride ourselves
may be only the symptoms of a slowly declining liberalism.
In our own era it is difficult to reconcile the militarism left
in the wake of two world wars and the prospect of a third,
with a philosophy of liberalism. Nor does the welfare state
in practice seem to bear out the idealistic hopes of many social democrats and reformers. At the same time, some unpopular minorities, always subject to ostracism and social
pressure, are now being discriminated against in law.

But the argument of the decline of liberalism can best be
understood in reference to the meaning of liberalism as it
has developed historically. It is the widespread misunder-
standing of historic liberalism, as well as the often vague and
misleading use of the term, that effectively conceals the decline of liberalism and explains much of the dilemma of the
modern liberal, confronted as he is with the obvious contradictions between liberalism in its classic and its modern
form.

Acknowledgments

In MY study of the American liberal tradition, I have received assistance from a number of individuals and institutions. William Neumann and Rudolph Von Abele deserve especial thanks for the care that they expended on the entire manuscript, making valuable detailed suggestions in regard to both style and content. Merle Curti gave me the benefit of his wise counsel, and Samuel Sharp criticized several of the chapters. My appreciation of their helpful advice is not meant, of course, to imply that these friends and colleagues necessarily agree with my frequently controversial interpretations.

The actual writing of the book was speeded up by a year free of teaching duties. For this I am indebted to the John Simon Guggenheim Memorial Foundation, which granted me a Fellowship, and to American University for a leave of absence. The Library of Congress furnished the bulk of the research materials, and I am grateful particularly to the personnel of its Stack and Reader Division. For permission to examine the rich and extensive collection of Oswald Garrison Villard Papers I am indebted to Konrad Mueller, and to the staff of the Houghton Library of Harvard University. I also wish to thank Mrs. Kermit L. Culver for typing the manuscript.

Contents

1

The European Experience

LIBERALISM has deep roots in the past. Historically its origins may be traced back to the Humanists of the Renaissance, to the religious reformers of the Reformation, and to the many seventeenth- and eighteenth-century advocates of the natural rights philosophy. In its early stages liberalism was in large part concerned with criticism of existing society and institutions. It tended to be destructive or even revolutionary; thus it sought to limit the authority of both church and state, and to protect certain fundamental individual rights from interference by the governing powers. Along with their assertion of the claims of the individual conscience, liberals favored self-government and national self-determination. Sympathetic to the rights of minority groups, liberals were suspicious of any effort to control or suppress freedom of thought and expression. On the economic side, liberalism emerged from the feudal economy of the Middle Ages and early became identified with the pretensions and outlook of the rising middle class, standing for a philosophy allowing the utmost economic freedom to the individual.[1]

In its emphasis upon the free individual, liberalism is closely allied with many of the tenets of modern democracy. But there are also important differences. Freedom of the individual, for example, conflicts with such democratic principles as equality and majority rule. Thus majorities are not always stanch guardians of minority rights, and the struggle for equality encroaches inevitably upon the privileges or rights of some individuals.[2] On the other hand, liberalism is not the same as anarchism. Libertarian in its stress on minority rights and individual freedom, liberalism nevertheless accepts the necessity of government and of certain social and economic restraints. Accordingly, though it may often tend logically in that direction, liberalism differs from philosophical anarchism. Perhaps it is best therefore if we think of liberalism, not as a well-defined political or economic system, but as a collection of ideas or principles which go to make up an attitude or "habit of mind." [3] But within this liberal climate of opinion, however broadly or narrowly it may be defined, it is necessary to include the concept of limited representative government and the widest possible freedom of the individual — both intellectually and economically. Although not a system, liberalism in such periods as the Age of the Enlightenment became an articulate and unified movement.

Side by side with the liberal idea of the freedom of the individual went the concept of his enlightenment. In Western Europe and in the American colonies by the time of the eighteenth century, man was breaking the bonds that tied him to a feudal serfdom, universal state church, or absolute national monarch. The first task of liberalism therefore was the largely negative one of freeing the individual from the various absolutes of state, church, and feudal economy. Though this destructive, critical function was immensely important to the liberal tradition, liberalism was also a philosophy or way of life that had its positive, constructive features. This side of liberalism received perhaps its most notable first expression in the Enlightenment of the eighteenth century. Although its roots lay in the scientific discoveries and nascent individualism of the sixteenth and seventeenth centuries, the Enlightenment reached its greatest extent and influence in the following century, when the leading scientists and philosophers of Western civilization achieved a virtual intellectual revolution in the history of mankind.

Of first importance, and stemming logically from the tremendous scientific discoveries of Newton and his predecessors, was the idea of a universe governed by natural laws. The scientists' increasing knowledge of the world and its relationship to other heavenly bodies inspired the hope that man might penetrate the mysteries of the universe and reduce the supernatural to natural and knowledgeable terms. Corollary to this hope was a faith in human reason and in the ability of the educated individual to understand the laws of nature and guide himself accordingly. From these beliefs in natural law and in human reason derived the concept of natural religion, in which religious truth conformed to the evidence of science and nature and was accepted as a matter of reason instead of by faith. In politics, economics, and even psychology, natural laws also determined the course of events. Accordingly, arbitrary state regulations not only interfered with the operation of natural laws, but also curbed the natural rights of the individual. It followed therefore that political economy was a science devoted to the discovery and better understanding of natural laws, while the state was limited in its scope of operations to the preservation and protection of the natural rights of its citizens.

Assuming that man would use his reason and obey the natural law, the philosophers of the Age of the Enlightenment envisioned a steady progress on the part of society toward the ultimate goal of the perfectibility of mankind. Realistically, however, it was apparent to even the most optimistic of utopians that a state of perfection was still in the offing. It was only natural therefore that enlightened thinkers should, in the meantime, maintain a keen humanitarian interest in reforming, or at least in alleviating, evils that currently oppressed the individual and slowed the progress of society. Negro slavery, for example, was in obvious contradiction to the theory of natural rights; and in other respects as well individuals suffered from the effects of their environment. The improvement of society through private and charitable efforts was thus often the most practical and immediate task of the eighteenth-century enlightened liberal.

As a way of life, European liberalism achieved its greatest popular influence and most widespread geographical extent during the middle of the nineteenth century. Along with its growth, however, came signs of decline, and after 1870 liberalism was no longer ascendant even in its cradle, England, though the beginnings of its decline in Europe may be traced back as far as the time of the French Revolution. Before the Revolution, and in the age of the eighteenth-century Enlightenment, liberals had prided themselves on their cosmopolitan, humanitarian outlook. Laying great stress on the efficacy of men's reason, they had valued education and the scientific method as the two chief instruments of progress. But this faith in progress by gradual, evolutionary steps, central to liberal hopes for the future, was rudely interrupted when the Reign of Terror, and ensuing Napoleonic military despotism, shattered the early idealism of the French Revolution.

At first the Revolution had seemed to promise the realization of the dreams of the French *philosophes* and *idéologues*. The Revolutionary cry of liberty, equality, and fraternity was the counterpart of the popular sovereignty, democracy, and republicanism of Rousseau's famous *Social Contract* (1761). But Rousseau's mystical and romantic concept of the general will, however well it agreed with the Revolutionary democracy of the French masses, was in conflict with much of eighteenth-century liberalism. Wars and violent revolutions, pushing people into extremes of thought, are always dangerous to a moderate point of view, and it was not surprising therefore that in the course of the French Revolution the liberalism of 1789 was stifled by the Terror of 1793. In order to maintain itself, the Revolution was forced to suppress, one by one, all the liberties it had previously proclaimed, until eventually it was confronted by Caesarism in the person of Napoleon. The tyranny of the many had culminated in the dictatorship of the First Consul and Emperor.[4]

The period of restoration, which followed in the wake of the defeat of the Napoleonic conscript armies, ushered in an age of reaction during which liberalism remained in eclipse. With disillusion over the perversion of the ideals of the French Revolution there also developed a strong feeling against the liberal principles of the Enlightenment. Europe was now embarked on "the search for a principle of authority," characterized by "a general and widespread weariness of intellectual analysis combined with an appeal to faith, to sentiment, to history, in fact to anything that ran counter to the ideals of the Enlightenment." Intellectuals were oppressed by the kind of spiritual vacuum symbolized in Goethe's Faust, while they sought something — almost anything — to believe in. This emotional reaction was exemplified by Pietism and Methodism in religion, by Burke's appeal to history and tradition, and by the general aura of Romanticism. It was also apparent in the construction of German idealism by Hegel and his followers.[5]

Yet, though liberalism seemed dying in 1815, it presently revived, even if in a somewhat less original or daring form. Jeremy Bentham, the English reformer, was a bridge between the old and the new in liberalism, and also a characteristic figure with his emphasis on liberty and utility —

words that soon became the motto of the rising English middle-class Liberals. By mid-century, such major components of liberalism as laissez-faire economics, constitutional government, national self-determination, and popular education seemed well on the road to realization. But liberalism, as Carlton Hayes has pointed out, was also becoming more conservative and was in grave danger of being a philosophy of all things to all men. There was even some doubt about its one historical constant — the liberty of the individual against all despotic authority. Most threatening of all, undoubtedly, was the disastrous effect on liberalism of a growing economic nationalism and imperialism, the seedbed of the totalitarian nationalisms of the twentieth century. After the 1870's, reforms carried out in Western Europe under the banners of liberalism and democracy occurred only at a rising cost in individual liberties. Plans for state education and social security were advanced side by side with the conscription of individuals for military service. It was not surprising therefore that liberals were occasionally wont to complain that the new solicitude of the national state for the physical and mental well-being of its citizens was merely the direct concomitant of its own selfish and warlike purposes.[6]

The impact of nationalism and the decline of liberalism were most apparent in the German states. In Prussia, after the failure of the revolutionary movements of 1848, the conservatives gained control and backed the king in his efforts to reform the army along militarist lines. The old citizen army, supported by units of state militia, had proved unreliable during the revolution and was now transformed into a professional body of regulars and reservists. When the liberals in parliament refused to vote the necessary credits, the king appointed Bismarck as his chief minister. Announcing a policy of "blood and iron," Bismarck proceeded to govern Prussia during the 1860's without a legal budget and without calling parliament into session.[7]

By 1871, under Bismarck's chancellorship, a militarist Prussian state had achieved domination over the German peoples and had defeated in swift succession Denmark, Austria, and France. The new German Empire of William I and Bismarck, which arose from these military victories, gave short shrift to liberalism. Though the imperial Reichstag had the right to vote the army credits, it had no influence over the management of military affairs. At the same time, opposition to Bismarck's domestic policies on the part of labor and socialist groups was overcome by a broad program of social security legislation. This was designed not only to lessen the economic grievances on which the Social Democratic party grew strong, but also to attach the masses more loyally to the German Empire and to ensure their physical fitness to serve in the imperial conscript army. Meanwhile German industry was tied more closely to the militarist program of rearmament. A half century later the Nazi state under Hitler wrote the final chapter of what Friedrich Meinecke has called *The German Catastrophe*.

In England, in contrast to Germany, the problems of political nationalism, except as they developed into overseas imperialism, were less intense. But by the last quarter of the nineteenth century there were growing symptoms of an economic decline in the British Isles and a rising discontent with the fruits of industrialism and the philosophy of liberalism. Earlier in the century, under the impact of the industrial revolution, the older eighteenth-century philosophical liberalism had won new practical support from business and the middle class. At the same time, the Manchester school of economists preached the doctrines of laissez faire, which Gladstone and his Liberal party translated into practical politics. The Reform bills, beginning with that of 1832, slowly widened the suffrage, but without giving full power to the masses. Nevertheless, the extension of the suffrage gradually transformed the personal relationship between members of Parliament and their constituents. The discipline of parties had to be substituted, while the tyranny of public opinion and despotism of the administrative state, so feared by John Stuart Mill, Lord Acton, and other nineteenth-century English liberals, hovered on the horizon. During these years certain English intellectuals became admirers of Bismarck's state socialism; while Hegel, according to the French historian Halévy, had more avowed followers in Britain than in Germany. Other Englishmen of the Victorian era became disillusioned with the inefficiency of liberal democracy and were prepared to welcome a coming era of strong executive administration.[8]

By the turn of the century, liberalism in England was faced with a growing pressure from two extremes. On the left, and in the ranks of labor, there were those demanding social legislation and economic reforms. On the right, the Conservative proponents of a greater empire were advocating the adoption of a protective tariff to support a larger navy. In theory the Liberals, occupying a middle ground, could have withheld these social reforms or, adhering to their traditional antimilitarism, have refused the demand for larger naval appropriations. As a practical matter, however, the Liberals gave up their individualism and instead turned to new taxes. The additional funds were to finance the navy and to pay for the program of social security legislation inaugurated for the English worker by the Lloyd George budget of 1909.[9]

In the realm of foreign policy, the Liberal leaders, Grey and Asquith, now sided with the imperialist and militarist Conservatives to such an extent that there "was a veritable

cult of the principle of continuity . . ." [10] Thus the English
Liberal ministers moved on the two planes of domestic reform and of preparation for a possible war. Unable to con-
fide in Parliament because of rank-and-file opposition to the
idea of war, Asquith and Grey bided their time until the
German invasion of Belgium furnished the occasion for a
decision. It was apparent then that a war decided upon by
the Liberal government, rather than by the Conservatives,
would be less unpopular with the masses and might also
serve as a release from the almost unbearable tensions that
had been building up to a near-revolutionary climax in
1914.[11] At the same time, however, the war was to wreck the
Liberal party and fatally undermine traditional English
liberalism.

The collapse of liberalism in England in the midst of
World War I brought to a close a century marked by a series
of crises in the history of the liberal tradition of Western
Europe. Beginning with its subversion in Revolutionary
France, liberalism finally succumbed to the nationalism and
imperialism rampant in Europe at the end of the nineteenth
century.

In the United States the rise and fall of the liberal tradition was marked by something of the same succession of recurrent crises and over-all decline that characterized its
course in Europe. A rising colonial and Revolutionary liberalism was modified by the conservative reaction after the
War of Independence. A reviving liberalism in the early
nineteenth century, exemplified in part by Jeffersonian and
Jacksonian democracy, and paralleling a similar development in Europe, foundered during the Civil War. Although
there seemed to be ample evidence of a liberal recovery early
in the twentieth century, progressivism in the United States
was actually as delusive as Lloyd George's reform program

in England, and World War I was as disastrous to liberalism in the New World as in the Old.

In the perspectives offered by time, it has been possible to see that liberalism has survived in the nineteenth and twentieth centuries in an increasingly attenuated form. Along with such precarious existence has gone a gradual loss of vitality. This seems clearer today than it did fifty years ago. But because historians, in such overwhelming numbers, have focused their attention on elements of strength and growth in the American liberal tradition, the other side has been almost completely ignored. It is the purpose of the following pages therefore to trace the factors in American life that have pointed toward a declining liberalism. This we can best do by examining first, and rather briefly, the establishment of a liberal society in colonial America.

2

The Hope of America

THE DISCOVERY of America, falling within the era of Western history known as the Renaissance and Reformation, helped to mark the transition from medieval to modern civilization. Following Columbus's epochal voyage in 1492, over a century elapsed before the first permanent English settlement in the New World was begun at Jamestown in 1607. But the next one hundred fifty years saw the building up of a colonial society that was also to contain the embryo of a new nation. It was during these years of the seventeenth and eighteenth centuries that the rise of modern liberalism took place, not only on the continent of Europe, but in colonial America as well. In the New World the development of this American liberalism depended upon both native and inherited factors.

In all the long story of liberalism, in its American and European phases, it is important to remember that the eighteenth century was its classic age. In the United States this classic period, accordingly, belongs largely to our prenational history, and it is not far from correct to say that liberalism and colonial America grew up together.

If we turn back to the beginnings of the American colonies we see that the motives that originally impelled private persons and nation-states to cross the Atlantic and build a new civilization were not always the same. In the case of the governments, the rival economic and strategic ambitions of the great European powers summarized their interest in overseas ventures. But in regard to individuals, motivations were more complex. Some who came, such as Negro slaves or deported criminals, had little choice in the matter, while, at the other extreme, were the considerable number who migrated from sheer love of change or adventure. Probably the majority of the settlers who came to America did so because of their longing to break away from the rigid class society and restraints of Europe. In one way or another the average settler was fleeing absolutism. Religious dissenters, hopeful of escaping the bonds of an authoritarian state church, were joined by political refugees of every description. Most important of all was the lure of free land and the desire on the part of virtually every settler to secure greater economic and social advantages, both for himself and for his children.

In their quest for an individual freedom based on religious, political, social, and economic liberties, the settlers along the North American coastline were not to be disappointed. The harsh struggle for existence in a wilderness environment, although at first serving to emphasize the cruder and more material aspects of life, was gradually modified by the richness of the natural resources available to the early settlers. An abundance of free land ensured the widespread diffusion of property, higher wages, and greater social equality. Feudal customs of restricted land tenure proved impossible of general application in the New World. No hereditary aristocracy of lords and ladies owned exclusive title to the land, and the Old World customs of primogeniture and entailed estates were never popular in the colonies. Prosperity bred economic individualism and, in a land of seemingly boundless potential wealth, mercantilist notions of political economy began to yield the economic stage to a rising laissez-faire capitalism.

At the same time, with the colonists apparently determined to fight all outside authority, centralized political and economic controls emanating from the mother country proved difficult to enforce. In the opinion of Adam Smith, the celebrated English economist, the wealth of the colonies depended upon one simple economic factor, "plenty of good land," and one political factor, "liberty to manage their own affairs in their own way." [1] In the matter of religion, also, the numerous dissenting sects that were able to find refuge in the American colonies, plus the need to attract more settlers, did much to ensure a large degree of toleration. Thus the longing for freedom, which drove the more enterprising and adventuresome minority to the New World, was largely satisfied by contact with the American environment. "All took a risk, and in large part their hopes were joined." [2]

In the emphasis upon the role of the American environment, one must not overlook the continued interaction between the colonies and the mother country. Indeed the growth of liberalism in the seventeenth and eighteenth centuries was a two-way process. At the same time that a native American liberalism was flourishing, and broadening the base of the intellectual inheritance carried from Europe, colonization and settlement of the New World were having a beneficent effect on the Old. By sloughing off the adventuresome, discontented, rebellious, or freedom-loving element of its population, Europe was able to support a more liberal economic climate for those who remained. Thus the wealth and example of the New World exercised a liberating influence on the Old, and the existence of the American colonies as a frontier outpost of Western Europe contributed to the prosperity of the whole.[3]

Among the most important legacies bequeathed by England to her colonies was the striving for political and religious liberty. The English people had come to pride themselves on their freedom, and in the years before colonization of America they had already acquired a strong hostility to any form of arbitrary power. Essential to the English political tradition was the belief that individuals had certain natural rights which government could not violate with impunity. This tradition, reinforced by the revolutions of the seventeenth century, was most eloquently expressed in the writings of John Locke. And it was Locke, also, who espoused publicly a policy of religious toleration. After the Glorious Revolution of 1689, the more extreme persecution of dissenters, either political or religious, declined in England, and personal freedom became part of the individual's rights as an English subject. These rights were also respected in the English overseas territories. In the royal charters drawn up for the various American colonies, the rights and privileges of an Englishman were considered as a part of his person to be taken wherever he went. Moreover, they were interpreted as applying equally well to all settlers of the New World, whatever their original nationality.

The continued development of colonial liberalism is a familiar story that does not need extensive elaboration in these pages. Essentially the colonial period witnessed the successful working out of the experiment of a free people living in a free land. Nowhere else were a people able to build a culture and civilization with so little native interference. The Indian tribes formed only a thin veneer across the continent, and the lands of North America were truly virgin soil open for exploitation and use. Thus the liberal ideas, already germinating in Europe in the seventeenth century, were able to grow even stronger in the free American territory and climate of opinion.

Most important of all to colonial liberalism was the fact that American society was fluid and constantly changing. It was a society that was open at both ends. From Western Europe in the eighteenth century a new stream of settlers came to join the original English migrants of the previous century, and America early became a melting pot and a haven of refuge. Meanwhile the colonial population was pushing westward in search of still cheaper and better lands along the frontier. In time, as the population grew, the means of securing decent land cheaply diminished. Especially in the South, a native landed aristocracy of wealthy planters was able to force out the small individual farmer. Fortunately, however, with the growth of towns and town life there were new opportunities for the displaced yeoman farmers as artisans or mechanics. Moreover, there was the ever-present possibility of moving on farther west. The significant fact therefore is not the various economic barriers that were thrown in the way of a more equalitarian social order, but the large field that remained open to the enterprising individual.

It is true, of course, that class distinctions continued to exist in America as they always had in Europe. Sometimes social and class conflict reached the point of open revolt, as in the instances of Bacon's Rebellion in 1675 and the later uprising in the New York colony led by Jacob Leisler. But the lines between aristocratic and democratic elements were seldom well defined, and many complex outside political and economic issues were involved in these domestic colonial struggles. Thus sectional rivalry between tidewater and back country was always present as an additional source of dispute, and finally, of course, there was the open bitterness between the mother country and the colonies. In the course of the eighteenth century the aristocracy of merchants and planters was often able to assume greater economic and political powers, but at the same time the more democratic elements in the back-country regions were being strengthened by continued immigration. By the eve of the American Revolution therefore, despite the continued servile status of a substantial minority, the American colonies, judged by European standards and customs, had advanced far in the direction of an equalitarian order.[4]

Class lines, however sharply drawn in America, were less rigid than those which divided the population of the European nations. The upper class in the colonies was less aristocratic than in Europe, and members of the middle class in America who tried to copy the manners and customs of the upper strata of society could more often hope to achieve a higher station in life. The middle class itself, comprising the small independent farmers, artisans, clerks, minor officials, and lesser merchants, as well as the lower clergy and teachers, was the most numerous class in America. In large part therefore the American colonial economy fulfilled liberal expectations, approximating closely the agrarian dream of a society in which property was widely diffused and divided on fairly equal terms. Only the presence of the lower class of Negro slaves and indentured white servants intervened to mar the picture of a free and liberal social system.

In the case of indentured servants, who are estimated to have made up one-half to two-thirds of all white immigrants, advancement though limited was not impossible. The labor contract, or indenture, enforcing a period of servitude of from four to seven years, soon became the chief means of securing settlers, especially in Pennsylvania and along the frontier. Conditions of work and legal protection for the indentured servant varied, but in any event his servile status was limited in time and he sometimes received a bonus in the form of land upon completion of his term of service. Once free, the former indentured servant passed into the ranks of the other settlers.

No such opportunities or inducements as attracted the indentured servants were held out to the Negroes brought to America from Africa and soon fastened into perpetual slav-

ery. Though a servile status described the situation of both
the Negro slave and the indentured white laborer, it was the
institution of Negro slavery that formed the great exception
to generalizations about colonial equality and severely compromised early American liberalism. The very circumstances
under which the Negro was brought to America, after first
being uprooted from his native culture and herded aboard
the slave ships, did violence to the liberal belief in the dignity and worth of the individual. Moreover, slavery entailed
the disadvantage of encouraging wasteful use of the soil, thus
making more difficult the lot of the small independent
farmer. In Virginia, for example, by the eighteenth century
masters and slaves dominated lands that had formerly belonged to free farmers.[5] Slavery therefore, conflicting on
both moral and economic grounds with the main tenets of
liberalism, represented a paradox which a liberty-loving
age could hardly well defend. On the other hand, it was a
tribute to the liberalism of the American colonies that, by
the time of the Revolution, the slave system was coming
under growing attack.

Also a factor in mitigating the conflict of slavery with
eighteenth-century liberalism was the continuing colonial
interest in educating and Christianizing the Negro. So long
as this was done there was some basis for the argument that
the slave was being prepared for eventual freedom, and such
colonial interest was in marked contrast to the indifference
or hostility to Negro education that later came to characterize the South.

Almost as unfortunate as the Negro slave was the American Indian, who, though not enslaved, was often warred
upon and divested of his lands and hunting grounds. American colonists were little inclined to accept the Indian as a
noble savage. Such an idealized and romanticized picture of
the American aborigines was popular chiefly among social

theorists and primitivists in Europe, who felt that the Indian was an unspoiled child of nature. But Americans, disillusioned by firsthand contact on the frontier battleground, soon gave up their early attempts to Christianize him, although the Puritans seem to have been the only group wholly to condemn the Indian as a savage incapable of civilization. In the settled areas along the seaboard, a few educated eighteenth-century Americans accepted the stylized European concept of the Indian, but the general colonial policy and attitude remained highly illiberal.[6]

Always remembering the exceptions of Indian and Negro, it was nevertheless true that, in the course of the eighteenth century, colonial America achieved the basic framework of a liberal society. Not democratic, and even in large part aristocratic, it was, however, liberal in the sense of the great freedom of opportunity available to the individual. The colonial aristocracy was frequently a natural aristocracy of talents and ability, rather than an upper class based on inheritance or title of nobility. In originality, or in depth of intellectual life, the American scholar, artist, or scientist was not the equal of his European counterpart, yet freedom of thought largely prevailed. And it was also true that the average American of the 1700's enjoyed more liberty than his seventeenth-century predecessor or his British contemporary.

In the political sphere, colonial assemblies were able to maintain their rights and privileges against the demands of autocratic royal governors. The colonial legislative bodies were particularly zealous in insisting upon their right to indulge in free discussion and debate. Underlying this right, in turn, was the whole cause of free speech and a free press for which a noteworthy victory against possible British interference was scored when a colonial jury in 1733 acquitted

John Peter Zenger, a German printer in New York, of the charge of libel.

Political liberty in the colonies was closely tied to the preservation of local government under representatives chosen by the people. It is true that the suffrage was much restricted by property qualifications so that only a minority, and often a very small minority, of the adult male population was able to vote. Also newly settled areas to the west were likely to be discriminated against and underrepresented in the colonial legislatures. But these limitations on democracy were partly overcome by such advantages as frequent elections and close ties between voters and elected representatives. The right of the people to instruct their delegates was a distinguishing feature of the colonial theory of representation, and "local self-government seemed to the colonial mind to demand that representation should always be under the close scrutiny of the community." [7] In the case of the New England town meeting, all the freemen could attend and exercise an equal voice in community matters. Though the more direct democracy that accompanied the town meeting was limited in extent to the New England colonies, American political institutions as a whole were decentralized and divided among colony, county, and town governments. Undemocratic in restrictions on the suffrage and absence of majority rule, the colonial political system had, however, its redeeming liberal features. Against the British desire for more centralization and a tighter imperial control, colonial liberals argued that government should remain close to the people, its powers being diminished as it grew more remote from the popular will.

Religious institutions in the American colonies also shared the liberal atmosphere of the eighteenth century. The desire for religious liberty, which impelled many of the

colonists to come to America, was on the whole enhanced in
the New World environment. The Puritans, holding to the
narrow dogma of complete freedom only for those who were
true believers of Calvinist doctrines, attempted to limit both
political and religious liberty to members of their own corporation and church. But Puritan doctrines came under attack almost from the very beginnings of the settlements at
Massachusetts Bay. Most prominent among early religious
liberals who criticized the Puritan concept of church and
state was Roger Williams. After his banishment from Massachusetts, Williams fled to Rhode Island, where he was able
to put into practice many of his ideas of religious toleration,
as well as to encourage a more democratic political and economic system. No other American of the seventeenth century went so far as Williams in his defense of individual liberty, or in carrying to its logical conclusion the Reformation
principle of the right of free enquiry.

Outside Rhode Island, religious toleration came closest to
complete freedom in the Middle Colonies. In contrast to the
South, where Negro slaves provided the labor force, or to
New England, where the Puritans discouraged outsiders, the
proprietors of the Middle Colonies pursued a liberal policy
designed to attract settlers in large numbers. Maryland
granted its well-known act of toleration in 1649, and in New
York the British allowed the Dutch population to continue
its own forms of worship. Pennsylvania's liberal policy was a
mixture of practical needs plus the real idealism of the Penn
family in providing a refuge for members of the Society of
Friends.

On the whole, therefore, the colonial period witnessed a
gradual but steady progress toward religious toleration. In
contrast to the French and Spanish colonies, where church
and state remained in close union, the ties that bound them
together in most of the English colonies were becoming

weaker. Final disestablishment of the churches awaited the American Revolution. Meanwhile it was true that Catholics, Jews, and atheists were subject to various restraints, but in general the eighteenth century saw a trend in the direction of greater religious liberalism. In New England the Puritan hold was relaxed, and the power of the theocracy waned after the loss of the old colonial charter in 1684. The final climax of religious hysteria and fanaticism in the Salem witchcraft delirium of 1692 quickly subsided after nineteen persons had been hanged and many more arrested and imprisoned. This persecution of numerous innocents in the witchcraft trials marked the last important instance of extreme religious intolerance in the colonies. In Virginia, where the Anglican Church was strongly established and supported by public taxation, dissent was nevertheless permitted. It was not without point therefore that the French husbandman Crèvecœur commented on the extraordinary religious diversity and toleration that characterized the melting pot of the colonial population on the eve of the Revolution.[8]

By mid-century, religious liberalism was also being strengthened by the two opposite strands of thought that flowed from the natural religion of deism and the countermovement of the Great Awakening. Deism, adhering to a concept of religion that was governed by natural rather than supernatural forces, emphasized the rational element in Christianity. The evangelists of the revival of the 1740's, known as the Great Awakening, on the other hand, stressed the emotional side of religion. But inherent in both approaches was a reaffirmation of the importance of the individual in religion and his emancipation from older and more conservative forms of worship.

The new trend in religious thought, with its emphasis on an individualistic and humanitarian approach, was an example of the more enlightened liberal attitude of the eighteenth century. In contrast to the harsh Calvinist view of man as essentially a depraved creature destined for eternal damnation, a more optimistic conception of human nature became popular during the Enlightenment. Holding with Locke's famous *Essay Concerning Human Understanding* (1690) the position that man was not born with innate ideas or a predetermined future, liberals argued that he was instead a product of his environment. From this plastic theory of human nature there followed naturally the conclusion that man's nature was subject to change and that reform could be achieved through an improvement of the environment. All of this went far toward making up a new psychology and philosophy of progress and reform. Such a faith was also able to derive added strength from a contemplation of the American environment, where even the most casual observer could see ample evidence of a very great change and improvement.

The same liberalism that characterized American religious and political institutions on the eve of the War of Independence also prevailed in social life and thought. Abundant lands and the opportunity to get ahead economically resulted in a natural faith in a laissez-faire, agrarian type of society. Middle-class, family virtues of thrift, hard work, and self-reliance were favored and, in response to the need for population, women and children enjoyed a more important role and were also better treated than was the case in Europe. Although Puritanism exercised certain frustrations and restraints upon body and soul, colonial society was not in general censorious of one's private life and conduct. There was little provocation to crime among a people not crowded in slums or cities, and at the same time a growing humanitarian feeling characterized the colonial attitude toward the criminal. Formal education was still largely the privilege of the aristocracy, but there was the possibility of self-culture, as

Benjamin Franklin's career so amply demonstrated. Generally speaking, it was true that in education, morals, and social outlook American colonial life was moving hopefully in the direction of a greater freedom and wider opportunity.

In many ways the typical figure of this liberalism and enlightenment was Benjamin Franklin, who served almost equally well as the child or the spokesman of his age. Yet it is doubtful whether so enormously talented and gifted an individual as Franklin could in any sense be called typical. In almost any age or society, he presumably would have become a leader, but it was nevertheless a happy circumstance that his many-sided genius was allowed to flourish in the free atmosphere of colonial America. A self-made man, Franklin never forgot his humble background, and throughout his life continued to identify himself with the middle class. He also maintained a keen humanitarian interest in the less fortunate and actively promoted a multiplicity of reform schemes. A true liberal in his philosophy and life, he was tolerant and not dogmatic. In Europe he commanded respect as an example of American simplicity, and of the natural society of the New World. On both sides of the Atlantic his politics and economics were of a liberal persuasion. An agrarian, he regarded agriculture as the true source of wealth, and he therefore opposed an industrial organization of society. Private property he respected as a right, but he also urged that this right be tempered by individuals devoting their surplus wealth to charity and the general welfare of mankind. In science and education he stressed the practical needs of society, but he also had a great faith in self-education and never therefore advocated universal public schooling. America's first social philosopher, Franklin, in his life and thinking, exemplified the dignity of the free individual in a liberal society.[9]

Franklin's long career spanned the colonial and Revolutionary eras of American history, the period of a rising liberalism. Beginning with the impulse that carried the settlers to the New World, and continuing to grow in the free environment of the American continent, the struggle for a liberal society, which Franklin helped to carry on, reached a crisis in the War for Independence waged against Great Britain.

3

A Revolutionary Shift
in Emphasis

THE AMERICAN REVOLUTION was an event of transcendent importance in the history of the liberal tradition. In America it brought to a climax the ideas of liberal society that had been slowly developing in the thirteen colonies during a century and a half of British rule, while in England and on the continent of Europe the Revolution became an inspiration to liberals, who saw in the fighting across the Atlantic the dawn of a new era in the Western world. The role of the American Revolution was thus twofold. On the one hand, it represented the culmination of the localized colonial demand for home rule and, on the other, it seemed the opening phase of a world-wide struggle for a more liberal and humane society.

But despite the liberal hopes that it inspired, the American Revolution nevertheless was not without its dangers so far as liberalism was concerned. However liberal in its general outlook and broader intentions, the actual Revolution was not always equally liberal in the means that it used to attain its goal. Taking the more optimistic view of its significance, the Beards in their *Rise of American Civilization* assert that "in nearly every branch of enlightened activity, in every sphere of liberal thought, the American Revolution marked the opening of a new humane epoch." [1] But against this dictum of the Beards is the severe judgment of another American scholar, Vernon L. Parrington. Although he recognized that the American Revolution had certain social consequences which gave an impetus to American liberalism, Parrington maintained that the Revolution on the whole indicated the triumph of the middle class and the encroachment of a new spirit of nationalism and Americanism upon the older, local frontiers of colonial days.

This marked the turning point in American development; the checking of the long movement of decentralization and the beginning of a counter movement of centralization — the most revolutionary change in three hundred years of American experience. The history of the rise of the coercive state in America, with the ultimate arrest of all centrifugal tendencies, was implicit in that momentous counter movement.[2]

The line of thought that led directly to the American Revolution first began to take definite form in the atmosphere of native liberalism pervading the colonies by the middle of the eighteenth century. In the decade before 1776 the unceasing colonial struggle for greater self-government turned into a demand for home rule, and then finally into an open attack upon the whole monarchical principle. In the political philosophy developed by various American spokesmen, ultimate reliance was placed upon the argument that individuals had certain natural rights which governments violated at their peril. Included among these rights, to which the colonials had grown accustomed, was not only political self-rule but also a large measure of economic freedom. On both the political and the economic side, the American position was thus frankly individualistic.

Though there was little explicit democratic thinking in the colonies on the eve of the Revolution, the colonial period was still one of progress toward democracy, especially

along individualist lines. The early Revolutionary leaders
— James Otis, Patrick Henry, and the Adamses — all denounced British interference with individual freedom and
appealed to the concept of the natural rights of man. Colonial patriots, in other words, were thinking in terms of the
negative side of government, and their liberalism was at first
critical, and even destructive, in its emphasis.

The most zealous of all the Revolutionary leaders in arguing the case for radical democracy was Samuel Adams, a professional agitator who came close to being a forerunner of
the modern political demagogue. His saving grace, however,
was his ardent belief in the principle of home rule. According to Parrington,

Love of the New England town-meeting democracy was bred
in his bones. More clearly than others he saw the danger of
erecting a governing class irresponsive to the popular will. He
was, in short, the embodiment of the rising spirit of the
eighteenth century that found expression in individualism,
that exalted liberty and hated tyranny — a spirit that had for its
ultimate purpose the reduction of the powers of the political
state.[3]

Adams used the Boston town meeting as his particular
forum, and through a network of local committees of correspondence helped to keep up intercolonial enthusiasm
for the Revolutionary cause. But the violent propaganda
that he directed against both the British and the American
aristocracy illustrated the danger that the Revolution represented for a more traditionally liberal course of action. An
extremist himself, Adams and his coworkers incited their
fellow Americans to instances of mob violence out of keeping with a liberal spirit of toleration, or with legal procedures.

Although liberals of a more conservative persuasion drew

back in alarm from such episodes as the Stamp Act riots or the Boston Tea Party, obviously a revolution could not be carried on as an entirely peaceful affair. Accordingly, no matter how liberal in its intentions or ends, the American Revolution was destined inevitably to invade the liberties of some individuals. Crèvecœur, the French agriculturist residing in America, complained bitterly and eloquently of this radical, terroristic side of the revolutionary process, and he himself suffered the fate of fellow moderates in losing his property and undergoing social ostracism.[4] Though the Revolution was thus in many ways also a civil war, including its moments of terror and brutality, still the important fact to be noted is that it was conducted with little violence to minority or dissenting opinion. Loyalists who insisted on their views were the most oppressed, but patriot leaders could hardly have been expected to countenance an outright opposition, or the extension of aid and sympathy to the British cause. Even so, trial and execution for treason was rare or even nonexistent, and those who kept their feelings to themselves, or who agreed to accept the various American tests of loyalty, were for the most part able to survive the Revolutionary crisis with their persons and property unimpaired.

Prerevolutionary radicalism and mob violence indicated in part that Americans were ready to take up the challenge of declaring their independence and thus formalize their Revolution. Political independence, expressed in a later age in terms of national self-determination, was an idea that Thomas Paine, a recent emigrant to the colonies, depicted most attractively for his fellow Americans. In his famous tract *Common Sense,* which he published opportunely in January 1776, Paine argued the justice and necessity of separation from Great Britain. Beginning with his well-known distinction between a society and a government — "Society in every state is a blessing, but Government, even in its best state, is but a necessary evil — " Paine attacked the theory and practice of the British monarchy. Scorning reconciliation as "a fallacious dream," he pictured the advantages of peace and prosperity which a separated America would enjoy. Declaring that a "Government of our own is our natural right," he also envisaged the America of the future as a refuge for freedom and as "an asylum for mankind." [5]

Paine's pioneering work struck a responsive chord throughout the colonies. Actual hostilities, of course, had already begun at Lexington and Concord, and it was therefore becoming daily more obvious that Americans could not long keep up the fiction of loyalty to the crown, while they were busily engaged in fighting the king's soldiers. Independence was in the air, and it was the particular glory of Paine's work that he expressed so well what many Americans felt but could not bring themselves to the point of avowing. The actual Declaration of Independence, however, was not formulated until six months later, when the Continental Congress approved the words written by Thomas Jefferson.

Better than any other single document, the Declaration of Independence stated the liberal political philosophy on which the ideology of the Revolution was based. In its celebrated opening sentences, Jefferson expressed the American faith in natural rights — "that all men are created equal, that they are endowed by their Creator with certain unalienable Rights, that among these are Life, Liberty and the pursuit of Happiness." Governments, deriving their just powers from the consent of the governed, were instituted to secure these rights. But whenever any government destroyed them, the people in turn had the right to alter or abolish the government — though the Declaration added: "Prudence, indeed, will dictate that Governments long established should not be changed for light and transient causes." [6]

The worthiness of the American cause was then further demonstrated in the Declaration by a long bill of particulars drawn up against the English crown. This familiar, and necessarily exaggerated, list of American grievances reduced itself in essence to the charge that the British had violated American liberties, not only the liberties of the colonial governments but also the personal freedom of the rank and file of the citizenry. Although the Declaration obviously stated the American case in the most favorable terms possible, it was nevertheless significant that Jefferson's language was basically mild and dignified. It partook the liberal spirit of the times and argued the cause of revolution in a rational and restrained manner. The Declaration accordingly had little of the flavor of the typical revolutionary manifesto. Instead of calling Americans to arms, it appealed to world opinion to recognize the justice and merits of the American position.

While the Declaration of Independence ably summarized the American philosophy of political liberalism, the task of translating that philosophy into action still remained. It was therefore in the constitutions drafted by the various states during the course of the Revolution that one sees the practical application of the principles expounded in the Declaration. These constitutions were an expression of the importance that Americans attached to having a definite written document, specifying the personal and property rights of the citizen and the limited powers allowed government. All of them included a declaration of rights based on the 1689 English bill of rights, and the major emphasis was on liberalism in the sense of freedom from government interference. The people were to retain their sovereignty, while government acted as their agent. "In every instance in these early state constitutions," as one historian later wrote, the state is presented as created by the people, and existing solely for the good of the individual. Its sole duty is stated to be to protect him in the full enjoyment of his natural and inalienable rights. Public officials are declared to be the trustees of the people; the right of revolution is inherent in society. In no instance is the state presented as the provider of office, the creator of monopolies.[7]

The powers of state governments were not only limited in extent, but they were also divided among governor, courts, and legislature. At the same time, the individual was guaranteed freedom of speech, press, and religion, and granted the right to bear arms, to petition peacefully, and to join together in associations of his own choosing. Although the stress in both Declaration of Independence and state constitutions was on the rights of the people, not all persons were included in the term — women, Negro slaves, and white servants being exceptions. This limitation troubled the conscience of some of the Revolutionary leaders, but the greater part probably thought in terms of freedom and equality only for those already free or of freedom for political man as he existed in the eighteenth century. Also, as T. V. Smith has pointed out, it was not so significant that the framers of the Declaration did not assert an absolute equality as it was "that they did not feel it necessary to say in what respects men are *not* equal." [8] In other words, the question of equality was at least left open. After Independence, the suffrage continued to be limited by property qualifications, so that perhaps only a quarter of the adult male population was able to vote. But in the eighteenth century this moderate concession to popular rule was regarded as a real advance toward democracy, and on the whole the state constitutions, especially those that were adopted in the early stages of Revolutionary enthusiasm, were looked upon as political documents radical for their time.

Surveying the provisions of these first state constitutions, a prominent modern historian has concluded:

Truly no governments on earth have ever been instituted with so little authority to do ill, as those of the American states. Yet, not content with that, the framers of constitutions even limited their governments' power to do good, lest it be perverted to their hurt.[9]

Accordingly, many of those who thought of the war in terms of a continuing social revolution were disappointed that the new constitutions did not go further in providing positive government intervention in regard to the abolition of slavery, the separation of church and state, or the support of public education. Moreover, most of the constitutions showed little recognition of the humanitarian ideals current in the midst of the Enlightenment, although state legislatures in the North were beginning to provide for gradual emancipation. Pennsylvania's constitution, perhaps the most liberal of all, contained clauses respecting the more humane treatment of criminals and protecting the rights of aliens. And in Virginia, George Mason was the author of a comprehensive bill of rights which served as a model for other states.

In the realm of property and economic rights, the Revolutionary constitutions and statutes went far to advance the tenets of liberalism. Restrictions on the land in the form of quitrents, entail, and primogeniture were abolished. British mercantilism, with its limits on colonial overseas trade, and its prohibition of American migration beyond the Appalachians was rendered obsolete by Independence. This emancipation of commerce and industry, plus the downfall of the older landed aristocracy, helped to accomplish an economic revolution in which the trend was toward a freer society of smaller estates and individual farms. Economic and social shifts of a leveling nature also were made possible by the intimidation or expulsion of the loyalists, with perhaps as many as one hundred thousand fleeing the United States.

The American Revolution was liberal in its assault on the political and economic privileges of the British and Tory aristocracy. But the social and economic revolution accompanying every wartime situation, while it liberates and elevates one group or class, only does so at the price of creating a new aristocracy. In the process of fighting the Revolution, economic advantage and social privilege were by no means eliminated. Much loyalist property, for example, found its way into the hands of a new group of wealthy landed proprietors. Such transfers sometimes did more to advance speculation in land prices than to further the achievement of an agrarian diffusion of property. Army contracting also resulted in the creation of new wartime fortunes, while merchants in addition were able to prosper from an expanded foreign commerce and from privateering. Trading with the enemy, especially by way of the British West Indies and Canada, was illegal, though not unusual. Throughout the war years American farmers helped to supply the British armies with foodstuffs. This unpatriotic practice, however, became unavoidable when farmers were enclosed within the British lines or threatened with confiscation of their goods if they refused to sell. Over the economic course of the war as a whole there was a heavy emphasis upon inflation, speculation, and profiteering, in which merchants as prominent as Robert Morris were implicated. Although there were attempts both in Congress and in the states to curb inflationary price increases, most governmental regulation of the period was favorable to business. In its social and economic effects, the war therefore had its selfish as well as its liberal side.[10]

Although it did not eliminate privilege, the Revolution sounded a liberal note in its avoidance of despotism or dictatorship. Certain students of the American Revolution, in their pains to stress the fact that it was a social revolution as well as a war for independence, have made the point that the Revolution was a real revolt with mob violence and a reign of terror. This was especially the case in respect to the harsh treatment meted out to avowed loyalists and British officeholders, but it was also a tribute to the essential moderation and liberalism of patriot leaders that they fought the Revolution with so little violation of individual rights. What was truly liberal about the Revolution was not the extent to which it had to resort to violence and terror in freeing Americans from British rule, but the way in which it was able to avoid the substitution of new American despotisms for old British tyrannies.

The parallels between the American and other revolutions are fascinating, but it is also important to remember that Washington did not become a Caesar, a Cromwell, or a Napoleon. Among revolutionary movements in general, the American struggle was unique in the degree to which it maintained a balance between military discipline and individual freedom. Protesting British authoritarian rule, Americans were careful to avoid giving their own government too much power in either civil or military affairs. It is true that there was much fear of a military dictatorship, but the civil authorities in both Congress and the state governments were ever watchful and suspicious of any indications of military encroachment upon their powers. Washington, though he complained bitterly of the lack of troops and supplies, was careful to avoid serious conflict with civilian leaders. At the close of the war, the "father of his country" retired gracefully to private life, while he used his influence to prevent a nascent *coup d'état* organized by a discontented group of ill-paid officers.

But, perhaps, nothing better illustrated the liberal climate of opinion during the War of Independence than the way in which many Americans, despite the state of hostilities, were able to carry on their normal peacetime interests and pursuits. This was true not only of those in regions unaffected by the war, but also applied to civilians caught within the lines of the embattled armies. In an age when total war was still off in the future, noncombatants were able to enjoy certain rights and immunities. American scientists, for example, continued to correspond with their colleagues in England. Thus a Harvard scholar in a letter to the secretary of the Royal Society in London maintained that "political disputes should not prevent communication in matters of mere science," nor did he see how anyone could "be injured by such an intercourse." Benjamin Franklin and other American patriots retained the good will of old acquaintances in England, and to Franklin, Sir Joseph Banks, the distinguished naturalist, affirmed: "I respect you as a Philosopher & solicit the continuance of your friendship." Moreover, American students, despite the war, continued to go abroad to study medicine in Scotland, or painting in London under the aegis of the American expatriate Benjamin West. One of West's students, Benjamin Trumbull, who went to England after a period of service in the Continental army, had the misfortune to be arrested and imprisoned, but he was finally released and allowed to proceed to the Continent and thence home. It seemed therefore that, as one authority has pointed out, "The associations of American liberals and intellectuals with their English counterparts were scarcely interrupted by the war." [11]

In general, loyalty to the patriot cause did not prevent

Americans from continuing the various international strands of their private lives or their own special intellectual interests. Despite the heightened nationalism and patriotism of the war years, Americans retained in a high degree an international and cosmopolitan outlook. George Washington called himself "a Citizen of the great republic of humanity at large," while Thomas Paine, Benjamin Franklin, Thomas Jefferson, and others held fast to the world-wide interests and views of the eighteenth-century Enlightenment. In the same fashion, European philosophers and statesmen paid tribute to the success of American arms and referred to the achievement of United States independence as the beginning of a new epoch in world affairs.[12]

Yet, in spite of final victory and the preservation in large measure of the forms of a liberal society, it has been suggested that many Americans found the war a disillusioning business.[13] The more radical political and economic thinkers were especially disappointed. The principles of freedom and equality that they had asserted with such confidence at the beginning of the struggle for independence had become tarnished by the seven dreary years of war and fighting. It had not always been possible to conduct the war by individualistic or democratic procedures, and the very fact that colonial liberalism had been carried to the point of rebellion and civil war involved a necessary conflict with such major strands of the liberal tradition as peaceful change, toleration of dissenting minorities, and supremacy of civil government. Fastening their attention on local self-government and social change, colonial liberals were not prepared for the conservative countermovement and nationalistic consolidation that followed the war. This reaction was most marked in the case of the army officers who threatened a *coup d'état* in 1783, but it was also to be reflected in the general decline of liberal principles after the war.

4

Federalist Centralization
and Consolidation

THAT the years succeeding the American Revolution represented a period of conservative reaction in United States
history has become a commonplace observation. But on what
this means in terms of the liberal tradition there is much less
agreement. Parrington's point that the Revolution was the
beginning of the decline of American liberalism has attracted little attention. In general, historians have regarded
the conservative reaction after the Revolution as a passing
phase of postwar stabilization. Subsequently, it is argued,
the trend toward liberalism was re-established in the Jeffersonian and Jacksonian eras.

It is true that the conservative postwar point of view underwent later modifications and that many of the older, liberal Revolutionary ideals were revived in the nineteenth
century. But the shift in American thought in the period
between the Declaration of Independence and the adoption
of the Constitution represented more than a temporary reaction. It was rather, as Parrington insisted, a turning point
of American history and a direct challenge to the liberal tradition.

American liberalism before the Revolution sought first
of all to destroy authority. But in the course of the struggle
for independence this side of liberalism had to yield to the

exigencies of revolution and to the practical necessity of consolidating and concentrating a measure of authority in the hands of a semi-centralized war government. For the vigorous prosecution of war and revolution, however, neither the government of the Second Continental Congress nor later that under the Articles of Confederation was a wholly satisfactory instrument. The American people, still under the influence of colonial patterns of eighteenth-century liberal thought, feared and distrusted any semblance of an oppressive, centralized state. Determined therefore to keep the mainsprings of power within their own hands, they preferred to abide the comparatively weak and inefficient government of the Congress and Confederation.

A government of this type appealed chiefly to those who accepted an agrarian view of society. In such a society, agriculture was the basic economic pursuit, while the majority of the people were small farmers, tilling their own land and living off the fruits of their labor. Though capitalists in the sense that they owned their land and the right to their labor, they were small capitalists whose interests were opposed to those of the aristocracy of large landholders or wealthy merchants. In a nation with an abundance of land and commensurate economic opportunities, the welfare of such a group required no positive interference or protection from the government. The economic outlines of this type of agrarian society were presented in their greatest detail in the writings of the French and English school of laissez-faire economists, who became widely known by the middle of the eighteenth century as the physiocrats. But the enthusiasm for the physiocrat doctrines, which was expressed by Benjamin Franklin, Thomas Jefferson, and many later-day followers of Jefferson, was based primarily on American conditions.

The physiocrats' agrarian ideal, already favored by the

natural environment in colonial America, seemed even closer to realization as a result of the American Revolution. The overthrow of the aristocracy of Tory landholders and the destruction of the whole network of British mercantilist restrictions removed important barriers to American enterprise. Despite the rise of state taxes upon the free flow of goods in interstate commerce, the Revolution smoothed the pathway to a more liberal national economy. Moreover, so long as there was a frontier of free lands to the west, Americans could entertain the goal of an agrarian society. But the agrarian ideal, while it was never to lose completely its influence over American thought, was nevertheless difficult to put into practice. Somehow the dreams of an agrarian society seemed always to come into conflict with the realities of American economic development.

Essential to agrarianism was the conception of limited government. This implied not only political and economic freedom from governmental interference, but also a kind of government that did not use its political powers to bestow economic favors upon a particular class of the community. Economic paternalism in behalf of certain privileged groups was regarded by Jefferson as the main source of the tyranny and political corruption that he saw in Europe. It was such a set of evils that American liberals desired, at all costs, to avoid.

Government should not only be prohibited from interfering with the rights of individuals and from creating a large bureaucratic class who could live at public expense; it should also be prevented from intervening in economic matters, since the effect of any such intervention was always to transfer property and to establish some form of economic privilege. The greatest of all dangers to democratic freedom and equality was the use of political power by an aristocracy, a bureaucracy, a mercantile oligarchy, a pressure group, or any other minority interest in order to increase their wealth or to obtain the privilege of living parasitically on other men's labor.[1]

This doctrine of the diminished state, to which liberals, democrats, and agrarians had given their enthusiastic support in the Revolutionary struggle, was weakened in the postwar period. In the first place, the war itself had helped to breed a new aristocracy of talents and wealth eager to avail itself of the privileges lost by the departed loyalist upper class. Then, in the course of prosecuting the war, Americans became familiar with the business of army contracting and supply. Manufacturing increased, and corporations for private profit were founded. While private enterprise was thus being stimulated, business also began to look to the government for economic support. And finally Congress, by reason of its wartime borrowings, became heavily indebted to its own citizens. The government's securities, in turn, offered additional opportunities for speculation and provided a new type of capital for private investment. In a variety of ways therefore the war had an educational effect upon American business thinking and practice, especially teaching businessmen to identify themselves with the policies and operations of the government. After the return of peace, it was only natural that the new generation of businessmen should strive to enlist the aid of the government in preserving and increasing their wartime gains.[2]

Unfortunately, from the point of view of many of those persons who had prospered during the Revolution, conditions favorable to large-scale business enterprise were jeopardized by the weaknesses of the government under the Articles of Confederation. In both state and national government, a large Revolutionary war debt remained outstanding, and holders of government securities were concerned over the fate of the principal and interest of their invest-ment. At the same time, speculators in western lands desired a stronger national government to institute aggressive mili-tary action against the Indians and to protect the frontier. Merchants and manufacturers sought relief from the discriminatory trade measures of the separate states and favored the establishment of a government able to levy uni-form tariffs. Also desired was a satisfactory commercial treaty with Britain to avert further restrictions against American overseas trade. None of these policies, it was feared, could be accomplished under the Articles of Confederation or by the separate state governments.

In the midst of their other worries, conservatives were everywhere taking fright over the possibility of a resurgence of the old Revolutionary spirit of radicalism among the lower classes. Debtor farmers, propertyless mechanics, and discontented ex-soldiers, favoring a policy of cheap land and more paper money, were beginning to unite in their opposi-tion to strong government and higher taxes. In 1786 radical discontent reached its postwar peak when the debtor farmers of western Massachusetts, under the leadership of Captain Daniel Shays, forcibly closed the courts and threatened to capture the Federal arsenal at Springfield. The business leaders of Boston, by now thoroughly alarmed, supplied funds to finance the suppression of the revolt by calling out the state militia, and General Henry Knox in a letter of ex-planation to George Washington stated: "Our government must be braced, changed, or altered to secure our lives and property." [3]

Badly frightened by the leveling tendencies of what seemed to be a radical majority, conservatives sought eco-nomic security through a stronger centralized government. Their chief political object, according to James Madison, was "to protect the minority of the opulent against the majority." [4] Adopting the old radical and Revolutionary technique of propaganda and organization, merchants and bondholders held meetings and petitioned state legislatures to seek revision of the Articles of Confederation. This movement culminated in the call for a convention to meet in Philadelphia in May 1787. At the convention, all fifty-five of the delegates were men of considerable and varied property holdings, ranging from the possession of slaves and lands to investments in government securities and far-flung business enterprises. Convinced of the weakness of the Articles of Confederation, they easily resolved to disregard the announced plan of submitting amendments and to prepare instead an entirely new frame of government.

Fundamental to an understanding of the Constitution adopted at Philadelphia is the realization that it represented a compromise made possible by the large areas of essential agreement among the delegates. Between the two poles of a colonial and Revolutionary radicalism — which favored democratic individualism and state rights — and a lingering British conservatism — which frankly preferred a constitutional monarchy and the rule of a propertied aristocracy — compromise was relatively easy to achieve. The delegates to the Philadelphia Convention were overwhelmingly agreed upon the necessity of a government that was national, yet republican, and there was little sentiment in behalf of either a monarchy or the kind of decentralized government illustrated by the Articles of Confederation. In accord therefore on the basic theory of the new government, the delegates fashioned a document whose meaning depended to a considerable extent upon how it was to be interpreted. The very vagueness and silences of the Constitution left much to be inferred and decided in the future.

Undergirding the superstructure of the Constitution were two major premises of government that bore directly on the liberal tradition. First, the Constitution continued the traditional English and American belief in the natural rights philosophy. These rights were later spelled out in detail in the first ten amendments to the Constitution, forming the Bill of Rights, but the original document also set forth the idea of a government of limited powers, with protection of individual rights. The danger of tyranny was further guarded against by creating a government of separate departments. Although this system of checks and balances reflected a basic distrust of direct popular rule, it could also serve as an obstacle to any form of despotic power. Complete democracy in the sense of a nationalized town meeting was in any case impossible, and the republican substitute of representative government, though not sufficiently localized or close to the average citizen, nevertheless provided the framework of a government that was liberal, if not democratic, in form.

The second basic premise underlying the Constitution, which was in sharp contrast to its political liberalism, was the decision to give government broad and far-reaching powers over the economic life of the nation. Here the purpose was to transfer authority from the states to the national government. The many examples in the Confederation period of the way in which various states interfered with trade and commerce, and the recent pressures upon the states to make paper money legal tender for all debts, were especially alarming to conservative interests. The men at Philadelphia were convinced that the economic powers hitherto wielded by the states would be safer in the hands of a centralized national government. To this end, Congress was given exclusive authority to coin money and to regulate both foreign and interstate commerce. Thus the stage was set for the abandonment of laissez-faire liberalism and the substitution of a policy of economic nationalism or government paternalism.[5]

On its economic side the Constitution marked the triumph of the principles of what might be called a Whig capitalism, a term that also described the alliance of merchants and landowners ruling over England in the eighteenth century. This meant a defeat for the agrarian principles of the American physiocrats, a defeat that was presently reinforced by the Federalists' assumption of control over the national government. Though the achievements of the Philadelphia Convention had been substantial, the full conservative implications of its work were not realized until the new government took office and until the Federalists were able to put into effect the major features of the Hamiltonian economic program.

As interpreted by the Federalists, who controlled the government during the first decade under the Constitution, liberalism in the sense of individualism and decentralization was definitely weakened; yet during this period state rights and individual liberties were by no means dead or completely subordinated to national power. Antifederalism continued to hold the affections of a strong minority, which by 1800 was transformed into the Jeffersonian majority. Moreover, the Constitution itself, though providing a skeleton for the further development of a strong paternalistic state, also emphasized the rule of law and the protection of the economic and political rights of the private citizen. With regard to the balance of powers between the national government and the states, or between the entire government and the citizenry, much would depend on future practice. Here the basic conflict between Federalists and Jeffersonians continued well into the nineteenth century. Although neither group was able to preserve a consistent liberal approach, the Jeffersonian Antifederalists adhered more closely to traditional liberal tenets. But as Jefferson himself later bitterly lamented, it was of the utmost importance for the future that the conservative and nationalistic Federalists enjoyed the advantage of being the first ones to govern the new nation.[6]

Of the Federalist leaders, Alexander Hamilton was easily the most significant. Despite a humble background, he early identified himself with the upper-class aristocracy, and his interest in the American Revolution was certainly not that of a doctrinaire radical. Without any of the extremist convictions that actuated Sam Adams, Hamilton nevertheless sensed the opportunity that a period of revolutionary change could bring for a young man of his talents and ambition. During the war he made himself invaluable to Washington, serving as his chief aide, and he also made his entrance into the ranks of the wealthy aristocracy by marrying the daughter of General Philip Schuyler. Unhampered by intellectual loyalty to radical or Revolutionary principles, Hamilton after the war readily adjusted to the growing conservatism of the 1780's, becoming one of the leaders in the movement for a new constitution. Invited by Washington to become secretary of the treasury, after Robert Morris had refused the position, Hamilton assumed leadership of the administration and won approval by Congress for his program of economic nationalism. In this way he was able to put into practice much of the conservative political philosophy that he had outlined at the Constitutional Convention.

Under the familiar Hamiltonian program, the Revolutionary debt, both foreign and domestic, was refunded and made payable at its face value. Moreover, the state debts were assumed as a national obligation, thus ensuring their repayment in full and winning for the Federal government the loyalty of a new group of creditors. Finally, and most important of all, Congress acceded to Hamilton's request to establish a national bank. When Jefferson objected to the idea of a bank on the grounds that it was not one of the constitutional powers delegated to Congress, Hamilton answered with his famous doctrine of implied or resulting powers — that certain powers are implied, or are the result of other powers specifically enumerated in the Constitution. Hamilton accordingly contended that the right of Congress to charter private corporations or a bank was clearly implied by the Constitution and was also a natural result of the power of Congress to coin money, raise taxes, and incur debts — powers that required the existence of a bank if they were to be efficiently carried out. This reasoning, which was accepted by Washington in approving the bank bill, became a key factor in the so-called broad or loose interpretation of the Constitution. As such it provided an important base for extending the scope of the activities of the Federal government in future years.

Meanwhile, the bank itself was a significant example of government paternalism. It received a monopoly of government business, and by loans to private interests was able also to provide new capital for the business expansion that Hamilton deemed vital to United States prosperity. By refusing to enact a protective tariff or otherwise directly subsidize American manufacturing, Congress rejected further Hamiltonian projects to aid the businessman. But the uniform customs duties, new Federal taxes, and general financial stability already achieved were highly encouraging to conservative, propertied interests. Illustrative of the business revival of the period was the fact that charters were issued in the 1790's to over one hundred joint stock corporations, in contrast to the few dozen such companies that had been in existence previously. Banks, canal companies, and a variety of manufacturing enterprises followed in due course.[7]

Hamilton's nationalistic economic policies were based on his belief in the virtues of a strong rather than a weak government. Among its friends and supporters, the powers of such a government could be used in paternalistic and beneficent fashion. But in the case of its enemies or opponents, strong government might mean a coercive state able to work its will by use of force and military power. This power of retribution was realized most fully during the Washington administration by the unfortunate Whisky rebels of 1794.

The ambitious plans for the funding and payment of the national debt, outlined by Hamilton, required a revenue beyond the amount that could be collected from the moderate tariff duties approved by the First Congress. The Secretary of the Treasury therefore suggested that Congress place an excise tax on whisky. Such a tax would hit the small farmers of the back country who had opposed the adoption of the Constitution and who remained dubious of the Federalist program, but it would avoid giving offense to the men of wealth and property whose support Hamilton deemed necessary to the success of the new national government. Distilling in the 1790's was a small-scale enterprise carried on chiefly by Westerners who were thereby able to change their bulky grain products into a form more easily transportable across the mountains to eastern markets. The tax, though small in monetary value — originally from nine to twenty-five cents a gallon — struck at the heart of the prosperity and manner of living of the frontier farmers, and resulted finally in the summer of 1794 in full-scale, violent resistance in the western counties of Pennsylvania. This challenge to the authority of the government was met by the Washington administration by calling out fifteen thousand militiamen. Faced with such a show of force, the Whisky rebels speedily melted away. Although the whole affair may have been politically damaging to the Federalists, it served to emphasize the power of the Federal government, and especially its ability to collect whatever taxes it needed for current expenses and repayment of the national debt.[8]

The suppression of the Whisky Rebellion was the most

dramatic instance of the use of national power by the Federalists, but the Washington administration generally overlooked no opportunity to enhance the prestige of the Federal government. General Knox, the Secretary of War, with the backing of Washington and Hamilton, sought to persuade Congress to create a large army reserve of trained and disciplined militia, with much of the control placed in Federal, rather than state, hands. Although Congress refused to approve Knox's plans, it had to provide a larger army in order to suppress Indian resistance in the Northwest. Foregoing any serious attempt at conciliation or compromise, the administration pursued a policy of unmitigated force and repression in regard to the Red Man.[9] This martial note in the administration was reinforced in the person of Washington as president. The living symbol of Revolutionary nationalism and patriotism, Washington carefully surrounded the office of the presidency with as much formality and ceremony as possible. Such practices, reminiscent of the British monarchy, were particularly annoying to Jeffersonian lovers of republican simplicity, but the pageantry associated with Washington's term in office helped to build the concept of national loyalty.

A patriotic adherence to the new United States seemed all the more necessary because, from the start of his administration, Washington was faced with the grave problems occasioned by strained diplomatic relations with both England and France. This situation was almost immediately rendered more complex by the outbreak of the French Revolution and its development after 1793 into a general European war. The trials of a neutral in wartime, never easy to bear, were even more grave for a young nation that had not yet won a respected position among the powers of the world. Moreover, the internal divisions of opinion, generated by the French Revolution and war in Europe, soon split the

American people into two opposing factions. In the intense fire of conflicting views, approximating closely the old bitterness of loyalist versus patriot in 1776, liberalism nearly vanished, and a wartime intolerance and hysteria came to characterize American feeling by the late 1790's.

At first, almost all Americans welcomed the outbreak of the French Revolution, which seemed after all to be a European application of the principles fought for by the American and French armies at Yorktown. But as the Revolution became more radical, sentiment in the United States underwent a change. The assault on private property, the execution of Louis XVI and Marie Antoinette, and the institution of the Reign of Terror were all profoundly disturbing, not only to conservatives but to many sensitive liberals as well. American anxiety was further increased as the Revolution broadened into a general war. In view of its treaty with France, which had helped make possible the success of the American Revolution, the United States faced the issue of whether it should come to her aid, even at the price of war with Britain.

In this situation, Washington's proclamation of United States neutrality, though disappointing to pro-French elements, probably reflected faithfully the general American desire to stay clear of the European maelstrom. Neutrality, however, did not settle the question of whether American sympathies should lie with France or England in their struggle for power. Looking back on events, liberals of a later day may agree that as between a Revolutionary France, degenerating into the Reign of Terror and eventual dictatorship, and an England, in the grip of an hysterical and despotic conservative reaction, there was indeed little to choose. But in the 1790's few Americans were able to preserve a wholly detached view of the situation in Europe. Conservative Federalists, aghast at the violence and destruction of lives and property in France, turned to England as an exemplification of law and order. Radical Jeffersonians, on the other hand, remembering Gallic aid to the infant United States and bearing in mind the grievances that had helped to bring about the French Revolution, minimized the Terror and thought of the events in France as stages toward a better future.

The split in American opinion in regard to Europe continued until 1815, when the conclusion of both the Napoleonic struggle and the War of 1812 finally brought to an end an era of close absorption in foreign affairs. Before these differences of opinion over a proper American foreign policy could be resolved, they became the cause of serious violations of individual liberties. Even Jefferson's administration was not immune to using coercive powers against the citizenry in an effort to enforce his unpopular embargo legislation. But the most damaging assault on the principles of liberalism came earlier in the Adams administration with the passage of the notorious Alien and Sedition Acts of 1798.

These acts were a product of American hysteria in regard to both the radical course of the French Revolution and the increasingly unfriendly conduct of the French government. The fact that the pro-English policy of the Federalists under Washington and Hamilton was partly responsible for the deterioration of French-American relations did not allay the fears of conservatives in the United States. They noted with aversion the founding of numerous Democratic-Republican societies by American sympathizers with the principles of the French Revolution, and found even more alarming the numbers of English and French refugees who were agitating their radical ideas in the United States. When the conflict with France finally reached the point of the undeclared naval war of 1798, the Federalists determined to act and, in addition to strengthening the navy, created a new large army with Washington and Hamilton in command. The whole

character of the Federalists' conduct of foreign policy provoked James Madison to the melancholy comment: "Perhaps it is a universal truth that the loss of liberty at home is
to be charged to provisions against danger, real or pre-
tended, from abroad." [10]

Under the Alien and Sedition Acts, the President of the
United States was given authority to deport dangerous aliens
and, in time of war, to imprison or expel enemy aliens. While
the Alien Acts could be condoned on grounds of the crisis
with France, the Sedition Act was a law with a much different import. The only such measure in United States history
until the passage of the sedition legislation of World Wars
I and II, the act of 1798 made it a crime to combine against or
conspire to oppose the operation of the government. Moreover, "if any person shall write, print, utter, or publish" or
cause or aid anyone else to write or publish "any false scan-
dalous and malicious writing" against the government, Congress, or President of the United States "with intent to
defame" or "to stir up sedition," he should be punished by
a fine not exceeding two thousand dollars and imprisonment
not exceeding two years. Finally, the act provided for its own
expiration by the provision that it should remain in force
only until March 3, 1801, "and no longer." [11]

In later years, both President Adams and Alexander Hamilton, leaders of rival wings of the Federalist party, attempted
to disclaim responsibility for the Sedition Act. But neither
seems to have spoken out publicly against the bill at the time
of its passage by Congress. Also, in contrast to the Alien Acts,
which were never put to use, the Sedition Act was enforced
in vindictive fashion by the Adams administration. The real
intent of the measure may be gathered from the fact that it
was Republican newspaper editors and politicians who were
singled out for prosecution. Matthew Lyon, a radical Republican congressman from the frontier state of Vermont,

was jailed along with Thomas Cooper, the English free-thinker and exile to the United States. Cooper, in addition, was a close friend of Jefferson and other Republican party leaders.

In the view of Jefferson and his associates, the Alien and Sedition Acts had as their real purpose the stifling of any criticism of the Adams administration, thereby undercutting the Republican party and going far to destroy the development of a two-party system in the United States. No other measure of the Federalists was so destructive of the rights of free speech and a free press nor so much in violation of the elements of political liberty. Alarmed as they were, the Jeffersonian Republicans had to make their protests with utmost care lest in the hysteria of the times they be prosecuted for infringing the very act they were protesting. Accordingly, Jefferson and Madison, without revealing their authorship, began the attack on the Federalist law by drafting the famous Virginia and Kentucky resolutions of 1798.[12]

In the Kentucky resolution, Jefferson reviewed the grounds for his increasing objection to the centralizing policies of his opponents. The Constitution, he maintained, was a compact between the states, in which certain of their powers were delegated to Congress. Beyond those powers, sovereignty was retained by the states. Crimes against the United States were confined to certain categories, adequately covered by provisions in the Constitution against treason, piracy, counterfeiting, etc. On the basis of his interpretation of the limited powers granted Congress, Jefferson argued that both the Alien and the Sedition Acts were in violation of the Constitution and therefore null and void.

The Jeffersonians were anxious to enlist the aid of as many of the states as possible in urging Congress to repeal the obnoxious legislation. But the appeals that were sent out by the Kentucky and Virginia legislatures, with their authorship by Jefferson and Madison kept secret, met with a cool response from the other states. So long as the danger of war with France continued, any widespread formal protest against the illiberal acts was difficult to achieve, and after the war threat subsided, the acts themselves lost much of their meaning. This was especially true of the Sedition Act, which was destined to expire automatically by the close of the Adams administration. It is not even sure that the resolutions of protest penned by Jefferson and Madison had very much direct effect in helping to make possible Jefferson's own victory in the 1800 presidential election. But whatever their practical results, it was of the highest importance that the protest had been made. Even if authorship of the resolutions was not avowed at the time, sponsorship by two state legislatures was an indication that the resolutions had a politically respectable origin. And the fact that the protests were formulated in the midst of the hysteria of 1798, when war was a definite possibility, indicated all the more the value of the resolutions as a defense of liberalism and a protest against tyranny. Adams himself underwent a change of heart in regard to the foreign crisis, and the war threat with France presently subsided, to the intense discomfort of the more reactionary elements in the Federalist ranks.

Adams's last-minute pacific retreat and Jefferson's victory in 1800 made it easier to forget the way in which the Federalists had pursued a constantly illiberal course during their twelve years of power. Although the Republican opposition deserved censure for its blindness to the illiberal features of the French Revolution, the Jeffersonians' optimism was in large part based on their idealistic hopes that the Revolution might carry further American principles of democracy and popular government. The Federalists were correct in pointing out the necessity of the rule of law, rather than of revolution, for the preservation of liberalism, but they erred in the way in which they interpreted the laws at home. Using the checks and balances of the Constitution to thwart popular control, they went on to violate their own concept of a balanced government, adopting a broad and elastic interpretation of the Constitution and using expanded powers of government and the vague concept of the general welfare for the benefit of a particular class — the commercial, propertied aristocracy. But, though overthrown in 1800, the remnants of the defeated Federalists later had the grim satisfaction of seeing their Jeffersonian opponents embrace many of the same consolidating principles that they had earlier so bitterly denied.

5

Jeffersonian Compromise

No PERIOD of American history has occasioned greater diversity in interpretation than the two decades divided by the year 1800. Heralded on the one hand as an era in which the ideals of the eighteenth-century Enlightenment were expanded as a result of the outbreak of the French Revolution, these years have also been referred to as an age of counter-revolution and conservative reaction. This paradox of Enlightenment and reaction is heightened when one looks at the period closely and perceives its even deeper inner contradictions. For example, how can the intellectual radicalism of the 1790's — popular deism, Democratic-Republican societies sympathetic with Revolutionary France, and the widespread circulation of Tom Paine's *Rights of Man* and *Age of Reason* — be reconciled with the political supremacy of the conservative Federalist party of Washington, Adams, and Hamilton — all bitter critics of the French Revolution and of Paine's radical views?

The problem of interpretation for this period becomes even greater when it is recalled that after the Federalists attempted in the Alien and Sedition Acts to extend their political powers into the realm of intellectual life, thus enforcing a complete conservative reaction, they were overthrown, and the liberal followers of Thomas Jefferson came into office in the so-called Revolution of 1800. But the triumph of the radical Jeffersonians was short-lived. Their electoral victory

55

had been achieved in an era of increasing intellectual and social conservatism, in which deism, revolutionary radicalism, and even many of the cherished values of the Enlightenment were yielding their place to the new forces of religious orthodoxy, economic nationalism, and patrician control of thought. Thus the 1800's, reversing the procedure of the 1790's, united political liberalism with intellectual conservatism.

This confusion, although more marked in the first quarter century of the American republic, has not been entirely lacking in subsequent periods of the nation's development. Usually it is explained in terms of a frank dualism, in which United States history is contemplated as a continual struggle between radical and conservative points of view. Since these two compartments are not always neatly arranged to include all their various elements of thought and action, there results, on occasion, the paradox of a political reaction in the midst of a lingering period of antecedent intellectual revolt. In any case, the concept of a permanent war between the radical and conservative, or democratic and aristocratic, positions, however confusing in detail, has had the popular merit of enforcing an optimistic, progressive interpretation of American history. For, Americans have seldom doubted that ultimate victory will lie with the radical or, as it is usually expressed, the liberal, democratic position.

One of the traditional landmarks along this democratic and liberal, or even radical, pathway was the Jeffersonian era, which began with the election of 1800. The Jeffersonian heritage rightly deserves a prominent place in United States history, but along with its great popularity in recent years has gone an extensive re-evaluation of its actual achievements. Students of our political and economic history have united to minimize the effect of the Revolution of 1800. The judgment of a later scholar that "Jefferson, anti-Hamiltonian out of supreme office, became in good part Hamiltonian as President," [1] repeated the shrewd contemporary opinion offered by Hamilton that "Mr. Jefferson's character warrants the expectation of a temporizing rather than a violent system." [2] And, of course, Jefferson in his inaugural address made the famous remark: "We are all Republicans — we are all Federalists."

The clue to the difficult problem of reconciling Jefferson, the liberal, and Jefferson, the Federalized Republican, lies in dissociating Jefferson, the intellectual and philosopher, from Jefferson, the President of the United States. Jefferson's liberalism and radicalism fell mainly within the periods when he was not holding an administrative public office — in other words, during the first years of the Revolution, again in the second Washington and the Adams administration, and finally in the last years of his life after his own presidency. The other consideration that bears on Jefferson's liberalism was the retreat or compromise forced by the external circumstances of war or the threat of war. John C. Calhoun, in his comment on the failure of Jefferson to undo the work of Hamilton and the Federalists, reiterated the view of the orthodox Jeffersonians — that troubles in foreign affairs were a large part of the reason. Jefferson himself probed deeper into the problem, giving an answer that came to grips with the heart of the liberal's dilemma. Familiar with the example of centralization in Europe, and sure that power always tends to corrupt those who possess it, he warned that there was danger that any government entrusted with authority would degenerate into one of force and tyranny. "I own, I am not a friend to a very energetic government," he wrote Madison in 1787. "It is always oppressive. It places the governors indeed more at their ease, at the expense of the people." [3]

In the eyes of his opponents and of many of his erstwhile

supporters, Jefferson as president illustrated his own dictum. But Jefferson, at least, recognized the problem and struggled harder perhaps than any other president to preserve the sinews of liberalism. His efforts point up the significance to American liberalism of the Jeffersonian tradition; his defeat was an early indication of the decline of that liberalism. The dichotomy is summed up in Parrington's belief that, although Jefferson was "by far the most vital and suggestive" of all thinkers of the early republic, "the one to whom later generations may return most hopefully," his efforts were "foredoomed to failure." [4]

The main outlines of Jefferson's liberal philosophy are well known and began with his very real contributions to the American Revolution. Author of the Declaration of Independence, Jefferson was also one of the leaders of the social revolution in Virginia that abolished primogeniture and entail, and disestablished the Anglican Church. His bill for religious freedom, which he had drafted as a part of a general revision of the laws of Virginia, was finally passed in 1786. Going beyond the simple enforcement of legal toleration for dissenters, it called for complete freedom of thought and worship. In the preamble to this justly famous Virginia Statute of Religious Freedom, Jefferson declared that governments should interfere with the expression of opinions only when they "break into overt acts against peace and good order." Meanwhile, toleration and truth provided the best defense against error. It was essential therefore that minority opinion be protected from assault if it was to have an equal chance to become, perhaps, the majority view of some future day.[5] Jefferson's other important ambition for his native state, the institution of a comprehensive system of public education, met with paltry results except in the case of the later founding of the University of Virginia.

Jefferson's contributions to the Revolution were largely

of an intellectual sort. Adhering to the traditions and tenets of the eighteenth-century Enlightenment, he used the typical weapons of a liberal intellectual — the pen and the legislative assembly — in his efforts to overthrow British rule and to lay the foundations for a more liberal American society. Thrust into the practical direction of affairs as war governor of Virginia from 1779 to 1781, Jefferson's experience was less happy and not especially successful. Then, after the death of his wife and conclusion of the Revolution, he undertook the important mission of following in Franklin's footsteps as United States minister to France. His sojourn in Europe not only gave him an excellent opportunity for intellectual stimulation but bestowed upon him as well a certain added maturity and breadth of view.

From his European experience Jefferson derived at first hand a number of conceptions that reinforced his own native liberal philosophy. As America's official representative in France, he was anxious to improve trade relations between the two countries. Here, however, he was confronted by the restrictions of French mercantilism, so exasperatingly reminiscent of the old British colonial trade regulations. Without being a doctrinaire physiocrat, Jefferson was nevertheless very critical of governmental restraints on trade and constantly compared the European practice in this regard with the more favorable situation of America. After an excursion to Great Britain in 1786, he found much to condemn in the system of land monopoly and the way in which industrialism in "scientific England" ground down the poor. Along with the wealth and civilization of Europe, Jefferson saw the grave dangers of its excessive centralization and consolidation. "What a cruel reflection," he wrote mournfully in 1785, "that a rich country can not long be a free one." [6]

Although doubtful that it would work in Europe, Jefferson felt that a republican form of government was best for the United States because it lent itself least to the centralization that characterized Old World countries. Yet, as he warned Madison, there was danger of any type of government degenerating into one of force and tyranny, and he feared that the large cities and corruption of Europe would be transferred to the New World as soon as the supply of vacant lands in America began to diminish. Jefferson's apprehension over a society predominantly urbanized and industrialized is well known and was often adverted to in his correspondence as well as in his *Notes on Virginia.* "When we get piled upon one another in large cities, as in Europe, we shall become corrupt as in Europe, and go to eating one another as they do there." Such a society ran counter to all his agrarian principles and to his belief in individualism. With people working in factories and clustered together in great metropolitan areas, the individual would lose his freedom to an employer, to a government, or to the pressure of mass opinion.[7]

Jefferson's ideal economy emphasized the self-sufficiency of the individual, living in a self-contained community, and enjoying the economic advantages that went with ownership of land. Allied with this agrarian ideal was his preference for a limited government, in which as many powers as possible would be exercised on the local level. Although he recognized the weaknesses of the Articles of Confederation and the need for a government able to defend the United States from threats abroad, he desired to see the state and local instrumentalities sovereign in domestic matters. Jefferson accordingly admired the democracy of New England towns, and he included a similar system of local government in his suggested plans for organizing the Northwest Territory. In Virginia, he urged adoption of a type of local government extending down to the ward level. In his Autobiography, which he began at the advanced age of seventy-seven, he complained bitterly over the way in which the Federal judiciary had consolidated power in the national administration, at the expense of the rights of state and local governments. Arguing that "it is not by the consolidation, or concentration of powers, but by their distribution, that good government is effected," Jefferson depicted as the ideal, a society in which

Every State again is divided into counties . . . ; each county again into townships or wards, to manage minuter details; and every ward into farms to be governed each by its individual proprietor. Were we directed from Washington when to sow, and when to reap, we should soon want bread.[8]

The strength of Jefferson's belief in local government and in participation by the citizen in the affairs of his "ward-republic" was illustrated by his remark to a correspondent that, like Cato, he could only conclude every bit of advice on government with the injunction "divide the counties into wards." [9] This stress on local government continued to be one of the major themes of Jefferson's letter writing during his later years. Although he coupled his views with a support of the national government's strong foreign policy during the crucial period of the Madison administration, his reiteration of the importance of local and state rights almost carried him to the point of repudiating many of the steps that he had taken in his own administration. Fearful that a centralized government would assume absolute powers, he placed increasing emphasis upon education and local government as the two hooks upon which the preservation of republican institutions depended. It was especially ironic therefore that, in his own state of Virginia, Jefferson had so little success in securing the adoption of a system either of widespread common schooling or of responsible local government. These failures on the local scene were matched by an even greater decline in Jeffersonian liberalism over the nation as a whole. In this decline, the greatest irony of all perhaps was that Jefferson's own presidency contributed so importantly to the defeat of his principles.

In his inaugural address on March 4, 1801, President Jefferson set forth in optimistic and conciliatory terms a philosophy of political liberalism that complemented his ideal agrarian economy. To the vision of a young nation, rich in resources, Jefferson added his confidence in the ability of the people to govern themselves under the Constitution and rule of law, and according to the "sacred principle, that though the will of the majority is in all cases to prevail, that will, to be rightful, must be reasonable; that the minority possess their equal rights, which equal laws must protect, and to violate which would be oppression." Spelling these rights out in detail, Jefferson proceeded to summarize the essential features of a liberal democratic government — equal justice, limited power, and freedom of the individual in all his pursuits.[10]

How well Jefferson's two administrations realized his high ideals has ever since been a matter of controversy, but there is little doubt that he began his task as president with a profound awareness of the dangers inherent in the exercise of national power. In a significant pre-election letter to Gideon Granger, a Connecticut politician who became postmaster general in the new administration, Jefferson expressed the opinion that widespread opposition in New England to Republican principles would compel the Jeffersonians, if victorious, to adopt a consolidated and enforced nationalism. This contradicted Jefferson's own view that an ideal government was one close to the citizenry, with its domestic affairs in the hands of the separate states. "Our country is too large to have all its affairs directed by a single government," he wrote, adding: "What an augmentation of the field for jobbing, speculating, plundering, office-building and office-hunting would be produced by an assumption of all the State powers into the hands of the General Government!" But a simple and economical government, he feared, could not be realized if New England persisted in its contrary-minded Federalism.[11]

Jefferson's letter to Granger was an interesting advance apology for some of the policies later pursued by his administration. Meanwhile, however, New Englanders abated their hysteria over Jefferson's election, and his first administration, at least, was able to move smoothly toward the achievement of most of the goals of Jeffersonian liberalism. Neither the Bank of the United States nor the national debt was repudiated, but taxes were cut, the hated whisky excise was repealed, and offenders under the Sedition Act were granted pardons and remission of their fines. Furthermore, the civil service, including especially the diplomatic establishment, and the personnel of the army and navy were both drastically trimmed. Although the Jeffersonians did not accomplish the complete administrative revolution they had threatened when in the opposition, there remained a Republican point of view that contrasted sharply with the Federalists' manner of operating the government. Greater emphasis was placed on the responsibility of the executive branch of the government to Congress, and there was more respect for the integrity and functions of the states and of the individual citizen. While accepting the structure of the government left by the Federalists, the Jeffersonians proposed to administer it in a different spirit.[12] But midway in Jefferson's first term this dream of an era of Republican tranquillity and agrarian virtue was rudely interrupted by events in Europe.

The rise of Napoleon from the ruins of the French Revolution's early idealism, his acquisition of Louisiana, and the threat that this offered to American trade down the Mississippi, plus the possibility of a renewal of the European war, all operated to dispel Jefferson's Utopian Arcadia of simplicity and economy. Forced by the pressures of the frontiersmen's "agricultural imperialism," Jefferson abandoned his strict constructionist interpretation of the Constitution and eagerly grasped Napoleon's sudden offer to sell all of Louisiana to the United States. Although Jefferson drafted an amendment to the Constitution covering the right to add new territories to the Union, the deal for Louisiana could not wait, and Congress accordingly gave its quick approval to the purchase price of some fifteen million dollars, thereby almost doubling the national debt, which Jefferson and Secretary of the Treasury Gallatin had been at such pains to reduce. One further embarrassment to Jefferson in connection with Louisiana resulted from protests of local inhabitants at the arbitrary nature of the American government imposed upon them without their consent and in violation of the treaty terms. This, however, was soon corrected by the establishment for the more settled areas of the vast region of a territorial government comparable to that of the Old Northwest Territory.

On the whole, the modifications in Jeffersonian principles resulting from the purchase of Louisiana were mild indeed compared to the changes and difficulties enforced by the new outbreak of hostilities in Europe in 1803. In the not unsympathetic judgment of the Beards, the events in Europe drew Jefferson and his supporters "into domestic policies more autocratic and sweeping than Hamilton's boldest enterprise; hurried them, pacific as they were in intention, into a struggle not of their own deliberate making; compelled them to resort to hated measures of revenue and finance . . ." [13] And to cap the climax, the Federalists now resorted to arguing a state rights position and to threatening secession, while the Jeffersonian Republicans adopted, one after another, the nationalistic measures of their hated opponents. The Embargo Act, forbidding all American vessels to sail for European ports, which was passed by Congress in December 1807, involved the greatest threat to American individual liberties. This soon became apparent when a series of enforcement acts gave Federal agents the right to search out and seize ships and goods suspected of being in violation of the law. The much-hated Embargo Act has, however, to be understood in the light of Jefferson's efforts to preserve American neutral rights without going to war. But, despite his love of peace, Jefferson in his anxiety over violations of American neutrality also turned to a policy of building gunboats for the navy and of enlarging the size of the standing army.

The degree of nationalism, expense, and coercion implied in these various measures of Jefferson's second administration aroused the wrath of many of his followers, and resulted in a curious political alliance of conservative Federalists and radical doctrinaire Jeffersonians. Of the latter, none was more bitter or savage in his criticism than John Randolph of Roanoke. Randolph, who has been called an aristocratic libertarian, gave as his own epigram: "I am an aristocrat; I love liberty, I hate equality." This last comment explains something of his differences with Jefferson, although Randolph, like Jefferson, accepted equality in the sense of equality of opportunity. A strict constructionist, Randolph nevertheless was realistic enough to view the Constitution as a political instrument and not as a final authority. Only power, he argued, could restrain power, and he therefore desired to see the agrarian interests of propertied farmers preserved as a bulwark against the commercial and manufacturing power. Like John Taylor of Caroline and the hard core of original Jeffersonians, Randolph was strongly opposed to the idea of a paternalistic, protectionist state. A government restricted in its powers, Randolph realized, could not furnish the degree of subsidy and protection required to build up an industrial order, which was precisely why he preferred a strict construction of the Constitution. Although no leveler, he held that government should not deliberately produce inequality through legislation favoring a particular interest or group.[14]

With help from a few of the old Republicans and the Federalist opposition, Randolph played a significant role in combating the centralizing tendencies in the Republican administrations of Jefferson and Madison. The embargo, foreign entanglements, preparedness legislation, War of 1812, tariff, internal improvements, and Second Bank of the United States all incurred his keen displeasure. But the war and expansionist policies of the Republicans were the especial targets of his sarcasm, Randolph complaining on one occasion in a typical speech in Congress: "We had vaunted of paying off the national debt, of retrenching useless establishments; and yet had now become as infatuated with standing armies, loans, taxes, navies, and war, as ever were the Essex Junto. What Republicanism is this?" [15]

In the opinion of his latest biographer, Randolph's liberalism was more limited than Jefferson's. While Jefferson changed with the times, preserved his optimism, and saved at least a part of the American dream, Randolph became increasingly embittered, retreating finally into an intransigent southern state rights position. In Randolph's case, the consistency of his old Jeffersonian liberalism was marred by his growing acceptance of the orthodox southern view in regard to Negro slavery. Although opposed to slavery on principle, Randolph was defensive about the institution in the South because of his fears of a slave insurrection and because of his firm opposition to Federal interference with state rights. Slavery, he came to feel, was a matter of life and death to the South.[16]

Jefferson, like Randolph, also perhaps yielded some of his earlier antislavery convictions, but more significant was the way in which he drew closer to Randolph in other respects, thus returning to the liberal attitudes that had characterized his philosophy before the troubled years of his presidency. While the bulk of the Jeffersonians embarked on the nationalistic policies of the postwar era of good feeling, Jefferson himself beat a retreat to some of his earlier allegiances. Endorsing a strict constructionist work by John Taylor, *Construction Construed and Constitutions Vindicated,* Jefferson wrote in 1822: "I acknowledge it has corrected some erring opinion into which I had slidden without sufficient examination." A correspondent of Randolph's, alluding to some Jefferson letters he had seen, noted in 1826: "The old gentleman seems from this correspondence, to be more alarmed at the rapid and increasing encroachments of the Federal government than I could have imagined." And Jefferson himself, in referring to his endorsement of the Taylor book, wrote to Nathaniel Macon, stressing the urgency of two measures:

1st, how to check these unconstitutional invasions of states rights by the federal judiciary. . . .

2. to cease borrowing money to pay off the national debt, if this cannot be done without dismissing the army and putting the ships out of commission, have them up high and dry, and reduce the army to the lowest point at which it was ever established.[17]

In the Beards' view, the policies of the Jefferson administration, with their seemingly anti-Jeffersonian nationalism, were "a reversal of means not ends."[18] Considered in economic terms, Jefferson was adapting his policies to the changed world situation — the broad Jeffersonian agrarian goal remaining the same. Thus the Louisiana Purchase was dictated by Jefferson's desire to keep the United States an agricultural nation. But, as Jefferson himself seemed to have realized after he relinquished office, the old liberal goals had been subverted by the illiberal means that the Republicans had taken over from their Federalist opponents. While his Republican successors pursued a policy of economic nationalism as both an instrument and a goal of Republican statecraft, Jefferson returned to his old loves of widespread education and local self-government.

The transformation in Republican policies during the presidential administration of Jefferson and Madison, whether viewed as a realistic adjustment to changing circumstances or as an abandonment of earlier ideals, was related to the fatal dilemma posed by the long drawn-out war in Europe. The more intransigent of the followers of Jefferson probably agreed with John Taylor that it would have been better to abandon American neutral rights and let the New England merchants fend for themselves. Certainly, under Jefferson and Madison, the attempt to preserve American rights abroad seemed to have led only to increasing restrictions on individual liberties at home. The eventual result of such a policy was the yielding of the older agrarian principles of simplicity and economy that came with formal American entrance into the War of 1812.

John C. Calhoun, one of the War Hawks of 1812, in looking back upon this period, noted how war had absorbed the attention of government and arrested the efforts of Republicans "to carry out the doctrines and policy which brought the party into power." But the greatest impact of the war lay in the future, for, as Calhoun wrote, "the war, however just and necessary, gave a strong impulse adverse to the federal, and favorable to the national line of policy." [19] Other observers also commented on the nationalistic effect of that war. Albert Gallatin, one of the peace commissioners and, as secretary of the treasury, an intimate associate of both Jefferson and Madison, believed that the war had exerted a beneficent influence in the impetus that it gave to patriotism and Americanism. On the other hand, Gallatin, perhaps recalling his own earlier efforts for peace and economy, was forced to admit that "the war has laid the foundation of permanent taxes and military establishments, which the Republicans had deemed unfavorable to the happiness and free institutions of the country." [20]

By the 1820's the adoption of the nationalistic philosophy that held that government had a positive responsibility for the economic well-being of its citizens was resulting in modifications of the older liberal individualism. There was now a strong demand for government action to extinguish Indian claims, build roads, and provide a satisfactory banking and credit system. Instead of the rapidly diminishing debt of Jefferson's first administration, the country found itself saddled with a huge postwar indebtedness of some one hundred twenty million dollars. The Bank of the United States, allowed to expire on the eve of the War of 1812, had to be rechartered to facilitate the management of this national debt. A protective tariff became necessary to protect the manufacturing that had sprung up in the period of isolation from European markets during the embargo and the war. An enlarged military and naval establishment was authorized upon the earnest recommendation of President Madison. And finally, to meet the challenge posed by the extensive area of the new American empire stretching beyond the Mississippi, Madison, like Jefferson, urged an amendment to the Constitution granting Congress the power to build roads, canals, and other internal improvements. Pending such an amendment, Madison was unable to overcome the remnants of his strict constructionist views, and in his last official act as president, he vetoed the bank bonus bill. Under the terms of this measure, which was introduced in Congress by Calhoun, the one and a half million dollars paid by the Second Bank of the United States as a bonus for its charter would have been set aside as a permanent fund for internal improvements.

Like his predecessor Madison, President James Monroe had difficulty adjusting his strict constructionist views to the nationalism of the postwar era. At the close of Jefferson's presidency, Monroe had reached the point of an open break with his superior over the nationalistic trend of the party's policies. And during his own term in office he vetoed a bill providing funds for the repair of the Cumberland Road, although he allowed the original construction to be completed. But any such inklings of a return to the older Jeffersonian state rights position were canceled by the nationalistic tenor of John Marshall's decisions as chief justice of the Supreme Court. In a period of Republican administrations, Marshall was a vital link in the chain that bound the older aristocracy of the Federalists to the later capitalism of the Whigs. Under his leadership, the Court seemed to bear out Jefferson's opinion that the judiciary was a "subtle corps of sappers and miners constantly working under ground to undermine the foundations of our confederated fabric. They are construing our Constitution from a co-ordination of a general and special government, to a general and supreme one alone." [21] In a series of notable decisions, climaxed by that in the famous *McCulloch* v. *Maryland* case of 1819, Marshall defended the national as against the state power. He included in his argument the nationalistic interpretation of the origins of the Constitution, as well as the broad constructionist views originally voiced by Alexander Hamilton.

However much Jefferson and his older followers such as

John Taylor decried Marshall's decisions, there was little difference between the constitutional interpretations of the Supreme Court and the nationalism of the younger Republican leaders who had come into prominence since the War of 1812. Henry Clay, for example, offered a scheme to unite differing class and sectional economic interests in one comprehensive program — his famous "American system." To the old idea of a fundamental antagonism between agrarian and commercial interests, Clay opposed his plan for joining all sections behind a national bank, protective tariff, internal improvements, and generous land policy. Each area, excepting only the Old South, was promised some advantage, and the American system, Clay hoped, would provide an economic basis for the new nationalism of the 1820's. Clay thus tried to broaden the old Hamiltonian economic program in order to give it a greater mass appeal.

Hamilton's Federalist party had collapsed after the War of 1812. But a decade later when John Quincy Adams, a Republican converted from the Federalism of his father, entered the White House, the doctrines of the American system of Hamilton and Clay received their most enthusiastic presidential support. In his first message to Congress, Adams surpassed all previous recommendations for internal improvements and suggested government aid for cultural as well as economic endeavors. This message, which went too far for American taste and was consequently politically unwise, proved alarming to even Adams's friends. Of all the cabinet, only Richard Rush, temporarily the Secretary of State, approved the message when it was first read to them. Jeffersonians believed the Adams program to be full of unconstitutional doctrines, and to most Americans the ideas must have seemed more European than American. They interpreted the message as advocating legislation for the benefit of a class, and Adams's concept of a planned economy they regarded as unmitigated consolidation and centralization. But if "The Message was, for its time, Caesarean," as a recent writer had put it, it was also fortunate that Adams "was the mildest of Caesars." [22] He sincerely believed in the merits of his far-reaching plans and later in life complained bitterly at the defeat of his comprehensive program for internal improvements.

> I fell and with me fell, I fear never to rise again, certainly never to rise again in my day, the system of internal improvement by means of national energies. The great object of my life therefore, as applied to the administration of the government of the United States, has failed.[23]

In the quarter century between John Quincy Adams's message to Congress in 1825 and Jefferson's first inaugural address in 1801, the course of American life and thought underwent amazing shifts. Disappointed though he was over the failure of his administration to put into effect his nationalistic measures, the son of old John Adams nevertheless stood as a notable example of the metamorphosis of American politics. The Jeffersonians had become Federalists, and the Federalists had followed John Quincy into the ranks of their opponents. From this strange union, the older liberals in the Jeffersonian circle could derive little comfort. Under the overriding compulsions of the new nationalism that characterized the era of good feeling after the War of 1812, an eighteenth-century agrarian liberalism received scant support.

6

Jacksonian Democracy: The Many and the Few

THE MIDDLE PERIOD of American history was an era that abounded in contrasts. The age of Jacksonian democracy, of romantic revolution, a golden age of American culture, the period of the flowering of New England and of the rise of the common man, the decades between the War of 1812 and the Civil War manifestly exhibited great strides in the direction of democracy, progress, and reform. Yet these same years witnessed the rise of a crude materialism, the degeneration of political democracy into a species of mob rule and intolerant nationalism, and most important of all, the failure to achieve the abolition of slavery except by a civil war.

In the face of such obviously conflicting tendencies, there is room for a reappraisal of the customary glowing accounts of this Middle Period of American history — the age of Jacksonian democracy. For example, many of the crudities of the Gilded Age after the Civil War, which have ever since drawn a generous measure of criticism, probably existed in embryonic form in the decades from Jackson to Lincoln. This was well recognized at the time, for though the antebellum decades were ones of great faith in progress, they were not entirely lacking in criticism: the New England transcendentalists and reformers, Alexis de Tocqueville in his celebrated *Democracy in America,* and others less well known were aware of the dangers of American progressive democracy. But because so much of their criticism was tempered by a large measure of sympathy and hope, its more pessimistic implications have been almost ignored. It would seem therefore that not enough attention has been given to the possibility that the democratic and nationalistic tendencies of this period may have developed at the expense of older liberal values.

It is in many ways difficult to interpret Jacksonian democracy as a liberal movement. Certainly an era that experienced mob attacks on Catholics, immigrants, and abolitionists, as well as a violent uprooting of Indians and Mexicans on the plea of manifest destiny, had its illiberal aspects. But the threat of slavery and western expansionism to liberalism was concealed by the resurgence of agrarian democracy that took place in the 1830's along with the entrance of Andrew Jackson into the White House. Although agrarianism, with all its promise for a liberal revolution, was destined to be short-lived, it was nevertheless true that the defeat of John Quincy Adams and election in 1828 of Andrew Jackson to the presidency paved the way for a return to older agrarian principles. In contrast to a policy of economic nationalism, which Republicans had proposed after the War of 1812, the Jacksonians revived in realistic and practical fashion much of the old Jeffersonian individualist philosophy. Of course, with revival went some revision. The Jacksonian democrats were less optimistic than the Jeffersonian apostles of the Enlightenment had been about the nature of man and the possibility of his achieving Utopia. As Arthur Schlesinger, Jr., has pointed out, the Jacksonians "moderated that side of Jeffersonianism which talked of agricultural virtue, independent proprietors, 'natural' property, abolition of industrialism, and expanded immensely that side which talked of economic equality, the laboring classes, human rights and the control of industrialism." [1]

But Jacksonian acceptance of industrialism and support of the working class did not outlaw the possibility of retaining agrarian goals, or the achievement of a type of agrarian society that would include small businessmen, petty traders, and prosperous artisans, as well as independent farmers. Perhaps the appeal of Jackson's program may be better understood if it is thought of as a program not of labor against capital, but as a program for the lower middle class, or the plain people, whether they resided in urban or in agricultural areas. This large and growing segment of the population stood to gain most from the Jacksonian war on monopoly and privilege. With the resources of the West beginning for the first time to be exploited on an extensive scale, and with manufacturing entering upon the threshold of a century of expansion, the lower middle class could afford to be capitalist in its inclinations and in its hopes for the future. Jacksonian laissez faire and equal rights were more allied to the needs and desires of the great mass of the people than the Whiggish economic theories of Henry Clay or John Quincy Adams. Although Clay and his nationalist school of later Jeffersonians sought to make the old Hamiltonian Federalist concept of economic paternalism popular by broadening its base, the Jacksonians' program had a greater appeal in an America that was still young, hopeful, and expanding, and in which social life had not yet become overwhelmingly institutionalized.[2]

While neither Jackson nor his followers left any great body of political or social philosophy comparable to the Jeffersonian literature, the main outlines of Jacksonian liberalism are easy to infer from the policies of his administration. The partial rejection of internal improvements at Federal expense, the war on the bank and monopolies, and the tacit sympathy for the small farmer and workingman were some of the important features of the Jacksonian program. At the outset of the administration, the check on the American system of internal improvements, announced in Jackson's veto of the Maysville Road bill, was an attack upon the policy of Federal largess for the speculative business elements moving into the West. Through the 1830's, the belief prevailed that the average pioneer's interests would be better served by reduced Federal spending, lower taxes, and a more liberal land policy. Thomas Hart Benton's graduation and pre-emption legislation therefore was closer to western desires than the plans of Henry Clay. Benton, a stanch supporter of Jackson, and long Missouri's representative in the Senate, sought by his proposals to make it easier for western pioneers to acquire lands, either pre-empting the good or gaining the inferior at a price graduated downwards. That the states and private enterprise, rather than the Federal government, then assumed the major responsibility for building roads and canals in no wise canceled the impact of Jackson's Maysville veto in so far as Federal policy was concerned. At least the President had restrained the Clay-Adams drive in the direction of a paternalistic economy, thereby postponing extensive Federal aid to transportation until the Civil War era.

In the same way, the Jacksonians' fight over the tariff and the bank during the 1830's served to check the policy of Federal legislation in the interests of a section or a class. Though Jackson firmly supported the Union against the South Carolina nullificationists, he also urged a lowering of the tariff. Finally, in the war on the bank he broke the very citadel of entrenched monopoly — the creature of the economic nationalists from the days of Hamilton to Clay. In the words of Frederick Jackson Turner, "The severance of official connection between the national government and the capitalist was one of the most important steps in American history. Thenceforth, the industrial interests were obliged to act by underground methods and by the lobby." [3] By their attack upon the whole Whig conception of an economic paternalism, the Jacksonians were able to preserve a large measure of American individuality while at the same time enhancing the trend toward equality and further minimizing distinctions of aristocracy, rank, or class.

The assaults on economic privilege in the form of subsidies, tariffs, and the bank especially won favor with the more radical members of the Jacksonian democracy. Making laissez faire a radical principle and adhering to a belief in a natural order of society, unclogged by the restraints of monopoly and privilege, the Jacksonians proposed to use the power of the state to enforce free competition. Such a policy was popular particularly in the large eastern cities where the small property owner's stake in society was being threatened by the growth of corporations and entrenched monopolies. In New York City, for example, the radical Jacksonians, or Locofocos, as they were called, were led by the picturesque journalist William Leggett, assistant to William Cullen Bryant as editor of the New York *Post*. Leggett's philosophy was a compound of his belief in laissez faire and his preference for agrarian democracy.

A disciple of Adam Smith and of John Taylor, Leggett ascribed the growth of inequality to interferences with the natural right of property by federal and state authorities, and declared that democracy could be maintained by narrowly limiting the powers of the government, by maintaining a regime of strict *laissez faire,* and by keeping the Western lands open for settlers and preventing them from becoming the property of wealthy speculators.[4]

The economic liberalism of the Jacksonian era — agrarian and small capitalist in its orientation — tended to prevail down to the Civil War, although the shift to a greater concentration of industry in the hands of a relatively few individuals was already becoming apparent by the 1850's. Until recently there has been little disposition to quarrel with the view that the United States, in the decades from Jackson to Lincoln, pursued the old Jeffersonian agrarian ideal in its economic life. But the growing volume of governmental intervention in all phases of the modern economy has prompted a re-examination of earlier periods of our history. Most of this research, while it has demonstrated an undoubted attempt on the part of government to regulate or aid private business, has also shown the failure of such efforts. This was the case during the American Revolution. Later, Alexander Hamilton's vision of economic paternalism was imperfectly realized in the 1790's, and again after the War of 1812, when it was unsuccessfully revived by Clay and Adams. Actually therefore Hamilton's ideas were never put into practice until the Republican party came to dominate the American scene after the Civil War.

Although a laissez-faire liberalism and individualism thus characterized most of United States national policy until the Civil War, the question has been raised as to whether this was equally true of the situation in the states during this period. In other words, does the thesis of an agrarian, liberal, laissez-faire tradition have general validity for the antebellum decades or was it merely a matter of the locus of governmental activity in the economy shifting back and forth between the states and the Federal government? For example, has too much been made of the reluctance of Jackson to approve Federal funds for internal improvements, since many of these same projects were then carried out by the states? And did the states before the Civil War undertake the same sort of activities that are today performed by the Federal government?

The most important evidence of state action in the economic sphere took place during the 1820's and 1830's when the rush to build canals and roads went to unreasonable lengths. Although the degree of such activity hardly rendered it necessary, some of the western states followed the example of Missouri and devoted a special article in their constitutions to the subject of internal improvements, providing for their encouragement and support through the application of state funds. To the newer states of the West, as well as the older states dependent on western trade, the improvement of the means of transportation took on the nature of a public enterprise. Precisely because it seemed to benefit the whole community, it had a widespread popular appeal in such states. Rather than contradicting the ideal of Jacksonian individualism, state aid to internal improvements was looked upon as a means of encouraging agriculture and of opening up new avenues of trade for a larger number of individuals. But the improvement of transportation facilities was the only economic enterprise widely supported by the states before the Civil War, and even in this area such support usually took the form of the states' subscribing to the stock of private companies. The very scarcity of large private accumulations of capital rendered state aid more necessary, although it was true that railroad promoters, for example, worked hard to attract the funds of small private investors. "As early as 1838 the Western Railroad in Massachusetts had 2,331 stockholders. The New York Central in 1853 had 2,445. The Pennsylvania, financed almost entirely by house to house sales of stock, had over 2,600." [5]

Outside the field of transportation, the role of state governments in the economy was not a vital one. And even in that there was a decided reaction, after the Panic of 1837, against state aid for internal improvements.[6] The decline of the concept of state intervention in the economic sphere was, perhaps, most marked in some of the eastern states. For example, a case study of the part that government played in the pre-Civil War American economy, made for Massachusetts, has demonstrated the extent to which state action was confined and limited. After the American Revolution, the old colonial concept of the commonwealth yielded before a surge of antigovernment pressures. Debtor farmers learned that the ultimate weight of numbers would count for them in a democracy, and the merchants realized that the state could not work for them alone and that they could not simply write their economic interests into an interpretation of the common interest. Despite a continued desire for state intervention in their own behalf on the part of various economic groups, the fear of taxes and a heavy state indebtedness blocked public expenditures for several decades. Instead of taking a more positive, direct role, the state granted its economic powers to private banks and bridge companies. Later this policy was broadened into the corporate device, and charters were granted in a steadily mounting number to a variety of business concerns. These corporations soon gained private rights and were freed of the responsibilities that went with government agencies, thus negating the early concept of the corporation as a semipublic device. "Democratic unwillingness to confine the corporation to a favored few had dispersed it among many holders and that in turn had separated it from the state." [7]

In their study of Massachusetts, the Handlins go on to show how the proliferation of corporations turned an original government agency into a business form, with multiplication destroying the state's capacity to direct production through a judicious bestowal of corporation charters. Moreover, each grant of a special privilege provoked the protests

of outsiders, while "fanatics in freedom" battled all government aid and regulation, thereby meshing together the
struggle for reform and the battle against privilege. This did
not always represent an unqualified approval of laissez faire,
but it did indicate a weakening of the European concept of
government as the director of productive enterprise. The
dynamic elements in American society weakened class distinctions, and at the same time the instruments of state action, like privilege and incorporation, became so widely
accessible that the state was relegated to the role of a policeman. Moreover, this "transition from the Commonwealth
to the police state, from mercantilism to liberalism, was not
peculiar to Massachusetts or to the United States." [8]

A similar analysis of the government's hand in the economy, for the state of Pennsylvania, shows that the crusade of
the Jacksonians and workingmen against the practice of
state-granted charters to private corporations made use of
the concept of the community against the corporation. Although the arguments took on to some extent an individualist and laissez-faire tinge, the point of view was not always
antigovernment. In some ways the arguments could be read
as a support of governmental enterprise as against private,
but state-chartered, corporations. Yet, in attacking these
charters as a part of its antimonopoly crusade in the 1830's,
labor at the same time sought legislation in its own behalf.
This paradox was accomplished when labor identified its
cause with that of the whole community — "labor the only
true interest" idea. But whether the point of view in Pennsylvania — probably the most business-oriented of all the
states — was primarily individualist and antigovernment, or
whether it was actuated by the concept of positive government action in behalf of the community, was hardly important in the light of the fact that "Far from being limited, the
objectives of the state in the economic field were usually so

broad that they were beyond its administrative power to achieve." [9] In other words, a stable and expert administrative system had not developed to the point where effective state regulation or action was possible, and therefore the question of its interference was as yet of no practical concern and not to be worried about.

On the basis of such studies as have appeared, there is evidence that economic liberalism of an agrarian, laissez-faire nature was as much a part of the states' policies as it was of the national government's from the 1830's until the Civil War. The very weakness of the state governments administratively was enough to preclude them from effectiveness in the economic realm. Any attempt therefore to read back into the history of the states before the Civil War an analogy to the vast economic powers invoked today by the Federal government rests on a distortion of the magnitude, purpose, and general efficiency of the economy activity of the states.

In the states as well as in the national government, agrarian principles pervaded the Jacksonian period. The cry of equal rights for all and special privileges for none suggested forcefully a program of political and economic liberalism. Elaborating upon the Jeffersonian tradition, the Jacksonians demanded a broader political equality and a more generous economic opportunity. But in their assertions of an equalitarian political and economic democracy, the Jacksonians often neglected such liberal tenets as the doctrine of limited government and preservation of minority rights. Just as Jefferson in power sought compromise between the extremes of his own radical followers and the conservative Federalists, so the Jacksonian Democrats attempted to unite prolabor and antimonopoly radicals in the North with proslavery conservatives in the South. In the resulting confusion, the Jackson movement, despite the liberalism of much of its political and economic program, proved itself far from liberal in other respects — particularly in the matter of minority rights when such rights came into conflict with the will of the majority. Thus the Jacksonians' insistence on equal rights was unfortunately not paralleled by a similar solicitude for individual liberties, and the period after 1830, despite the promise that it held out for an agrarian order, was also an era in which liberalism in many ways declined.[10]

Personally Jackson, though often charming to an inner circle of friends and associates, had little of the philosophical or intellectual qualities of a Jefferson. Instead, he had a reputation for abrupt and arbitrary action, which aroused the concern not only of his political enemies but also of his liberal friends, who would have preferred a stricter adherence to legal methods. Much of this anxiety over Jackson's ways was traceable to stories of his military career and his indifference as an army officer to civil authority. Thus, after the victory of New Orleans, Jackson became embroiled with the local citizenry and flatly refused to honor a writ of habeas corpus issued in behalf of one of their number by Federal Judge Dominick A. Hall. Instead, Jackson ordered the arrest of the judge on charges of aiding and abetting a mutiny. Justifying his imperious actions, for which he was later fined one thousand dollars, Jackson admitted the violation of constitutional rights, but argued: "The laws must sometimes be silent when necessity speaks." [11]

This and other instances in which Jackson ignored inconvenient War Department orders and violated civil authority or foreign jurisdiction were responsible for much criticism of his candidacy for the presidency. On the other hand, once clothed with the powers of the highest office, Jackson in large part forsook his military ways, supporting, for example, in best Jeffersonian fashion, reductions in the army and navy. Only toward the close of his second term, in the midst of diplomatic troubles with France over the spoliation claims due the United States, did Jackson exert pressure upon Congress for larger military appropriations.[12]

Though not militaristic, Jackson was often autocratic and dictatorial in his conduct as president. The Whig opposition and the Congressional leaders, Clay, Calhoun, and Webster, all distrusted the way in which he used the powers of his office. The mental image of the President, astride a white horse, leading a Federal army against the nullificationists in South Carolina may have been partly responsible for Congressional willingness to push through the Compromise Tariff bill of 1833. At the same time, southern state-rights Democrats, who had assumed the mantle of Jefferson, were antagonized by the nationalism of Jackson's methods even when they agreed with his agrarian goals. To the National Republicans, who feared the Jacksonian ends as well as the means, the President was a tyrant reminiscent of George III, and so they labeled him King Andrew I and took for themselves the name Whig, after the English liberals. Though he hardly justified the title King Andrew, Jackson did at times act with seeming indifference to much of the liberal tradition. Rejecting therefore the interpretation of Jackson as a liberal, a later critic has issued the severe judgment that "If his had been the last great influence in the formation of the American character, American democracy might have become associated with ignorance, recklessness, and violence." [13]

The indictment of Jackson on the basis of "ignorance, recklessness, and violence," though an extreme and in some ways unfair view, was precisely the reason why so many of the liberal intellectuals of the time were repelled by Jacksonian democracy. This was especially the case among the literati and transcendentalists of New England, very few of whom exhibited any real enthusiasm for the Jacksonian cause. While the transcendentalists shared the romantic in-

dividualism of the Enlightenment, the Jacksonians thought
more in terms of practical economic and political reforms.
Basically, Jacksonian democracy accepted industrialism,
modifying its worse effects with an equalitarian program.
Although occasionally, as in the case of Emerson, impressed
by the new world of machinery, New England reformers and
transcendentalists on the whole rejected industrialism and a
democracy based on the large urban masses of workingmen
and businessmen. Thoreau's denial of all this was, of course,
the most thoroughgoing, but Thoreau was also among the
least political-minded of the Concord group. In general,
however, the skepticism of so many of the leading intellectuals and reformers, particularly the New England transcendentalists, to Jacksonian democracy illustrated its limitations as a liberal movement. To most liberals it had
less appeal than Jeffersonian thought and philosophy, and
even its agrarianism was too nationalistic and equalitarian
to gain the favor of individualist believers in a transcendental heaven.[14]

A critical, and yet dispassionate, view of Jacksonian democracy was that set forth by the famous contemporary
foreign observer of the American scene, Alexis de Tocqueville, in his celebrated volumes on *Democracy in America*
(1838–1840). A student who was a sympathetic and even at
times flattering interpreter, Tocqueville in his *Democracy*
nevertheless "more than hinted of corruption in the American Eden." [15] Confessing that "in America I saw more than
America; I sought the image of democracy itself, with its
inclinations; its character, its prejudices, and its passions, in
order to learn what we have to fear or to hope from its progress," Tocqueville struggled with the problem of whether
the Jacksonian movement was liberal as well as democratic
in its outlook. The American form of government, with the
checks provided by the Constitution and the Federal system,

was, he believed, best suited to the interests of the majority of the people. Although nothing was more striking to the foreign visitor — or more commented upon by the host of travelers in the United States — than the absence of the visible signs of government and its accompanying quota of useless functionaries and soldiers, there was nevertheless a centralized government in the United States in the sense of a common set of interests among the people. But there was no centralized administration controlling local as well as national matters.[16]

Tocqueville did not agree with those who deduced from this that the government of the United States was of necessity weak and would therefore in time fall prey to the liberties of its citizens. The chief danger to American democracy, he warned, did not stem from the decentralization of its government or from an excess of individual liberty, but from the "inadequate securities which exist against tyranny." Though serious evidence of tyranny was not present in the United States, Tocqueville feared the power of the legislative majority and the decrees of the magistrates as possible threats to freedom of opinion. Believing that the American people had a passion for equality more than for liberty, he noted that there was little true independence of mind or freedom of discussion in the United States. From this he concluded that, if freedom were destroyed in the United States, it would be by the tyranny of the majority rather than by a minority. Also, a sizable war, which always augmented the powers of the government, was a formidable threat to liberty. "A long war," he pointed out, "almost always reduces nations to the wretched alternative of being abandoned to ruin by defeat or to despotism by success. . . . No protracted war can fail to endanger the freedom of a democratic country." [17]

Running through Tocqueville's account of *Democracy in America* was his attempt to distinguish between freedom and equality, and to resolve the dilemma of preserving individual liberties in the midst of a growing democratic tendency toward centralization and uniformity. The danger of individualism lay in the possibility that self-interest, improperly understood and applied, might further encourage the inordinate American desire for wealth and material prosperity. Although there was no apparent likelihood of a landed aristocracy springing up in the American states, Tocqueville was apprehensive of the pretensions and power of the rising industrial class. Dissenting from the view that the majority will had absolute sway in the United States over the individual, he nevertheless saw a threat to personal freedom in the excessive stress that democracy placed upon equality. While freedom was necessary for equality, there was always the danger that, with equality once attained, liberty would be ignored.

The more equal the conditions of men become and the less strong men individually are, the more easily they give way to the current of the multitude and the more difficult it is for them to adhere by themselves to an opinion which the multitude discard. . . .

As the conditions of men become equal among a people, individuals seem of less and society of greater importance; or rather every citizen, being assimilated to all the rest, is lost in the crowd, and nothing stands conspicuous but the great and imposing image of the people at large. This naturally gives the men of democratic periods a lofty opinion of the privileges of society and a very humble notion of the rights of individuals. . . .[18]

The solicitude for the future of American democracy exhibited by Tocqueville and others was based essentially on their realization of its potentially illiberal aspects. Despite the efforts of the Jeffersonians, the decades following the

American Revolution had continued to be conservative, nationalistic, and antiliberal in politics and economics. The renewal of agrarian liberal tendencies, touched off by the Jacksonian triumph, was temporarily decisive in reversing a paternalistic Whiggish trend in American government after the War of 1812. But Jacksonian democracy, nationalistic and popular in its appeal and program, also became illiberal in respect to minority rights and civil liberties. Yielding to the demands of a proslavery South and an expansionist West, the Jacksonians found themselves supporting the suppression of free speech and free thought and justifying the manifest destiny of the nation at the expense of the rights of Indians and Mexicans.

Of great importance to liberalism in the Jackson era, in both a positive and a negative sense, was the great American West. Throughout the Middle Period, this West, as both myth and reality, continued to exert a vital influence, paralleling and also helping to mold Jacksonian democracy. Although the conquest of the frontier, in successive waves of westward migration, involved such features as Indian warfare, with its accompanying lapse into barbarism, the sense of opportunity and liberation offered by the West was compensation for the temporary decline in civilization.

On the whole there was comparatively little conflict between early American westward expansion and the ideals of liberalism and democratic government. The West continued to be a reservoir of individualism and the domain of the self-made man. Although individualism did not preclude a measure of neighborly cooperation nor increasing agitation for government aid in bettering transportation facilities, the image of the frontiersman as a free and self-reliant individual, subsisting largely by his own efforts, remained a valid picture. Thus during the 1830's the West exemplified Jacksonian doctrines of individualism and shared in the Jacksonian belief in equality of political and economic opportunity, as against the Whig policies of economic subsidies for business and speculative interests.

But outside the domain of economics, the West did not always have the same liberal import. As the pioneers went west they became more nationalistic in some ways. The rigors of the frontier often enforced a way of life that was degrading and inhumane. Whatever the ideal, in practice civilized qualities frequently yielded before the cruder barbarism of the West. Even though much of this was only temporary, soon passing before the new surge of civilized values emanating from the East, it meanwhile fostered a kind of bumptious equalitarianism and heightened nationalism. In the West everything was exaggerated — the good and the bad alike. And it was this exaggerated, boastful egalitarianism and superpatriotic nationalism, emblazoned as manifest destiny, which seemed often to threaten American liberalism.

Whether the expansionism of the West, however rationalized in terms of manifest destiny or the American mission, was compatible with earlier pacific and republican ideals was a question that could not be avoided indefinitely in the United States. For example, were republican government and expansionism suited to each other? Could the American Constitution and liberal ideals be stretched to cover a vast empire? Anxiety over these issues, which was at first strongly felt by the Jeffersonian Republicans, became instead the special concern of old-line Federalists, who resented the purchase of Louisiana and the prospect of seeing New England degenerate into a section inferior to the rising West. Other Americans, Republicans as well as Federalists, were dismayed lest individual liberties become the price paid for such expansionism. These fears, partly altruistic and partly selfish, had to be dissipated before democracy and expansionism could be linked. This union, which took form only gradually, was first made explicit during the thirties under the aggressive frontier nationalism of the Jacksonians. Jacksonian Democrats talked the language of expansionism, initially in regard to the Indians of Georgia, but later in reference to the Mexicans in Texas and California and the British in Oregon. Summing up popular feeling, an essay in the *Democratic Review* of 1839 depicted America as "The Great Nation of Futurity," and a later article in the same journal first used the phrase "manifest destiny." [19]

In the case of the Indians, the conflict between their rights and the demands of the white settlers reached a crisis in the 1830's when the Jackson administration determined to move the Red Men residing within the state of Georgia to new lands beyond the Mississippi. The problem was aggravated by the fact that the Creeks, Cherokees, and other Indian tribes of the Southwest had attained a considerable degree of civilization and asked only to be left alone on their lands as guaranteed by previous treaties with the United States. To a large extent these Indians had fulfilled one of the cherished dreams of the eighteenth-century Enlightenment. According to this view, which was shared by Jefferson and others, the Indians would in time achieve a higher level of civilization through proximity to the white man's society. Of course, the pioneer backwoodsman seldom accepted the humanitarian liberal's sympathetic feelings toward the Red Man, but continued to be governed in his thinking by the frontier adage that the only good Indian was a dead one.

Despite a background of hostility and numerous clashes with the Indian on the part of both private citizens and contingents of the regular army and militia, the removal policy of the 1830's undertaken by the Jackson administration marked the first official abandonment of the hopeful ideal of a progress in civilization for the Indian. In disregard of the actual improvement already attained by the Indian nations in Georgia, statesmen of the South and West justified the removal policy on grounds of the Indians' inflexible barbarism. Jackson himself took the lead in rationalizing the justice of the removal policy by calling it an inevitable step in the progress of civilization. In a message to Congress he declared:

Humanity has often wept over the fate of the aborigines of this country, and Philanthropy has been long busily employed in devising means to avert it, but its progress has never for a moment been arrested, and one by one have many powerful tribes disappeared from the earth.[20]

President Jackson's argument, repeated by a host of land-hungry expansionists, led naturally to the concept that it was the manifest destiny of the American people to cross the continent and pre-empt the soil from ocean to ocean. Thus, by the 1840's, former apprehensions of an incompatibility between democracy and expansionism largely disappeared as the American people, to the slogan of "Fifty-four forty or fight," and calls for the reannexation of Texas and reoccupation of Oregon, marched to their manifest destiny in the Far West. Young Democrats united with the older Jacksonian statesmen in their enthusiasm for expansion. Although the bulk of the advocates of manifest destiny were congregated in the West and in the newer areas of the South, labor leaders of the East saw a more than incidental connection between renewed increments of cheap land and higher wages. The chief doubts accordingly came from the remnants of an older liberalism, the idealists and humanitarian reformers of the Northeast, the abolitionists who called the Mexican War a slaveholders' plot, and the conservative Whig leaders in both the North and the South who feared the implications of an aggressive, expansionist war.

Expansionism carried to the point of war, no matter how democratic or popular the reasons, marked a retreat from the principles of American liberalism. Individual liberals saw in the Mexican War the danger that the United States would turn to pursuing a military policy, and they warned that this was the traditional means by which personal liberties were subverted. In contrast to the philosophy of many of the advocates of manifest destiny, antiexpansionists argued that United States influence on the world was greatest when it confined itself to peaceful teaching by example. The popular association of democracy and expansionism only increased the fears of the small minority of liberals who questioned the nation-wide tendency of the times. Thoreau, for example, was provoked by the Mexican War to write his celebrated essay *Civil Disobedience*, with its criticism of the whole doctrine of majority rule as against the liberty of the individual's own free conscience. Observing the fruits of the war he had opposed, Thoreau complained:

The whole enterprise of this nation, which is not an upward, but a westward one, toward Oregon, California, Japan, etc., is totally devoid of interest to me, whether performed on foot, or by a Pacific railroad. It is not illustrated by a thought; it is not warmed by a sentiment; there is nothing in which one should lay down his life for, nor even his gloves, — hardly which one should take up a newspaper for. It is perfectly heathenish, — a filibustering *toward* heaven by the great western route. No; they may go their way to their manifest destiny, which I trust is not mine.[21]

Joining forces with Thoreau, Herman Melville, famous in his own time as the novelist of the South Seas, and later renowned as the author of *Moby Dick,* raised his philosophical objections to the manifest destiny of his fellow countrymen. Democracy he linked to the youth of the nation and to the richness of the West, but there was also a danger to a liberal democracy in the pursuit of a policy of conquest.

Free horses need wide prairies; and fortunate for you, sovereign kings! that you have room enough, wherein to be free.

And, may it please you, you are free, partly because you are young. Your nation is like a fine, florid youth, full of fiery impulses, and hard to restrain; his strong hand nobly championing his heart. On all sides, freely he gives, and still seeks to acquire.

But years elapse. . . . The maxims once trampled under foot, are now printed on his front; and he who hated oppressors, is become an oppressor himself.

Thus often with men; thus, often, with nations. Then marvel not, sovereign kings! that old states are different from yours; and think not, your own must forever remain liberal as now.[22]

The manifest destiny of the United States was to carry the American people ever farther from the agrarian dreams of the Jacksonians and their liberal followers. The pressures of western nationalism had led to the War with Mexico, and expansionism in the fifties by becoming tied to the aggressive designs of the southern slavocracy was to pave the way for the Civil War. Among the results of that struggle was the demise of an agrarian economy. This involved a subtle paradox, because in large measure it was the agricultural imperialism of the more expansionist-minded agrarians that had linked democracy to expansionism and so made possible both the Mexican and the Civil War.

In the midst of a growing national democracy, the Jacksonians became in a sense the prisoners of the idea of the rise of the common man. The democracy and majority rule that they espoused was in many ways inimical to an older traditional liberalism that emphasized the freedom of the individual and the right of minority dissent. Intent on their goal of an agrarian utopia for the plain people under a mild republican government, the Jacksonians resented the intrusion of single-minded, radical reformers. And so liberalism, in the sense of individualism or of free enquiry, was largely left to transcendental critics in New England, to abolitionists and other radical reformers, and to a handful of left-wing democrats. Retaining only its economic program, the Democratic party of Jackson worked out an alliance among southern slaveholders, western expansionists, and the urban and immigrant masses of the North. National unity was thus preserved at the price of liberal values. While the ideal of peace and the rights of Indians and Mexicans were rudely brushed aside in the westward surge of manifest destiny, an even greater violation of individual freedom was being perpetuated in the spread of the institution of Negro slavery.

7

The Curse of Slavery

By THE middle of the nineteenth century the institution of Negro slavery, with all its attendant problems, stood out as the most direct challenge to American liberalism. Neither the liberalism of Jefferson nor the agrarian democracy of Jackson had provided a solution to this troublesome issue. Instead of remaining the dying institution of the late eighteenth century, localized in the tidewater areas of the Old South, it had managed to achieve a new vitality in the early part of the nineteenth century. At the same time, the acquisition of Federal territories in the trans-Mississippi West made slavery a national problem, subject to increasing debate in the halls of Congress. Keeping pace in its expansion with the march of the American people across the continent, the westward extension of slavery led ultimately to the Civil War.

Thus the institution of slavery, ardently defended by its beneficiaries as the foundation stone of an ideal Greek democracy in the South, was also the greatest single factor in the decline of nineteenth-century American liberalism. A curse to both the whites and the blacks, it had a disastrous effect upon the North as well as the South. In the latter section, especially, the intensification of the proslavery argument accompanied a steady decline in freedom of thought and in the other liberal ideals of Jefferson's day.

The increasing aggressiveness of the southern defense of slavery in the nineteenth century was in marked contrast to the liberal attitude of leaders of the South at the time of the American Revolution. In the late eighteenth century, the aristocrats who dominated life in Virginia and other parts of the Old South had presented, as Clement Eaton has pointed out, a striking paradox "in their combination of the habits and tastes of patricians with the possession of liberal views concerning religion, slavery, and politics." "Aristocrats with liberal views," they shared the values of the eighteenth-century Enlightenment, with its cosmopolitan and international outlook, its antislavery attitude, its emphasis on reason, and its espousal of deism.[1]

In Virginia, for example, nearly every one of the prominent statesmen of the Revolutionary period was on record as favoring some form of emancipation, and a not-inconsiderable number of large planters from George Washington to John Randolph actually provided in their wills for the manumission of their slaves. Typical of many others in his attitude was George Mason, author of the famous Virginia Bill of Rights and the aristocratic owner of three hundred slaves at the time of his death in 1792. Mason described slavery as a slow poison, not only for the Negroes but for the slaveowners as well. Contaminating the mind and morals of the owners, it stood as an example of tyranny for future legislators. "Taught to regard a part of our own Species in the most abject & contemptible Degree below us," he wrote, "we lose that Idea of the Dignity of Man, which the hand of Nature had planted in us, for great and useful purposes." Henry St. George Tucker, the widely respected professor of law at William and Mary College, argued that slavery was inconsistent with the Bill of Rights and should be eradicated. In addition, he attempted to stir the Virginia legislature into action by delivering a series of antislavery lectures and by the publication in 1796 of an important antislavery pamphlet proposing gradual emancipation. The postponement of the problem, he warned his fellow citizens, would only render more difficult its eventual solution. In the neighboring state of Maryland, the cause of emancipation was championed by two of the leading aristocrats, William Pinkney and Charles Carroll of Carrollton, but the latter's plan for emancipation was voted down by the legislature.[2]

The turning point in the feelings of the South regarding slavery, and the accompanying decline of southern liberalism, fell within the period between the waning of the eighteenth-century Enlightenment and the triumph of Jacksonian democracy in the 1830's. These decades witnessed a conservative reaction in American thought that was only partially counteracted by the Jeffersonian victory of 1800. In addition to the general impact of conservative modes of thinking in this period, the economy of the South was being drastically altered by the invention of the cotton gin and by the rise of cotton factories in England and in the northeastern states. The demands of the industrial revolution for more raw cotton, and hence more labor and land, created a new attitude toward slavery on the part of the South. This was especially true in the cotton-growing areas of the lower South, where the planters now became militant exponents of the expansion of slavery. Just as economics helped to dictate the abolition of slavery in the North, so the cotton gin and industrial revolution helped to assure its continuance in the South. New economic pressures, in conjunction with the more conservative temper in American political and intellectual life, accordingly accomplished a major transformation in southern thinking on the slavery issue.

Evidence that the enlightened liberal attitude toward slavery on the part of the Revolutionary generation of the South was undergoing a change can be seen in the course of events that began in the late 1780's. During the deliberations of the Constitutional Convention at Philadelphia in 1787 there was strong disagreement between some northern and southern delegates as to whether Negro slaves should be considered as property subject to taxation or as persons to be included in fixing the quota of a state's membership in the House of Representatives. Southern delegates desired the Negro to be counted equally with the whites for purposes of representation, though not of taxation, while most Northerners argued that the slaves were property, liable to taxation, but not deserving of representation. Although one of the delegates, Rufus King of Massachusetts, condemned any proposal that would recognize slavery in the Constitution, the members of the Convention were for the most part more concerned with the practical questions of direct taxation and representation in proportion to population. The famous three-fifths compromise, which was written into the Constitution to govern both of these questions, was perhaps satisfactory to no one, but it demonstrated the strength of pro-slavery interests at the Convention and also gave the practical victory to the South, since the Federal government did not use its power to levy direct taxes in proportion to population.

The other important action of the Convention relating to slavery was in the matter of the foreign slave trade. By the time of the Revolution, this trade was being subjected to a growing volume of criticism, first, on humanitarian grounds and, second, because British merchants were the chief beneficiaries. Although Jefferson's denunciation of the trade was expunged from the Declaration of Independence's list of grievances against the crown, several of the states prohibited its continuance. Opponents of this traffic in human beings hoped that the Constitutional Convention would completely outlaw the evil, but when the matter came up for discussion a bitter debate ensued. The southern states were divided. While Virginia, Maryland, and North Carolina had already

THE CURSE OF SLAVERY

acted to end the slave trade, South Carolina and Georgia, having no surplus of Negroes, felt differently. Charles Pinckney of South Carolina pointed out that his state would never adopt the Constitution if it prohibited the slave trade. His cousin Charles Cotesworth Pinckney asserted that Virginia and Maryland would gain higher prices for their slaves if the trade was stopped, but that South Carolina and Georgia, faced with a labor shortage, would be forced to confederate on unequal terms. In deference to these arguments, the foreign slave trade was permitted to continue until 1808.[3]

Fundamentally, the Constitution extended the same protection to slavery that it accorded other property rights, an action that was a serious check to the antislavery movement. To the Quakers and other strong antislavery groups, it seemed as if the Constitution was a document devoid of protection for human liberties. Moreover, the failure to achieve emancipation in the high tide of Revolutionary, eighteenth-century liberalism was to cast a pall on the liberalism of succeeding years. "Ironically enough," as one historian has written, "America's freedom was the means of giving slavery itself a longer life than it was to have in the British empire."[4]

The renewed guarantees for the protection of slavery written into the Federal Constitution were illustrative of the changed feelings on the subject that were beginning to characterize much of American sentiment by the 1790's. That provision of the Northwest Ordinance which prohibited slavery in the territory north of the Ohio River incurred criticism in the South and was even openly flouted by Southerners who brought their slaves into the region. The general agreement in the Constitutional Convention that a Negro slave was property, which should be returned to its owner, was reinforced by the passage of the Fugitive Slave Act of 1793. A decade later, the purchase of Louisiana opened the

way for the creation of new slave states and territories and
set the stage for the forthcoming bitter political struggles
over the extension of slavery. At the same time, the antislavery movement gradually lost its early hopefulness in regard to eventual abolition. Instead, antislavery spokesmen
turned more and more to the illiberal panacea of colonizing
freed Negroes in Africa; and in the South emancipation was
considered only in connection with colonization. Meanwhile, discrimination in the North against the free Negro
increased, with separate churches being established and difficulties placed in the way of Negro education. Hostility to
Negro education reached a climax in the North in the famous case of Prudence Crandall's school for Negro children
in Canterbury, Connecticut. Established in 1831, the school
was broken up three years later after much litigation against
and persecution of the owner.[5]

The popularity of the colonization movement, and the
corresponding loss of interest in educating or Christianizing
the Negro, reflected a decline in idealism and liberalism.
The argument that slavery was a step on the ladder from
barbarism to freedom had little force if the Negro was not to
receive any of the benefits of civilization. Also the older faith
of the Enlightenment in the natural rights of man, and in
the possibility of progress and reform through changes in the
environment, was discarded by a policy that discouraged
education and self-improvement. Most important of all, the
espousal of colonization in place of education for the Negro
was an admission of failure on the part of free society. It indicated a belief that younger Negroes could not be educated
and brought to a position of equality with the white population.

The North, as we have seen, was by no means exempt from
taking an increasingly illiberal attitude toward the Negro.
There, as well as in the South, people shared in the conserva-

tive reaction from the ideals of the Enlightenment, of which a changed sentiment about slavery was part. The diversity of feeling between the two sections over the question of slavery seemed consequently to rest more on economic than on intellectual or humanitarian differences. In any case, the sectional clash did not reach serious proportions until economic rivalry for the West began to drive a strong wedge between the states to the north and those to the south of the Mason-Dixon line. Even then it was not so much the profitableness of slavery in the South, in contrast to its economic extinction in the North, as it was the fact that the profits of slavery were coming to depend on the expansion of the institution westward. Slavery confined to the states of the Old South could be treated as a local institution that would in time die out. Slavery carried into the newer states of the West, and united with an aggressive foreign policy, raised the specter of a slave imperialism in place of the older agricultural imperialism of the Jeffersonians. Furthermore, the slave plantations in the Southwest had few of the redeeming, civilizing features of the easygoing Virginia estates. As the plantation moved west, aristocracy often yielded to plutocracy, while liberalism succumbed to harsh intolerance.

Meanwhile, it was becoming apparent that no amount of state rights talk in the South could obscure the fact that slavery, when carried into the Federal territories of the West, was a national problem of mounting seriousness. The national issue came to the forefront in 1819 when Missouri, the first organized territory beyond the Mississippi, applied for admission into the Union as a slave state. An amendment to the enabling act, permitting statehood only if slavery were prohibited, touched off a debate in Congress and the nation, which Thomas Jefferson described as sounding "like a firebell in the night." [6] His alarm seemed not without reason as bitter northern attacks were answered by a no less vehement southern defense of the peculiar institution. As the struggle over Missouri turned liberal aristocrats, already skeptical over emancipation, into ardent defenders of slavery, Jefferson's criticisms of the institution were no longer acceptable in the South. Nathaniel Macon, John Taylor, and John Randolph were among the older disciples of Jefferson who now justified slavery in terms of the needs of their section. Going still further in his defense of slavery, Thomas Cooper, a protégé of Jefferson's, and a stanch radical in his youth, frankly repudiated the whole philosophy of natural rights and the equality of man, becoming "among the first of the former followers of the great Virginia democrat publicly to deny the validity of the social doctrines of the Declaration of Independence." [7]

For the South as a whole, Jefferson's death in 1826 symbolized the passing of the older liberal aristocracy. The new generation of southern statesmen, which achieved political leadership by the second quarter of the nineteenth century, was frankly conservative and aggressively proslavery. It repudiated much of the Jeffersonian heritage and attacked the philosophy of the Declaration of Independence with its assertion of the equality and natural rights of man. Even Jacksonian democracy, which might have broadened the base of the older Jeffersonian variety of aristocratic liberalism, served only to popularize and extend the illiberal side of southern thinking, helping to rally nonslaveholders as well as planters to the defense of white society.

In theory, the triumph of Andrew Jackson in 1828, with the encouragement that it offered to the movement for greater political and economic democracy, seemed to threaten the position of the plantation aristocracy. But any such threat was easily countered after 1830 by the plea of the need of southern unity to meet the attacks of northern abolitionists. Thus the plain people of the South, instead of

serving as a force for southern democracy and a greater liberalism on the slavery question, were coerced into support
of the peculiar institution. However much he may have suffered from the economic competition of slave labor, the
common man was nevertheless persuaded to join in a defense
of the system, accepting the romantic picture of life and
labor in the Old South that was fostered by the large slaveholders. Indeed, in this process of tightening southern unity,
the nonslaveholding masses were often less tolerant of the
Negro than the upper-class slaveowners. Convinced that
slavery was necessary to preserve white supremacy, majority
opinion was swayed by emotion and propaganda and diverted into a defense of slavery. Thus Jacksonian democracy
and the repudiation of eighteenth-century liberalism
achieved a synthesis in connection with the slavery question,
and "The Jacksonian democrats made no effort to disturb
the vast complex of property rights involved in the institution of slavery." [8]

In Virginia, a celebrated instance of the defeat of the
antislavery and democratic forces occurred in the Constitutional Convention of 1829–1830. There the older eastern
aristocracy of the state was able to maintain its control
against the democratic and antislavery western counties.
Moreover, this Virginia aristocracy of 1830, retaining little
of its earlier liberalism, voted down measures for universal
white manhood suffrage, local self-government, and adequate representation of the West. The failure of the liberal
element to effect reforms was given further illustration in
1832, when the state legislature refused to approve a plan for
gradual emancipation.

The question of emancipation had already been precipitated in Virginia by the famous Nat Turner insurrection of
August 1831, in which sixty-one whites were killed and over
a hundred Negroes put to death in revenge for the slave out-

break. Thoroughly alarmed, many Virginians favored immediate emancipation and colonization as an alternative to further slave revolts, but the tidewater planters countered all such schemes with a vigorous defense of slavery. Instead of offering any compromise to modify the institution of slavery and appease the Negroes, legislatures in the South responded to the challenge of possible future uprisings by making their slave codes more severe. When Thomas R. Dew, professor of political economy at William and Mary College, promptly published his *Review of the Debates in the Virginia Legislature,* the proslavery argument was launched in earnest and the future course of the South became clear.[9]

Hitherto there had been a certain division of opinion in the South on the slavery question, with many of the back-country, nonslaveholding areas favoring some form of gradual emancipation. But now events, in the North as well as in the South, united to accomplish the final breakdown of any such liberal feeling. In the midst of the hysteria over the Turner revolt, the South took note of the rising abolitionist sentiment in the North. In January 1831, in Boston, William Lloyd Garrison had already issued the first number of his *Liberator,* with its radical manifesto of immediate and unconditional abolition. Garrison's paper soon became anathema to the South, serving as a symbol of northern radicalness on the slavery issue. And Garrison's voice, united with others, also became a clarion call for converts into the antislavery ranks.

Embittered by the evil of slavery, the abolitionists of the North proposed its immediate and absolute end, regardless of the consequences. Provoking a stronger defense of the institution by the very intensity of their attacks, the abolitionists hastened the decline of liberal and antislavery sentiment in the South. At the same time there were many persons in the North who resented the way in which the abolitionists upset the political balance between the sections. Turning to mob action, people in both the North and the South attempted to silence, and in some cases actually martyred, the more unyielding critics of slavery, thus further weakening liberalism and the rights of free speech and a free press. The abolitionists were frequently accused of inciting such mob action in order to attract sympathy for their cause. Thus they may well have contributed to the decline of a liberal climate of opinion by the very manner in which they invoked the right of freedom.

At the opposite extreme from the abolitionist view of slavery was the favorable picture of southern life drawn by proslavery spokesmen. After 1831, the romantic concept of plantation life became a stereotype generally accepted in the South, and the small minority who enjoyed its fruits was able to dominate the section's thinking. Intellectually, the isolation of the plantation and farm fastened a conservative outlook upon large parts of the South, while at the same time the growing provincialism and stagnation of much of southern life made the section as a whole extremely sensitive to hostile northern criticism. The aura of romantic nationalism and feudal chivalry was illustrated by the Southerner's protective attitude toward white women in contrast to Negro women, and by his fostering of a military cult among the youth of the region. But underlying this romantic picture were such grim realities as miscegenation, illiteracy and disfranchisement of the poor whites, and continual fear on the part of all whites of a servile insurrection. Even though the latter danger was exaggerated, revolt and rumors of revolt played an important part in the decline of any vestiges of southern liberalism on the slavery issue. And in the case of the poor whites, though there were signs of improvement in common schooling and of a greater democracy in politics by

the 1840's and 1850's, illiteracy and political disability remained powerful allies in the maintenance of upper-class
control.[10]

Despite the strong prejudices of the common man in the
South against the Negro, basically it was the dominant
planter class that enforced a conspiracy of silence in regard
to any criticism of slavery. The great Whig planters, and an
occasional cultivated Democrat like Joel Poinsett, were
therefore exceptional in their attempt to exercise a tolerant,
moderating influence on the slavery question. Aroused by
the denunciations of their institutions in the abolitionist
press, the leaders of the South countenanced the destruction
of vast quantities of antislavery literature and the passage of
legislation restricting any free discussion of the slavery issue.

In Andrew Jackson's second administration, the question
of censorship in connection with slavery reached a crisis over
the right of petition and the privilege of the mails. On both
of these questions the Jacksonians deferred to the wishes of
the South, and to the generally hostile feelings of the populace toward the abolitionist minority. Although the latter
frankly proposed to stir up agitation by deluging Congress
with petitions against slavery, and through the mailing of
antislavery tracts into the South, interference with their legal rights stirred the protests of many nonabolitionist liberals in the North. In the House of Representatives, John
Quincy Adams led an eight-year fight against the gag rule of
1836, which provided that all abolitionist petitions be laid
on the table without being read. In the case of the mails,
President Jackson approved the policy of Postmaster General Kendall in allowing southern postmasters to refuse to
deliver the hated antislavery literature. Going even further
in his effort to conciliate the South, Jackson in his message
to Congress in December 1836 advised the passage of a Fed-

eral law forbidding the circulation of "incendiary publications intended to instigate the slaves to insurrection." [11]

Jackson's evident willingness to deny the mails to abolitionists aroused criticism, and ultimately it was "a factor of some importance in building favor in the North for the abolitionist movement." [12] But that his action was not unpopular with the mass of the people at the time was suggested by the wave of mob violence that was visited upon antislavery advocates in the thirties and early forties. This reign of mob law, although characteristic of many parts of the North as well as of the South, did not, however, result in any such lasting suppression of liberty there as it did in the South.

The refusal of United States mails to abolitionist literature was paralleled by similar restrictive measures adopted by southern states. In Virginia, to meet the menace of abolitionist publications, the state legislature passed in 1836 what has been termed "the most intolerant law that was ever placed on its statute books." [13] Severe penalties were provided for any abolitionist who should come into the state and maintain "that the owners of slaves have no property in the same, or advocate or advise the abolition of slavery." Any person who should print or circulate literature to this effect would be deemed guilty of a felony, and postmasters and justices of the peace were given inquisitorial power over the mails. Other border states passed similar laws in an attempt to resist the tide of abolitionist propaganda. Only Kentucky refrained from legislation infringing freedom of speech or press, and there a substitute for legislation was found in the mob action that forced James G. Birney, Cassius M. Clay, and other antislavery editors to abandon their presses and flee the state.

Birney, after his failure to establish an abolitionist newspaper in Kentucky, moved across the Ohio to Cincinnati, where in January 1836 he founded the *Philanthropist*. Soon after the first issues began to appear, a strong local opposition developed to the continuance of his paper. Southern feeling was intense in Cincinnati, and Birney was subjected to increasing threats of violence and mob action. Finally, on July 30, 1836, the storm of disapproval broke and a mob destroyed the press on which the hated *Philanthropist* was printed. Birney was forced into hiding, while the populace vented its wrath in raiding the Negro section of the city. Public reaction to the events in Cincinnati varied. The South saw no issue involving freedom of the press, and there was also considerable sentiment in the North for the passage of state legislation to curb the freedom of the abolitionists. But in the midst of the controversy inspired by Birney there occurred the most significant of all the cases involving freedom of the antislavery press.

On November 5, 1837, Elijah Lovejoy was killed by a mob while protecting the press and shop of his newspaper in Alton, Illinois. Lovejoy, a graduate of Princeton Theological Seminary, had been forced to leave St. Louis, Missouri, because of the increasing aggressiveness with which he maintained both his antislavery opinions and the principle of a free press. Transferring his paper to Alton, he suffered the destruction of three presses before his death defending the fourth. The tragedy at Alton stirred the feelings of the North, inspiring countless sermons, editorials, and protest meetings. In contrast to the growing censorship practiced in the South, abolitionism and freedom of the press now tended to merge in the North into a single cause. "The long-continued argument of the abolitionists that slavery would either engulf liberty, or freedom snuff out slavery, was beginning to bear fruit. To many who had condemned the abolitionists as radical, they were now not merely agitators for black freedom, but defenders of traditional American rights." [14]

The threat to the freedom of the northern antislavery press, beginning with the destruction of Birney's newspaper at Cincinnati and culminating in the action of the mob at Alton, was relatively short-lived, but it was extremely important and long-lasting in its effects upon the abolition movement and northern opinion. As Russell Nye has pointed out in his study of civil liberties and the slavery controversy, the death of Lovejoy and its repercussions gave the abolitionists "the opportunity of reaching, without fear of reprisal, a wider audience than before, plus the added protection of the right to cry 'martyr' if expression or circulation were stopped or hindered." Although the abolitionists remained in the minority in the North down to the outbreak of the Civil War, after 1840 opinion shifted in their direction, and they were no longer subjected to threats of mob violence or denied the right of free speech.[15]

In the South the suppression of any semblance of free discussion of slavery in the pages of the press after the middle of the 1830's was paralleled by the same denial of free thought in other aspects of intellectual life. Although the section boasted that its institutions of higher learning were better supported and attended than those of the North, there was little academic freedom on any phase of the slavery issue. The dismissal of professors suspected of antislavery views and the general spirit of intolerance that prevailed could not help but weaken southern colleges and universities. Northern teachers, upon whom the South was heavily dependent, kept silent or were forced to leave their positions. At the same time the South, with some success by the 1850's, endeavored to keep its youths from attending northern colleges and also began to boycott textbooks written by Yankees. In religious life, as in education, an extreme orthodoxy was enforced. The liberal views and outright skepticism of the Jeffersonian period were succeeded by a general conservatism among the churches. Thus the liberal Unitarians were reduced to three congregations in all of the South, and even so mildly liberal a group as the Episcopal Church lost favor and had only sixty thousand members on the eve of the Civil War. By the middle of the 1840's the dominant churches in the South — the Methodist, Baptist, and Presbyterian — had all separated from their northern brethren, largely because of a divergence of views on the compatibility of slavery with Christian teachings.

Along with orthodoxy in church and school went a general intellectual conservatism that struck down any hint of radicalism. In contrast to the wave of reform, and the various fads and fancies that captured the imagination of liberal opinion in the North, the South set its face not only against most of the popular reform schemes of the era but also against the concept of change in any way. Progress was interpreted along strictly conservative lines, and reform was equated with revolution.

Under the leadership of John C. Calhoun, the statesmen and intellectuals of the South tried to work out an exposition of liberalism in terms of the defense of slavery. In its espousal of state rights, free trade, and an agricultural type of society, the proslavery argument, it was true, adhered to many of the basic tenets of Jeffersonian liberalism. But southern liberalism as a theory could not be squared with the practice of slavery, and by the time of Jefferson's death, in 1826, the South was turning against the basic principles of the natural rights philosophy and its corollaries of liberty and equality. In the next decade the South stood ready to accept Calhoun's argument that slavery was "a good — a positive good . . . the most safe and stable basis for free institutions in the world." In similar fashion, Calhoun's friend Senator James H. Hammond of South Carolina maintained that slavery was the "corner-stone" of any good republican edifice. "In all social systems," he told his colleagues in Congress, "there must be a class to do the menial duties, to perform the drudgery of life." Such a class constituted "the very mud-sill of society. . . . Fortunately for the South," he observed, "she has found a race adapted to that purpose to her hand . . ." [16]

In the 1850's two of the first treatises on sociology published in the United States, each written by a Southerner, defended the slavery system and contrasted it favorably with a free society. George Fitzhugh, in his *Sociology for the South, or the Failure of Free Society,* argued that personal liberty and freedom were synonymous with barbarism. A free society was impractical because of the threat of a labor surplus and of revolution. In a later work, entitled *Cannibals All! or, Slaves Without Masters,* Fitzhugh maintained that democracy and liberty were alike antagonistic to civilization. Liberty encouraged the weak to rise up and overthrow the strong, while democracy offered equality to all. Denouncing what he termed the laissez-faire, white-slave society of the North and of England, Fitzhugh called upon the South to preserve Negro slavery and government based on force. In a work similar to Fitzhugh's, Henry Hughes announced his intention of expressing some of the views of the southern people on slavery. Conceiving of perfection in terms of an authoritarian, socialist order, Hughes criticized the confusion inherent in a free society. In contrast, he depicted a future utopia for the South under a system that he called, not slavery but "warranteeism with the ethnical qualification." [17]

But it was Calhoun, to a greater extent than any other antebellum statesman or thinker, who attempted to reconcile a liberal philosophy with the defense of slavery. A realist in his views on politics and economics, Calhoun had no patience with the classic liberalism of Jefferson or the romantic liberalism exemplified in the revolutions of 1848 in Central

Europe. Essentially he tried to erect a structure that would safeguard the slave aristocracy of the South and ensure its voice within the Federal government. Evolving his doctrine of the concurrent majority, a scheme by which controversial measures would have to receive a geographical as well as a numerical majority before becoming law, Calhoun came to grips with the problem of minority rights and majority rule.

There is a wide gap between the evaluation of Calhoun as "the Marx of the Master Class" and the judgment that Thoreau and Calhoun were the two outstanding defenders of the free individual against the all-pervasive interests of the national state. Despite his repudiation of the Jeffersonian heritage and his ardent defense of the interests of the slav-ocracy, Calhoun in contrast to most of his contemporaries sensed the danger to liberalism inherent in the power of the Jacksonian majority, and in the nationalizing tendency of manifest destiny. Bold and imaginative though he was in his solution of the concurrent majority, Calhoun's flaw lay in his associating his principle of minority rights with the illiberal cause of slavery.[18]

The conservatism of the South was in many ways a natural phenomenon in a people intent on the preservation of their institutions and way of life against what they regarded as out-side criticism and attack. But defense alone was unsatisfac-tory. As Calhoun and the other southern leaders realized, the South could maintain its slave system only if it was al-lowed to grow. To deny the positive good, and need for ex-pansion, of slavery was to acquiesce in its eventual dissolu-tion by gradual emancipation.[19] Ultimately, therefore, the existence of slavery within the framework of a liberal society was impossible. Calhoun and the later generation of south-ern leaders accordingly were forced to abandon, one by one, the postulates of an earlier southern liberalism, embracing in their place a militant and aggressive proslavery philosophy.

Tragic enough for the South, slavery worked a further tragedy in that the North also was not immune to its illiberal influences. The evils of slavery were a part of the institution and not any special attribute of the southern people. In the North slavery was more vulnerable to attack, but there as well as in the South the Negro was subject to exploitation. In the treatment of the free Negro, for example, the harsh restrictions imposed by the South after 1830 were almost being matched in some parts of the North by the 1850's. Universally discriminated against, and regarded as inferior beings, the free Negroes were allowed to vote only in Massachusetts, Maine, and New Hampshire, while Illinois and Iowa forbade even their entry into the state. In the words of Allan Nevins, "Nothing better illustrated the impasse reached by the country than the harsh and increasingly harsher lot of the free Negro; a lot darkest in the South, but sad enough throughout the North." [20]

Other minority groups in the North also suffered the attacks of bigotry and occasional mob violence because they did not express or accept the majority point of view — the waves of nativist uprising against immigrants and Catholics being conspicuous instances of such mass prejudice. But, except in the case of the Negro, and especially the Negro slave, there was little in the way of official, legal discrimination in the United States. Inequality, after all, as a contemporary student of free institutions sagely observed in 1848, was no reason for disbelieving in "the maxim that all men are equal."

First. Because to teach and to act upon it is the only way of attaining equality, to the extent to which it is actually attained.

Second. Because it is not in the power of government to make anything like an accurate discrimination between the inequalities of different men.[21]

By the 1850's, despite its refusal to accord equality to the Negro, the North was becoming alive to the slavery issue. The passage of the Compromise of 1850, with its hated provision of a stronger Fugitive Slave Law, made converts to the abolitionist cause. The denial of a jury trial to the alleged fugitive slave obviously weighted the scales of justice against him. And in other ways as well, the law aroused the antislavery feelings of the North and touched the consciences of men who had hitherto dismissed the abolitionists as visionary radicals. The mob violence in the North that had once been directed against this unpopular minority now turned its power to freeing fugitive slaves from the reaches of the law. Emerson, the serene philosopher, who had been reluctant to give himself over wholly to any reform movement, enlisted in the antislavery crusade along with such Massachusetts extremists as Theodore Parker and Thomas Wentworth Higginson. And in 1859, Emerson's transcendental partner, Henry Thoreau, became the first public defender of John Brown following his raid on Harpers Ferry.

Although the abolitionist and antislavery forces of the North were able to relate in dramatic fashion the cause of freedom for the Negro to the entire cause of freedom and of civil liberty, the North too shared in the guilt of what had become a national problem. The liberalism of the North on the slavery question first became suspect when it mobbed the abolitionists, thereby helping to provoke further radicalism and a weakening of toleration and moderate measures. And, secondly, the sincerity of the North could legitimately be called into question when it attacked slavery in the South while it discriminated against the free Negro in the North.

In their all-important goal the abolitionists were of course to be successful, though only after a tremendous civil struggle. Always a small minority until the final freeing of the Negroes in the course of the Civil War, the abolitionists by the close of the 1850's had nevertheless won the northern population to an acceptance of the wrong of slavery. Although the primary purpose of the North in the secession crisis of 1861 was to preserve the Union on terms advantageous to free society, the antislavery cause was a powerful moral bulwark to the northern cause throughout the four long years of bitter fighting. And yet, in almost all other respects, the Civil War was to occasion a setback for traditional liberal values.

8

An American Tragedy

THE ROAR of the guns opening fire on Fort Sumter in the early morning hours of April 12, 1861, drowned out the voices of conciliation and moderation in the United States. The long and bitter sectional struggle between North and South had finally reached the point of violence, and the American experiment in united self-government was threatened with dissolution. Also challenged by the prospect of war were many of the values and ideals associated with traditional liberalism in the United States. It is true that any war, even one fought over some great moral principle, involves the use of methods essentially illiberal; for the very substance of liberalism — its emphasis on reason, on toleration and respect for individual and minority rights, and on progress by evolution instead of revolution — is bound to suffer in wartime. But this incompatibility of war and liberalism becomes even more true in the case of a vast internal conflict such as the American Civil War. All this, obvious enough in retrospect, was no answer to the problems for which the pre-Civil War generation vainly sought a solution.

Perhaps it was too much to expect that statesmanship could prevent a call to arms in a nation so badly torn and divided. Each succeeding event of the fifties had served only to strengthen the hand of the radicals on both sides of the Mason-Dixon line. Cultural and economic cleavages were paralleled by the breakup of the two national parties — first the Whigs and then, in 1860, the Democrats. Meanwhile, in the South the search for some drastic solution was encouraged by a sense of impending defeat in a lost cause. Southern extremists therefore were able to argue the advantages of attempting secession and southern patriots could feel that in the struggle to achieve a more glorious southern nationalism they were fighting for liberty and independence. The southern radicals, combining in a curious way the defeatism of the older state rights argument with the new vision of an expanding southern nation, were thus able to prevail against the moderate and liberal opinion which stood out against withdrawal from the Union.

As a section the South was a minority within the United States. In its adherence to Negro slavery it ran counter to the weight of enlightened world opinion, while its plantation economy was in conflict with the realities of an expanding northern industrialism. Unless the South could somehow preserve its isolated agrarian economy and outmoded social institution, its cause was indeed doomed. But the minority position of the South, so clearly apparent to us today, was only beginning to be perceived by the 1850's. The fruits of manifest destiny, exemplified in the territories gained from the Mexican War, were less bountiful than the South had expected. Meanwhile, California had come into the Union as a free state and, despite the rearguard action fought by the South in Kansas, it seemed probable that virtually all of the national domain would become free territory in which slavery would be excluded by climate and geography, if not by statute. At the same time the new railroad trunk lines, constantly being pushed to the west, were tying the Upper Mississippi Valley securely to the North. Moreover, in 1850, for the first time, the value of manufactured goods had exceeded the output of agriculture. This triumph of northern industrialism, despite all the cries of "Cotton Is King," meant that the political and economic demands of the North, as well as of the West, would have to be given greater recognition than they had hitherto received from the pro-southern Democratic administrations of Presidents Pierce and Buchanan.

While the South was embracing secession as a desperate means of overcoming its minority status, and the probable ensuing demise of the slavery system, the North was showing signs of a growing and restive self-confidence. Although the Republican party avoided the extremism of the abolitionists on the slavery issue, its stand against the further extension of slavery in the territories admitted of no real compromise or reconciliation with the South. In the election campaign of 1860, the Republican party under Lincoln made antislavery views, for the first time in American history, both respectable and popular. Moreover, the fact that the now victorious Republicans would hold national power and therefore be in a position to satisfy northern desires in economic legislation as well as in the matter of the extension of slavery indicated a greater potential threat to the South than all the agitation of a generation of abolitionists.

Although Lincoln's election thus signified the eventual triumph of the northern point of view in regard to slavery, a protective tariff, homestead legislation, and other measures, northern opinion was by no means united in favor of a policy entailing the coercion of the seceding states of the lower South. Until Sumter, compromise and peace sentiment prevailed throughout the North, and Lincoln in his first inaugural address was careful to avoid giving offense to the southern people. In general, however, though there was a strong desire in the North and in the border states for some peaceful solution to the problems of secession and the extension of slavery, neither the Republican party nor the secessionists were willing to retreat or compromise on these issues. This essentially radical inflexibility on both sides encouraged the outbreak of hostilities, which came with the firing on Fort Sumter. While the states of the upper South now joined the Confederacy, the northern states collected their resources and prepared to undertake the grave task of preserving the Union.

Among the ironies of the struggle to maintain the American Union was the fact that nothing seemed to effect so great a transformation in the fundamental character of that Union as did the Civil War. The question arises, of course, as to what extent the Civil War should be interpreted as the fundamental cause of the changes that came over American life during the war and postwar periods. The Beards, for example, in their interpretation of the war as a "Second American Revolution," have been accused of attributing too much to the war's influence. Seeing in such a thesis a nostalgic preference for the agrarian ways of antebellum society, in contrast to the new postwar industrialism, some critics have argued that the war only accelerated a tendency already well marked. The growing industrialization of the United States, they point out, was, after all, irrevocable. But in either event, whether it was a fundamental cause or only an acceleration of the inevitable, the Civil War nevertheless played a vital role in the course of American liberalism.

In a broad sense, the Civil War was an expression of a decline in liberalism that was already taking place to the accompaniment of the spread of slavery, the expansion of the country westward, and the rise of the common man. The war thus was merely continuing and bringing to fruition trends in being since 1830. Yet it was also true that it was the war primarily that shattered all hope of peaceful change — "the first major interruption in the process of material and social reconstruction with which the Americans had been occupied since the founding of the first colonies." [1] The reform movements of the era from Jackson to Lincoln and the literary activity of the late 1840's and early 1850's were equally cut off by the war and the concentration on the slavery issue that had preceded hostilities. Thus, before the Civil War resulted in the liberation of a single slave it first dealt a powerful blow to many of the prized attributes of liberalism in the United States.

The subordination of virtually all reform efforts and liberal endeavors to the one great cause of the eradication of the slavery evil created an uneasy feeling among many of the idealistic crusaders of the era. Pacifists, in particular, were upset by the prospect of actual warfare between the states. More than any other single group of liberals, the adherents of the peace movement were faced by a conflict of loyalties between their abolitionism and patriotism and their rejection of the means of war. United States Senator Charles Sumner of Massachusetts, who had spoken out against the Mexican War in vigorous fashion, and who had belatedly worked for peace and reconciliation in the last days before the attack on Fort Sumter, voiced the doubts of many of those who hated both war and slavery. In an interesting letter to Richard Cobden, the English liberal and pacifist, Sumner tried to justify his course of action. Agreeing with Cobden that he would never "have counseled a war for emancipation," Sumner argued that he could nevertheless "not surrender to slavery." The chance of peaceful secession had been lost, and now Sumner felt that the North had no choice but to prosecute the war. "This is sad enough to me!" he wrote.

It costs me a pang to give up early visions, and to see my country filled with armies, while the military spirit prevails everywhere. Everywhere soldiers come forward for offices of all kinds, from the presidency to the post of constable; and this will be the case from this time during my life.[2]

Wendell Phillips, the stanch abolitionist orator and agitator, was assailed by similar doubts and misgivings. Originally in favor of letting the South depart in peace, he, however, soon came to accept the war as necessary.

The war is better than the past, but there is not an element of good in it. I mean, there is nothing in it which we might not have gotten better, fuller, and more perfectly in other ways. . . .

Neither will I remind you that, when we go out of this war, we go out with an immense disbanded army, an intense military spirit embodied in two thirds of a million of soldiers, the fruitful, the inevitable source of fresh debts and new wars.[3]

Phillips, alarmed over Lincoln's suspension of the writ of habeas corpus, warned his lecture audience that "We live to-day, every one of us, under martial law." Though he preferred what he called the despotism of Washington to that of Richmond, he concluded sadly that the United States was "tending toward that strong government which frightened Jefferson; toward that unlimited debt, that endless army." Phillips's typically abolitionist solution for these problems was for the North to free the slaves, organize them to aid the Union, and thus bring about a speedy conclusion to the war.[4]

Although a minority of the believers in peace held fast to its pacifism, for most the prospect that the Civil War might fulfill their long-felt hopes for the abolition of slavery proved too strong to resist. Also carried away by the war spirit was a majority of the literary and professional people of the country. Seeing in the war a great moral crusade to preserve the Union and free the slaves, quiet intellectuals, liberal philosophers, and leading churchmen became suddenly bellicose. The clergy and the churches with few exceptions saw the war, once it had begun, as a holy crusade against the

Southland. "Peace will do for angels," declared the Reverend Horace Bushnell, "but war is God's ordinance for sinners." [5] Even those with an ingrained dislike of the war and its militarizing effects could not escape the new martial air. Nathaniel Hawthorne, describing a visit to wartime Washington, complained bitterly of the ever-present numbers of soldiers and the prospect that "One bullet-headed general will succeed another in the Presidential chair . . ." But Hawthorne also wrote that the atmosphere of the camp and the smoke of the battlefield were morally invigorating, causing the more enervating effects of civilization to vanish away.[6]

Much of the spirit of new nationalism generated in the North by the great civil struggle between the states was celebrated in poetry and song. Emerson, Lowell, Whitman, and others caught the finer side of the war and helped perpetuate its memory in epic terms. Whitman, in particular, discouraged by the political and economic temper of the fifties, saw in the Civil War a great surge of idealistic nationalism. Deeply concerned over the suffering of his fellow men in wartime, Whitman was nevertheless confident that the fighting would be a step toward the achievement of a more thorough popular democracy. In general, it is this heroic picture of the Civil War that has come down in history, but there was also a side of the war that can be painted in darker hues. Along with the terrible destruction of life and property suffered in four long years of fighting went tremendous changes in American life and thought, especially a decline in liberalism on all questions save that of slavery. As every cause yielded to the demands of the war and the drive for victory, the way was opened for the loss of civil liberties in wartime and for the conservative reaction of the postwar years.

Thus "the fierce storm of war" was to pose a dilemma for many of the liberal idealists who responded to "the battle cry of freedom." Emerson, the calm transcendental philosopher of the prewar years, was a conspicuous example of their plight. Long a man of peace who had hoped that war would someday be abolished, Emerson, however, readily joined his fellow citizens in the struggle to preserve the Union and free the slaves. Occasionally troubled by some of the madness of the war years, Emerson, like Whitman, nevertheless hoped and believed that the conflict would free the nation from an excessive reliance on a crude materialism and infuse it with a new ethical and idealistic purpose. Giving patriotic addresses across the country, he won new respect and social prestige during the war, but he also yielded his real occupation as a thinker. "He had had to retreat too far from his prized position as a philosophical observer." At the end of the war, therefore, he found it hard to get the poison of hate out of his system. In the words of his most scholarly biographer, "His thinking did not thrive so well as before. He no longer enjoyed a sphere of almost limitless intellectual liberty. For him the idea of liberty had become too much constricted in the symbol of the manumitted slave. It was hard even for so puissant a liberal as Emerson to free himself from the narrowing boundaries of his postwar world." [7]

It was unfortunate that the Civil War, in which both sides avowed that they were fighting for freedom and democracy, should have resulted in such widespread violation of fundamental civil liberties. Partly this was a result of the bitterness of a conflict in which families were divided and in which brother fought brother. But, even more, it was due to the fact that the Civil War was the first modern total war — a conflict fought to the point of exhaustion which embraces most of the energies of the participants. Thus, although neither Lincoln nor Jefferson Davis aspired to become a dictator in the twentieth-century sense of the term, before the close of their long struggle the governments of both the

North and the South verged closely upon military despot-isms.

At the outset of the Civil War the United States, despite a degree of martial ardor displayed on earlier occasions in its history, was hardly a militarist nation. Yet, in the course of the four years of grim fighting the ideal of a liberal and anti-militarist democracy was often undermined. The Anglo-Saxon heritage, which emphasized the rule of law and held the military in strict subserviency to the civil power, was challenged by the argument that the Constitution no longer operated and that "military necessity knows no law." Also posing a threat to liberalism was Lincoln's assumption that the war was a rebellion that should be put down by the ex-clusive authority of the President. Accordingly, without summoning Congress into special session, he issued an ex-ecutive proclamation calling for volunteers and, in violation of the Constitution, directed an increase in the size of the regular army.

Faced with a tremendous civil upheaval, the Lincoln administration was from the first embarrassed and harassed by the large number of active and vocal proponents of the cause of the Confederacy, as well as by a sizable loyal opposi-tion that questioned the efficacy of various Republican war measures. In theory, the war might have been expected to lead to an attempt at prosecuting certain individuals for treason, but actually little use was made of the treason clause of the Constitution. Instead, the Republican party leaders, anxious to curb dissenting opinion as well as outright dis-loyalty, went beyond the lawful prosecution in the courts of actual cases of treasonable activities. Through a policy of arbitrary arrests made possible by Lincoln's suspension of the writ of habeas corpus, persons were seized and confined on the suspicion of disloyalty or of sympathy with the south-ern cause. Thus, in the course of the Civil War, a total of thirteen thousand civilians was estimated to have been held as political prisoners, often without any sort of trial or after only cursory hearings before a military tribunal.[8]

In his exercise of extraordinary war powers Lincoln was for the most part modest and circumspect, but the policy of arbitrary military arrest was nevertheless allowed to continue throughout the war. Among the many caught in the administration dragnet, the best known was the antiwar Democrat Clement L. Vallandigham. Labeled a Copperhead, Vallandigham spoke out vigorously in denunciation of the military dictatorship of Lincoln, combining his attacks with a plea for a "VIGOROUS PROSECUTION OF PEACE FOR THE UNION." [9] During the war, the effort of Vallandigham and others to secure Supreme Court protection and redress from the decisions of the military commissions was unsuccessful. But in 1866, after the war was over, the Supreme Court, in the somewhat similar Milligan case, passed upon the power of military commissions to try civilians in areas, not in the immediate vicinity of the war, where the civil courts were still functioning. In its decision the Court declared that "Martial rule can never exist where the courts are open and in the proper and unobstructed exercise of their jurisdiction." Nor could martial law be invoked in the case of threatened invasion, but "The necessity must be actual and present; the invasion real, such as effectually closes the courts and deposes the civil administration." [10]

The arbitrary arrest and imprisonment of civilians by the military and executive departments of the government was the chief violation of civil liberties during the Civil War, but the rights of individuals were also invaded in other ways. In the South, the Northern Confiscation Acts resulted in the seizure of private property on the ground that it was being used to aid the cause of the Confederacy. Thus, for the first time in modern history, war was officially waged against individual citizens, an illiberal tactic destined to become a commonplace of total warfare. In the matter of a free press there was some suppression of newspapers and considerable censorship of individual correspondents by denying them the use of telegraph lines controlled by the military. The latter exercise of governmental authority was justified by the war power, but the assault on antiadministration newspapers bore the mark of political reprisal and oppression. Meanwhile, the schools also were invaded by wartime hysteria, and there were instances of teachers dismissed or being forced to resign for alleged disloyalty or because of a lack of what was deemed a proper enthusiasm for the northern cause.[11]

Exceeding all other measures in its effect on the individual citizen was military conscription, put into practice on a large scale for the first time in American history during the Civil War. Although defended as a just and necessary exercise of the war power, the imposition of compulsory military service, first by the South and later by the North, was much assailed as infringing upon the liberties of the individual. In the Confederacy, Vice-President Alexander H. Stephens, a liberal of the state rights school, was a particularly bitter opponent of conscription. Stephens never accepted the argument that a conscription law was necessary to save the South nor changed his conviction that it had any other purpose than to give the government greater control over its own citizens. If the measure was actually imperative, then Stephens believed that the true goal of the war for the South was lost and the whole struggle would be better given up, because conscripts "never have been, and never will be the means of establishing Free Institutions or maintaining them." [12]

In the North, the draft laws served the same nationalistic purpose of transferring control over recruiting from the states to the Federal government. Although only a limited success from the military standpoint, the Conscription Acts of the North — providing the first systematic, long-term military draft in American history — were significant in encouraging the idea that the rights of the individual should be subordinated to the needs of the state. Conscription also furnished a basis for further criticism of the Lincoln administration and its conduct of the war. In contrast to the arbitrary arrests or the censorship and suppression of news, the draft law affected virtually every American household. Going far beyond the degree of compulsion exacted in theory by the state militia laws, the national conscription act was without precedent in the annals of either the United States or Great Britain. James Ford Rhodes, in his account of the widespread Civil War draft opposition, expressed doubt that so untraditional a course enjoyed the support of American public opinion. Horace Greeley, the famous editor of the New York *Tribune,* complained to Secretary of War Stanton:

It is folly to close our eyes to the signs of the times. The people have been educated to the idea of individual sovereignty, & the principle of conscription is repugnant to their feelings and cannot be carried out except at great peril to the free States. . . .

Drafting is an anomaly in a free State; it oppresses the masses. Like imprisonment for debt . . . it must and will be reformed out of our systems of political economy.[18]

Conscription and the violation of civil liberties were only two of the more obvious instances in which traditional liberalism yielded to the wartime forces of nationalism and militarism. In a variety of other and lesser ways, the war also threatened the spirit of liberalism. Although the governments attempted little in the way of direct censorship or propaganda, such agencies as the Loyal Publication Societies and the Union Leagues stirred popular enthusiasm for the cause of the Union. A whole generation grew up to the sound of marching feet and was educated in an atmosphere of heightened nationalism. Military education flourished for the first time outside the South, and the Morrill Act, passed in the heat of war, laid the basis for Federal support of such training in the land-grant colleges. Finally, there was the tremendous impact that the thousands of officers and men who had served in the war would exert upon peacetime society in the years to come. Although not militaristic in a European sense, the Civil War veteran had to some extent lost his individuality and become institutionalized. The carry-over of the war experience was also illustrated by the founding of the Grand Army of the Republic. Stimulated by this pressure group, which they had helped to establish, a host of ambitious Republican politicians would be able to refight the Civil War in their election campaigns.

In economic matters the war also occasioned a tremendous expansion of the role of the Federal government. Along with the obvious part played by official Washington in contracting for the purchase of army supplies there was the important financial legislation passed by the new Republican administration. In place of the low duties current in the era from Jackson to Lincoln, the Republican Congress returned to the Whig theory of a protective tariff for American manufacturers. At the same time the business and agricultural interests of the West were rewarded for their support of the party by the passage of a homestead law, and by the granting of Federal lands and funds for railroad building. Labor also felt the force of government intervention as a result of official encouragement of the wave of immigration that poured into the United States to fill wartime jobs and join in the westward movement. Even more alarming to American workers

was the use of the Civil War army to suppress labor disturbances.[14] Finally, the position of the Federal government as
against the individual or the separate states was strengthened
by such wartime legislation as the National Bank Act, an
unprecedented income tax, and a variety of excise taxes
which were the equivalent almost of a univeral sales tax.

The requirements of the armies and Republican policies
favorable to business combined to make the war years great
in economic progress and consolidation. This was particularly true of the railroads, which were able to integrate
smaller systems into the long trunk lines extending west.
But other industries also enjoyed a boom, with new mass
production techniques and processes being developed to
meet inflated wartime needs. Later, in the postwar period, it
would be forgotten that many of the national problems associated with the rise of big business and monopoly had had
their origins in this earlier era of expansion and consolidation during the Civil War.

A growing nationalism and centralization, accompanied
by a diminishing liberalism and individualism, was one of
the important results of the Civil War. It was not surprising,
however, that such a tremendous struggle should have a
revolutionary impact upon American life. In the South,
even more than the North, the war had wrought an upheaval.
There the abolition of slavery and the destruction of the
social system and economy of the antebellum period were
prime examples of the war's more direct effects. In the
North, on the other hand, people could rejoice that the
major ends of the war had been served, even if at a heavy
cost and at the expense of many of the values of traditional
liberalism. In the words of a later historian:

The heirs of the Jeffersonian tradition and the surviving followers of Jackson were compelled to work for the victory of the

North in order that slavery might be abolished; yet in the final outcome that victory meant the triumph of Hamiltonian economics and, in large measure, the destruction of the agrarian way of life upon which American democracy had been founded.[15]

Vernon L. Parrington in his interpretation of the war was even more gloomy. Along with the abolition of slavery in the lost cause of the South went the defeat of "the old ideal of decentralized democracies, of individual liberty; and with the overthrow of the traditional principles in their last refuge, the nation hurried along the path of an unquestioning and uncritical consolidation, that was to throw the coercive powers of a centralizing state into the hands of the new industrialism." [16]

Still celebrated as the great American epic, with a vast literature devoted to portraying its more heroic aspects, the Civil War is also the supreme American tragedy. This was obviously so for the South. To the failure of its bid for independence were added all the economic losses and psychological indignities that are the customary but nonetheless bitter fruits of military defeat. However, the downfall of the lost cause was not the real tragedy of the Civil War, for the South in its perfervid defense of slavery had long since ceased to be the champion of liberalism. The essential tragedy of the Civil War was rather the failure of free society in the North to follow up the liberal ends implied by its wartime goals of the preservation of the Union and the abolition of slavery. In the aftermath of the fighting, both of these goals were diverted to crasser purposes. Thus, the saving of the Union made possible a degree of integral nationalism inconceivable in the older federalized United States. And this new nationalism, involving a frank repudiation of a former American liberalism, was to become synonymous with the crude materialism and selfish exploitation of the postwar Gilded Age.

9

New Nationalism and New South

WITH THE close of the Civil War, North and South alike turned to the necessary task of reconstruction. In both a material and a spiritual sense the nation had to be reconstituted. Unfortunately, the statesmen and leaders of the North, who had the major political responsibility of reconstruction, felt called upon to adopt a vindictive program that was hardly in keeping with Lincoln's injunction of "malice toward none; with charity for all."

Just as the opening of the war had silenced those who continued to urge moderation and compromise, so the four long years of hard fighting made difficult a return to a policy of toleration and reconciliation. Lincoln's own reported advice in his last cabinet meeting — "We must extinguish our resentment if we expect harmony and union — "[1] was ignored as the Radical Republicans of the North proceeded with their calculated program for the subjugation of the South. In this beleaguered land, now governed as a conquered province, there was small hope that a long-discarded, native liberalism could be revived. The extremist course of the Civil War appeared to have achieved its logical reward, but the results were hardly those envisaged by either the secessionists of the South or the abolitionists of the North.

The fate of the abolitionists' great accomplishment in helping to end slavery provides an instructive example of the way in which a noble cause can be subjected to distortion and decline. As Vernon L. Parrington pointed out, the abolitionists were the type of militant and single-minded reformers who, by "marshaling the discontent of their generation, sometimes do succeed in removing mountains; but unfortunately they leave a great scar, and the débris litters the whole countryside. Other mountains may even arise from the waste of the leveling." Thus, after emancipation came the Fourteenth Amendment, opening the way for the triumph of nationalism and big business under the gospel of the due process clause. The Civil War was succeeded by the Gilded Age, and the postwar era presently took on the nature of a great political barbecue, with Republicans waving the bloody shirt and bestowing favors on the business community. Parrington, with these results in mind, was moved to the cynical comment:

The devil understands the ways of the world too well to become discouraged at a temporary set-back, for if righteousness succeed in breaking the bonds that bind a generation, he knows that the market place carries an ample stock of new cords to replace those that are broken.[2]

The emancipation of the Negro, promulgated originally as a means of helping to win the war, continued to serve ulterior ends during the years of peace. The question, of course, no longer involved slavery. As James Russell Lowell explained in 1865, "We take it for granted at the outset, that the mind of the country is made up as to making no terms with slavery in any way, large or limited, open or covert." But, he added, if the Negro received his freedom, "Must we not make them voters also, that they may have the power of self protection . . . ?"[3] Lowell and many others in the North believed that the Negro must have the vote if he was to secure an education plus simple economic and social justice. Admittedly, the mass of Negro freedmen were not ready for the suffrage, but in a democracy an excluded class without political rights became a discontented element subject to exploitation and dangerous to the community. This dilemma had been pointed out very clearly more than a decade before the Civil War by Frederick Grimké, a distinguished nonabolitionist member of the famous antislavery family. Whether or not the Negroes were an inferior race, Grimké believed their long years of bondage had made them unready to exercise the privilege of the suffrage. Granting this, would it be possible, he asked, to give them their freedom and at the same time deny them their equal rights under the Constitution?

How could we refuse to impart the benefit of those institutions, whose existence is the very thing which has suggested the change. And yet on the other hand, how could we consent to commit violence upon those institutions, by placing them in the power of a race who have no comprehension of their uses.[4]

The disastrous effects of universal emancipation, Grimké predicted in 1848, would not come immediately. Eventually, however, the free Negro would be reduced to a status not far removed from that of slavery.

Ideally, either a system of gradual emancipation or of immediate abolition in a spirit of self-sacrifice and genuine idealism by the people of the North as well as the South would have been preferable to freedom as a result of a bitter Civil War. In any case, a meaningful freedom would have required extensive economic aid and education to enable the Negro to eradicate the blight of slavery and take his place on equal terms with the white man. The more sincere among the Radical Republicans probably had in mind just such needs with their proposals of a land distribution in the

South and economic benefits and education through the Freedmen's Bureau. But the Bureau's aid was susceptible of political abuse and was liable to the danger of encouraging the freedman to believe that he was a privileged ward of the Federal government. At the same time the attempt to solve the South's problems by the political means of the Fourteenth and Fifteenth Amendments, extending civil rights and the suffrage to the Negro freedmen, was as fruitless as it would have been superfluous had the intent of the Thirteenth Amendment been honestly carried out. Unfortunately, however, while the South sought to minimize the effect of Negro freedom, the North was not unselfish in its demand of full civil rights and equality for the Negro.

A possible compromise in this matter would have been to grant the suffrage only to educated Negroes. This solution was advocated by President Johnson and had the support of E. L. Godkin, editor of the *Nation*. But a moderate or liberal program for the South and for the Negro was not desired by the Radical Republicans, who needed a sizable and immediate Negro vote if they were to stay in power. Charles Sumner, Republican senator from Massachusetts, and a stanch advocate of the Negro freedman's rights, explained the practical political situation facing his party. In a letter to his friend John Bright, the English liberal, Sumner admitted frankly:

Without the colored vote the white Unionists would have been left in the hands of the rebels; loyal governments could not be organized. The colored vote was a necessity; this I saw at the beginning, and insisted pertinaciously that it should be secured. It was on this ground, rather than principle, that I relied most; but the argument of principle was like a reinforcement.[5]

In the long run it was certainly open to question whether the Radical program, even when sincerely motivated by a concern for his welfare, actually benefited the Negro. Examining it in the context of the other Radical Republican measures, it is difficult to escape the conclusion that the rights of all individuals and groups were regarded as inferior to the overriding demands of a victorious nationalism and statism. Friends of the freedmen believed that the national government had to take over many of the powers hitherto exercised by the states in order to enable the Negro to enjoy the advantages of emancipation. But the Republican party also favored a stronger national government in order to forestall the return of the South and the Democrats to the seats of political authority. If the southern states were allowed to rejoin the Union without the restraints imposed by the new amendments to the Constitution, what was to prevent them from disfranchising the freedmen, joining hands with the Democrats of the North, and overthrowing the Republican saviors of the nation?

The enlarged scope of the powers of the Federal government was reflected in the political theory of the generation after the Civil War. The remnants of the older natural rights and state rights philosophies of government were now replaced by the new teachings of nationalism. For all practical purposes the Civil War had ended the arguments of nullification and secession. The question of whether sovereignty lay in the Federal or in the state governments had been resolved by force of arms, and the victors of the North were ready to consider themselves as constituting the new nation. Although Jefferson Davis, the late President of the Confederacy, would admit only that the war showed secession "to be impracticable," the state rights argument was now useful chiefly as a means of preserving white supremacy in the South and of preventing Federal civil rights legislation.[6]

The last important defense of the principle of secession therefore was Alexander H. Stephens's *A Constitutional View of the Late War Between the States* (1868–1870), a superior amplification of Calhoun's older *Disquisition on Government.* In his book, Stephens contended that the Constitution was the supreme law of the land only in judicial matters. Nullification of a law by a state was accordingly illegal, but secession of a state from the Union was justified because the Constitution rested upon a compact between the states.[7] Whatever the merits of his argument, which depended in the last analysis upon the motives of the founding fathers at the Constitutional Convention at Philadelphia, the weight of events, as well as the sheer volume of the writings of his opponents, ran heavily against him.

In contrast to Stephens's justification of the lost cause, the northern view of the nature of the Union and of the location of sovereignty rested on an expansion of the classic nationalist position maintained by Daniel Webster and taken over by Lincoln during the war. According to this theory, the Constitution was a perpetual contract, while the Union in its origins went back to the common struggle of the people during the American Revolution and as such was older than the separate states. Sovereignty resided in the people as a whole and not in the states or in the people of the separate states. With minor variations, northern writers on politics now located sovereignty in the Federal government, while the Supreme Court in an artful decision ruled that, though sovereignty was divided between the states and the Federal government, it was the latter which drew the borderline between their powers. The Court refused to recognize the secession of the southern states, which consequently were regarded as never legally out of the Union. The war had been fought by a rebel element only, and the nature of the Union, defined as "an indestructible Union, composed of indestructible States," remained unimpaired.[8]

With the development of a new nationalistic political theory to keep pace with the reconstitution of the Union, American thinkers forsook the liberal heritage of English and French thought. In place of John Locke and other philosophers of the natural rights and compact theories of government, American political theorists now turned to Hegel and the German idealists, whose philosophy glorified the role of the state. A pioneer American work in presenting a Hegelian interpretation of the state was *The Nation* published in 1870 by Elisha Mulford, a graduate of Yale and an Episcopal clergyman. Mulford followed Hegel in giving the state the human characteristics of personality and conscience. A moral organism, the state was not a necessary evil but a means toward the realization of a more perfect freedom. Ultimately all rights descended to man from God, and the state was God's chosen instrument. It followed therefore that there were no absolute, inalienable rights of the individual. Mulford took essentially the position presented earlier by Orestes Brownson, the Catholic layman, whose *American Republic,* published in 1865, was one of the first works to repudiate democratic individualism and the natural rights theory.[9]

In the colleges and universities, academic philosophers of the state also popularized the new theories of nationalism. At Yale, Theodore Dwight Woolsey, though he accepted in part the doctrine of inalienable rights and of passive resistance to the state, nevertheless pointed out that individual rights were meaningful only if they were protected by the state.[10] Woolsey was in many respects a disciple of the German-American scholar Francis Lieber, professor of political science and history at Columbia College in New York and an outstanding pioneer in the shift away from the natural rights theory. Born in Germany, but resident in the United States after 1827, Lieber in the years before the Civil War had been a liberal nationalist, teaching in the uncongenial

atmosphere of the antebellum South. Transferring to Columbia, Lieber did yeoman work for the North during the
Civil War as an author of numerous propaganda tracts and
of a standard manual on the laws of war, which he wrote for
the army.

Lieber's many war and postwar activities provided an especially interesting contrast with the liberal leanings of his
antebellum works on political science. For example, in his
important book *On Civil Liberty,* first published in 1853,
Lieber maintained that rule by the propertyless masses, or
"democratic absolutism," was the very antithesis of liberty.
True liberty was embodied in institutions, the main function of which was to protect the rights of the minority. Like
Tocqueville, Lieber feared the great powers of a democratic
popular majority, and his *Civil Liberty* "was a lengthy and
elaborate paean for limited government." In his early writings, Lieber was careful to distinguish between the nationalization of peoples and the centralization of governments,
which he feared. His latest biographer, Frank Freidel, has
argued that Lieber's anxiety over the aggrandizement of the
powers of government, and the popularity of such a view
with liberals after the Civil War, "led to an equally ominous
hegemony of the industrial leaders." [11] But this interpretation seems to hold that industrialism in the North had
nothing to gain from the nationalism of the victorious Republicans, and it also overlooks the extent to which Lieber's
own philosophy became attuned to the thinking of the Civil
War era. His acceptance of the place of war as a normal part
of a nation's growth and the vindictive, nationalizing policy
that he came to advocate were actually much more congenial
to the new generation of business and political leaders than
his earlier writings on liberty and limited government.

For the change in his views, and for his defense of such

northern war measures as the suspension of the writ of habeas corpus and the policy of arbitrary arrest, Lieber was frequently charged with inconsistency. In reply, he argued that the great and unprecedented nature of the struggle to preserve the Union justified the arbitrary means invoked, and he himself, it may be noted, labored mightily during the Civil War to bring about the triumph of his nationalistic concepts. After Appomattox, Lieber accepted enthusiastically the extremist attitude of the Radicals in regard to Reconstruction policy, at the same time contributing his own advice to such influential friends as Senator Sumner. For these activities one of Lieber's correspondents, a distinguished Louisiana physician and an admirer of his earlier works, wrote asking him: "Can you reconcile your teachings and your practice? How can *you* lend yourself to the policy of the most unscrupulous, cruel and vindictive party that ever existed?" [12]

Lieber, however, paid little heed to such admonitions and, continuing to oppose reconciliation with the South, he took a position with the War Department as archivist of Confederate records, searching for evidence that would convict Jefferson Davis of treason. His new employment was an amazing contradiction of the passage in his *Civil Liberty* in which he asserted: "The trial for treason is a gauge of liberty. Tell us how they try people for treason, and we will tell you whether they are free." But Lieber was soon disappointed in his work. After sifting through some two hundred seventy thousand Confederate letters, he found a good bit of vague material but none of the sort needed by the Radical Republicans if they were to hang Jefferson Davis. As he came to realize this fact, Lieber lamented late in the spring of 1866: "The trial of Jeff. Davis will be a terrible thing — volumes, a library of the most infernal treason will be belched forth — Davis will not be found guilty and we shall stand there as completely beaten. The time was lost, and can never be recovered." [13]

In his teaching position at Columbia, Lieber was succeeded by a southern Unionist from eastern Tennessee, John W. Burgess. Burgess carried much further Lieber's nationalism, joining with it a profound admiration for the "Teutonic political genius" and Germanic conception of the state. For this Burgess has been compared to Treitschke, the German navalist and imperialist.[14] The very possibility of such a comparison illustrates the extent to which the theory of nationalism was carried by American scholars in the era after the Civil War. Although ultimately this nationalism would help effect a reconciliation between the two sections, healing the wounds of war, its first and most potent influence was in the North, "where the older and stabler trilogy of aristocracy, decentralization, and agriculture were sacrificed to the newer and more experimental trilogy of democracy, nationalism, and industrialism." [15]

In theory the South after the Civil War continued to adhere to many of the tenets of its historic state rights position. In practice, however, the new nationalism of the North was not without influence in the former Confederate states. Of course, there were "bitter-enders" like Jefferson Davis who could not reconcile themselves to the defeat of the Confederacy. But at the other extreme were Southerners whose adjustment was so complete that they cooperated with the Radical Reconstruction policies of the Republicans or became the proponents of the New South, a term redolent of industrialism and nationalism. In either case, the impact of the Civil War experience on the South resulted in no reversal of the trend away from liberalism. In the first place, the Reconstruction policy of the North, based on force and military occupation of the former Confederacy, was the opposite of liberal. Apart from the small number of those who were thinking in terms of the Negro freedmen's welfare, it was folly for Northerners to argue that their program for the South was liberal, either in its eventual ends or in its actual means. But, if the North was far from magnanimous in victory, neither was the South particularly noble in defeat. A dignified and gentlemanly adjustment undoubtedly would have involved great difficulties for most Southerners. After all, few had the opportunity of Robert E. Lee, who was able to achieve a worthy new career as the president of Washington College, now Washington and Lee University. More characteristic therefore were, on the one hand, the bitter laments and recriminations of those who could not accept defeat and, on the other hand, the surrender of the so-called Scalawags and Bourbon aristocrats who were willing to make their peace with the businessmen and politicians of the victorious North.

One of the most unfortunate features of the Reconstruction period was the encouragement that it offered to extremist and extralegal methods. Deprived of home rule and of any legal recourse by the policy of military control, the worst elements of the South turned to such devices as the Ku-Klux Klan and the black codes. The attempt to control the Negro via these notorious codes, so reminiscent of the old slave laws, and the accompanying resort to violence and intimidation by the Klan are well known. Also a familiar story is the history of the northern Carpetbag and Negro governments which were established in most of the southern states. Corrupt and inefficient, these governments nevertheless accomplished some good in such relatively virgin fields in the South as public education. In addition, many Reconstruction officials in their violation of the principles of good government had the unsavory example of similar developments in the North, where political corruption reached the national administration under President Grant. Much of the corruption of the Carpetbaggers, moreover, took place with the connivance of the better elements in the South, as Bourbon aristocrats availed themselves of the lush contracts dispensed by the Reconstruction governments.

For all its illiberalisms, however, the process of Radical Reconstruction was strictly limited in time. In no southern state did Radical or Carpetbag rule endure for so long as a decade, and in most the period was far shorter. In any event, the return of the South to the Union was inevitable and the only question was on whose terms the reconstitution was to be accomplished. This was settled when the final defeat of Radical Reconstruction in 1877 ensured the "redemption" of the South to home rule and white domination. The conservative white leaders, who had accomplished this redemption and who were to dominate the new governments, represented an aristocracy, sometimes called Bourbon, but which more recently has been given the expressive term "Redeemers." As C. Vann Woodward has pointed out in his writings on the New South, the Redeemers came to terms with the new nationalism and industrialism of the North. In comparison with the brief period of the years of control by those who governed during the Confederacy and Reconstruction, the Redeemers enjoyed a rule that was more lasting and more important in the history of the South. The intellectual descendants of the antebellum Whigs, the Redeemers were dedicated to the building of a business civilization on the ruins of the Old South. Welcoming northern manufacturing and capital and actively seeking government support and subsidization, the Redeemers of the New South were the counterparts of the Republican nationalists and business barons of the industrialized North.

The New South wanted all the private capital that the North could supply and after that as much in the way of Federal subsidies as possible. While the South favored laissez faire in the sense of the giving up of Radical Reconstruction, it had no patience "with state rights and *laissez faire* if they implied abandonment of Federal subsidies, loans of credit, and internal improvements." The compromise of 1877 and end of Radical Reconstruction in return for southern support of Hayes's clouded title to the presidency had as an added feature a promise of Federal subsidies for construction of railroad trunk lines into the South and Southwest. In the parlance of the Gilded Age, a lot of the talk of sectional reconciliation therefore had as its basis an economic bargain.[16]

Of course, the South did not entirely yield its older traditions. In the works of the local color school of writers, and in much of the popular literature about the South by both northern and southern authors, the antebellum South lived on replete with magnolias, columned porticoes, and chivalry. But the Old South was interlaced with the New. In the perfervid words of her chief orator, Henry W. Grady, editor of the Atlanta *Constitution:*

The Old South rested on slavery and agriculture, unconscious that these could neither give nor maintain healthy growth. The new South presents a perfect Democracy, the oligarchs leading in the popular movement — a social system compact and closely knitted, less splendid on the surface but stronger at the core, a hundred farms for every plantation, fifty homes for every palace, and a diversified industry that meets the complex needs of this complex age.[17]

Stripped of its rhetoric, the New South of the Redeemers had its less pleasant features. Poor despite the influx of northern capital, which was used largely to maintain absentee control of the southern economy, the South had little money for public services, social legislation, or even its common schools. Public education, stigmatized in the minds of many as a Carpetbag measure, was the first to suffer, and the "average length of the common school term in the South fell off approximately 20 per cent after Redemption, and the 100-day term, the highest average attained during Reconstruction, was not restored until after 1900." Expenditure per pupil also declined and remained far below the national average. Assisted by small northern endowments, such as the Peabody and Slater Funds, a minority carried on a struggle for better schools in the South. Northern teachers, however, were suspect because of the role they had played in Reconstruction days in their work among the Negroes. Thus, the teaching of Negroes after the Civil War continued to invite hostility and repression in the South. This was partly a southern resentment against northern intrusion, but in the North there were also many who still objected to having Negro children educated at public expense.[18]

Particularly damaging to the Redeemers' claim of paternalistic justice to the Negro was the establishment after the Civil War of the brutal convict lease system. The old penitentiaries were hopelessly inadequate to take care of offenders formerly confined on the plantations, and the convict lease system also fitted in with the policy of financial retrenchment, which precluded the construction of adequate jails. Moreover, the system was well adapted to the requirements of the harsh penalties inflicted upon Negroes under the new criminal codes of the South. A recent historian has concluded, "The degradation and brutality produced by this system would be incredible but for the amount of evidence from official sources." And another modern scholar can find a parallel for the southern convict lease system "only in the persecutions of the Middle Ages or in the prison camps of Nazi Germany." [19]

Although the Redeemers left no doubt of the Negroes' inferior place in southern society, racial discrimination in the sense of Jim Crow laws was not prevalent in the South until the conservative and aristocratic Redeemers lost their political hold before the tide of Populism in the 1890's. Discrimination was more a demand of the poorer white elements of the population, which felt keenly the threat of Negro competition. The reactionary regimes of the Redeemers, on the other hand, had even allowed Negroes the suffrage when their votes could be controlled, and for twenty years after 1865 no southern state had segregation laws in respect to railroad travel. But, beginning in 1887, such laws multiplied as the anti-Negro Populists gained influence in the South. "The barriers of racial discrimination mounted in direct ratio with the tide of political democracy among whites." An example of the bitter racism of the period was the rise of lynching, with a peak reached in the 1890's. In place of the improvement in race relations promised by Reconstruction, there had been a deterioration by the close of the nineteenth century. Progressivism was for whites only, and the Negro was forced to accept the compromise policy of acquiescence and adjustment suggested by Booker T. Washington. Though the South boasted that a frank paternalism would settle the Negro problem, there was little doubt that its policy meant keeping the Negro at the bottom rail of society. And, in the abandonment of the Reconstruction goal of civil rights for the Negro, the North largely went along. The Supreme Court's decision in October 1883, declaring the Civil Rights Act unconstitutional, provided judicial sanction for discrimination laws that southern states were beginning to place on their statute books.[20]

On all sides, in the North as well as in the South, the new nationalism that succeeded the Civil War marked a further retreat from liberalism. In its political theory, and in its practical ramifications for the Reconstruction of the South, this nationalism was coercive and extremist. Economically, the rising industrial order of the North had its counterpart in the gospel of the New South. North and South the alliance of government and business had been much strengthened by the Civil War and its aftermath. Although business interests occasionally espoused a philosophy of laissez faire, basically they relied upon the favors and subsidies of the government. Especially in the North, Whiggery became the order of the day. Minority groups that seemed to represent an exception to the dominant nationalism — the Negroes, Indians, and immigrants — underwent an enforced assimilation, while only a handful of older liberals or philosophical anarchists stood out against the nationalizing forces engendered by the times.[21]

Before the close of the nineteenth century the reconstitution of nationalism was to be achieved beyond all dispute. The trend away from liberalism, of which this new nationalism was an important part, surmounted all criticism. Throughout the Western world, in the last third of the century, there was an intensification of nationalism and a weakening of the older patterns of an eighteenth- and early nineteenth-century liberalism. The United States, as well as most of Europe, seemed to be entering a new age. An unprecedented industrialization, urbanization, and immigration, plus the rapid exploitation of the resources of the West, were transforming the face and thinking of the older pre-Civil War America, thereby creating a host of new problems to challenge liberalism and democracy.

10

Pre-emption, Exploitation, Progress

THE CONCENTRATION of powers in the national government, so well designed to serve the ends of Radical Reconstruction, also appealed to the developing business and financial interests of the North. "A supreme national government, controlled by Republicans friendly to industry and finance, could insure favors to corporations, protective tariffs, a centralized banking system, the redemption of government securities, and subsidies to railroads. A national government could also provide the rank and file with free homesteads on the public domain and insure for the clamoring veterans of the late war adequate pensions from the exchequer." [1] Not the least among the results of the Civil War was the way in which, as the Beards have maintained, "The Second American Revolution, while destroying the economic foundations of the slave-owning aristocracy, assured the triumph of business enterprise. As if to add irony to defeat, the very war which the planters precipitated in an effort to avoid their doom augmented the fortunes of the capitalist class from whose jurisdiction they had tried to escape." [2]

But the classic picture of the American scene during the 1870's is that penned by Parrington in the final volume of his *Main Currents in American Thought*. According to Parrington, the Civil War removed the check of an agrarian order, and "In the years following the war, exploitation for the first time was provided with adequate resources and a competent technique." The social philosophy of the age "was summed up in three words — preëmption, exploitation, progress." Although America, as it moved forward to conquer the last frontiers to the west, still accounted itself individualistic and democratic, individualism was being simplified to "the acquisitive instinct," while progress was becoming synonymous with the pre-emption and exploitation of the public domain by large-scale business interests aided by government subsidies. The nationalistic ideas of Alexander Hamilton and Henry Clay had been revived, while "Under the nominal leadership of the easy-going Grant a loose rein was given to Whiggish ambitions and the Republican party became a political instrument worthy of the Gilded Age."

Parrington likened these postwar years to a great barbecue. "It was sound Gilded Age doctrine. To a frontier people what was more democratic than a barbecue, and to a paternalistic age what was more fitting than that the state should provide the beeves for roasting." Loyal citizens had saved the government during the trying days of the Civil War, and it was only fair in return that the government should give some tangible reward to their patriotism. Thus the theory of Whiggery "asserts that it is a duty of the state to help its citizens make money, and it conceives of the political state as a useful instrument for effective exploitation. . . . But unhappily," as Parrington pointed out, "there is a fly in the Whiggish honey. In a competitive order, government is forced to make its choices. It cannot serve both Peter and Paul. If it gives with one hand it must take away with the other. And so the persuasive ideal of paternalism in the common interest degenerates in practice into legalized favoritism. Governmental gifts go to the largest investments." [3]

With the South crushed by defeat, and the North enjoying its victory in the form of a postwar boom, the rivalry of competing economic interests for government favors did not at once reach the stage of a serious struggle for political power. Spurred on by the opening up of the vast reaches of public domain in the West and by the tremendous industrial expansion of the Northeast, the American economy seemed able to produce more than enough for everyone, including the hundreds of thousands of immigrants who continued to cross the Atlantic. These years following the Civil War were unquestionably years of great material development, and the dominant note in politics was one of encouraging this expansion. Beginning with the economic legislation of the war years, the Republican party gave the business interests of the North the protection and encouragement they desired. Thus, the Morrill Act of 1862 inaugurated a succession of protective tariff measures — each higher in its rates than the preceding one — that continued virtually unbroken down to World War I, only to be resumed again in the 1920's. Industry favored by high tariffs, which often went beyond any justifiable need for protection from foreign competition, also benefited from an easy Federal immigration policy, the maintenance of a gold standard and sound currency, and the willingness of the government to intervene, with the regular army if necessary, in the labor disputes that marked the last quarter of the century.

Instead of the limited state desired by Jeffersonian believers in an agrarian society, the post-Civil War era was characterized by the passage of a stream of tariffs, taxes, and subsidies unprecedented in their volume and scope. The result of all this was that, as the biographer of Mark Hanna pointed out: "For the most part all that business needed in order to become more prosperous was to be let alone. Existing legislation both national and state was encouraging it in almost every possible way." [4] In the West, however, there was discontent and the Chicago *Tribune,* speaking for agricultural interests, warned that the idea of republican government as an agent of the people had yielded to the feudal notion of an oppressive government which engaged in all sorts of paternal tasks, including internal improvements, education, the regulation of wages and hours of labor and of crops and prices. "With the close of the war, during which so many unwonted powers were exercised, the theory of paternal government has been revived among us." This, the *Tribune* pointed out, had been accomplished largely through the taxing power, taking away from one and giving to another.[5]

The effect of taxes and government debt upon traditional liberalism had already been noted by Francis Bowen, the well-known Harvard economist and philosopher. Calling attention to the fact that the United States in four years of fighting had accumulated a war debt greater than England's as a result of her twenty-two-year struggle against the French Revolution and Napoleon, Bowen lamented that there was now a tax on everything, although "Hitherto, in this country, our boast has been that we were free from all great burdens imposed by the government. . . . Hitherto with us the tax-gatherer has been but an infrequent visitant and one whose hunger was easily appeased." [6]

Liberals believed that the solution was a return to Jeffersonian principles of limited government. For example, Samuel J. Tilden, Democratic and liberal reform candidate for president in the election of 1876, voiced the opinion that the general situation of the United States after the Civil War was reminiscent of conditions on the eve of the Jeffersonian revolution of 1800.

The demoralizations of war — a spirit of gambling adventure, engendered by false systems of public finance; a grasping centralism, absorbing all functions from the local authorities, and assuming to control the industries of individuals by largesses to favored classes from the public treasury of moneys wrung from the body of the people by taxation — were then, as now, characteristics of the period.

But the danger to the country now was greater. "The classes who desire pecuniary profit from existing governmental abuses have become numerous and powerful beyond any example in our country. . . . For the first time in our national history," Tilden concluded, "such classes have become powerful enough to aspire to be in America the ruling classes, as they have been and are in the corrupt societies of the Old World." [7] Echoing Tilden's point of view, Edwin Lawrence Godkin, editor of the liberal New York *Nation,* in an article on the Crédit Mobilier scandal, called for a return to honesty in government. Confident that the country was enjoying enough prosperity, Godkin asserted that the answer to bribery and corruption was to end the power of members of Congress to bestow great privileges upon private individuals and business corporations. "The remedy is simple. The Government must get out of the 'protective' business and the 'subsidy' business and the 'improvement' and the 'development' business. It must let trade, and commerce, and manufactures, and steamboats, and railroads, and telegraphs alone. It cannot touch them without breeding corruption." [8]

Popular with Godkin, Tilden, and other eastern liberals was the idea of reform from the top under the leadership of the patrician or aristocratic classes of the community. This was the element that took the leadership of the Liberal Republican movement of 1872 and of the comparable reform wave in the Democratic ranks under Tilden in 1876. The reformers particularly emphasized the necessity of a civil service merit system. Better men in public positions, they hoped, would result in improved government. In the era of corruption after the Civil War there was a transparent need for honesty in government, and the civil service reform cause gradually won popular support. After the passage of the Pendleton Act of 1883, establishing a bipartisan Civil Service Commission, the United States prepared to move in the European direction of establishing a permanent body of public officeholders, and in time the civil service of the New World republic would come to surpass the bureaucracies of monarchical Europe. Generally overlooked, however, in the American enthusiasm for civil service reform, were those few individuals who complained that a class of Federal officeholders, guaranteed permanent tenure, might become an insolent aristocracy comparable to the bureaucracies of the Old World. Godkin admitted that there was no objection to civil service reform more serious than this. Although he felt on the whole that "the danger of an office-holding aristocracy" in the United States was based on mere conjecture, he noted that the evil effects of bureaucratic government were already clearly apparent in Europe.[9]

While the liberal movement in the East concerned itself with such questions as the tariff, taxation, a sound currency, and the purity of the civil service, in the West the focal point of the Federal government's relationship to its citizens lay in the administration of the public domain. Cries for cheap land and protests against land monopoly had been stock-in-trade arguments of various agrarian and utopian reform movements in the half century before the Civil War. In 1860 more than half the area of the country — over a billion acres — was under public ownership. Thirty years later half of this half, or one-quarter of the whole United States, still remained in the public domain, but much of the land was non-arable or reserved for some specific use.

The speeded-up process of disposing of public lands began

seriously in the midst of the Civil War, when the government under the Homestead Act of 1862 adopted a policy of granting free farms, of one hundred sixty acres each, to settlers who would cultivate the land for five years. The law also declared that within six months the settler, instead of waiting to secure the patent to his land by homesteading it for five years, could purchase the property at one dollar and a quarter an acre. By failing, under this alternate arrangement, to provide for cancellation of the patent if the farm was sold to anyone but the government, the Homestead Act opened the way for speculators to buy up vast quantities of land, worth far more than the minimum fee per acre, by the simple device of providing dummy "settlers" with the requisite purchase price of one dollar twenty-five cents per acre. Thus, authentic homesteaders, eager to avail themselves of a farm by fulfilling the terms of cultivating the soil for five years, were often forced to move beyond the range of the more desirable lands, which had already been pre-empted by speculators or dummy settlers. While approximately fifty million homestead acres were distributed in the first twenty years after 1862, much of this land soon found its way into the hands of speculators and was available to farmers only at considerable cost. The same limitation applied to land held for a profit by colleges endowed under the Morrill Act or sold by railroads for a good sum on the promise of providing transportation facilities.[10]

"By the very act that offered 'land to the landless poor,' Congress thus had nullified its apparent gift," is the conclusion of one historian of American economic life. And the force of his statement was further illustrated by the Federal government's policy of granting vast tracts of the public domain to railroads and to the states. Under the Morrill Act of 1862, Congress gave the states thirty thousand acres for each of their senators and representatives, the income from the sale of the land to be used to establish a college for instruction in the agricultural and mechanic arts. At the same time, Congress embarked on a policy of subsidizing the construction of rail lines in the West by extending direct loans and by the grant of sizable territories along the railroad right of way. In the decade after the passage of the Homestead Act, the railroads received over one hundred million acres from Congress. Under the various Federal land acts, some three hundred million acres were actually disposed of by 1934, with the railroads getting one hundred thirty million acres from the Federal government and an additional fifty million acres through the intermediary action of the states or, as in Texas, by the state itself. In addition, the states secured from the Federal government around two hundred million acres.[11]

Although the government was thus most generous in its disposition of the public domain, the small independent farmer was not the chief beneficiary of the Federal largess. "The homesteaders, even including those who acted as tools of speculators, got just about one acre out of every six or seven that the government gave up. Those who took free farms to keep received about one acre in ten." [12]

The homesteaders' struggle, in competition with railroads and various other business interests, for good arable lands in the West intensified the white man's pressure upon Indian lands. This pressure was responsible in large part for the recurrent Indian wars of the period from 1862 to 1877, and it continued to result in a mad scramble for Indian territory until most of this land was pre-empted for sale to advancing settlers. To the frontiersman the Indian had always been an obstacle in the path of westward progress, while to the Red Man the coming of civilization spelled the doom of the buffalo and other game on which he depended for his food. In 1871, an act of Congress stipulated that no more treaties be made between Indian tribes and the Federal government. Yielding the fiction of a separate nation status, the Indians now became the wards of the United States government, allowed for the present to occupy lands which they did not own under the white man's title, but not permitted to make individual entries on the public domain. Although Presidents Grant and Hayes and other high officials were sympathetic to the plight of the Indian, the old tribal lands, in violation of earlier treaty rights and agreements, were constantly being added to the public domain and opened up for white settlement. Finally by the 1880's, through the publication of such exposés of American Indian policy as Helen Hunt Jackson's *Century of Dishonor,* the public became aware of the way in which the Indians, as wards of the government, had been exploited by the very instrumentalities and agencies designed for their protection.[13]

The demands for reform in the treatment of the Indian resulted in 1887 in the passage of the Dawes Severalty Act. This measure provided the means by which the communal organization of the Indian tribes could be dissolved, the reservations broken up, and the Indians themselves admitted as American citizens qualified to take up land in individual ownership. Reservation lands not granted to Indian families could be sold to white settlers with the provision that an adequate payment be made to the remaining members of the tribe. Although the Dawes Act ended the anomalous status of the Indian as a ward of the government and opened the way to citizenship, it also served as a means of pre-empting large portions of Indian reservations for white settlement. Thus a recent historian of the public domain has concluded:

The operation of the Dawes Act of 1887 confirmed the expectations of its proponents. By 1892 agreements had been negotiated with fourteen Indian tribes, restoring to the public domain

26,000,000 acres most of which was already open to settlement. The greatest of the Indian reservations — that of the once powerful Sioux of the plains — consisting of 9,000,000 acres had already been opened to sale and settlement; the 21,000 Sioux Indians had accepted five other separate and very-much reduced reservations.[14]

Even the old Oklahoma Indian territory did not escape the pressure of the grasping whites, and in 1889 the extensive areas formerly owned by the Five Civilized Tribes were opened up for settlement. This completed the process of displacement that had begun back in Jackson's presidency when the so-called Five Nations had been forced to leave their homes in Georgia and cross the Mississippi. "By 1906, through the breaking up of the reservation system, some 75,000,000 acres, or about three-fifths of the whole amount of Indian land released by the Dawes Act of 1887, had been appropriated by the whites." [15]

The fate of the Indian foretold the passing of the frontier. In the course of exhausting the free land to the west, nothing cast more doubt on the possibility of the United States' achieving the old Jeffersonian dream of a liberal agrarian society than the way in which the government's land grants served the cause of monopoly and big business. It was not surprising therefore that the last of the followers of Jeffersonian liberalism to attain any widespread degree of public support in the United States should launch an attack upon Federal land policies. Henry George, the apostle of the agrarian ideas of a long succession of reformers, excelled them all in the popular attention that he was able to attract by his writings and lectures. Yet, it was the fate of George to advocate a system of agrarian reform in an age when increasing industrialization and governmental regulation of the economy had already diverted attention from the land. The title of George's great work, *Progress and Poverty,* stated the fundamental problem with which he wrestled throughout his life — the problem of want or poverty in the midst of plenty or so-called progress.

The child of a poor but respectable and religious Philadelphia family, George had his education cut off at an early age when he went to sea. In 1855 he reached San Francisco, then in the last stages of the gold rush. Under the impetus of the discovery of gold, California had telescoped the American frontier process into a matter of only a few years. It thus gave George an excellent laboratory for investigation, where he was able to observe at first hand the pre-emption of the state's wealth by speculative elements and the consequent failure of the gold to bring any general or lasting prosperity. George himself became an inveterate plunger into risky mining ventures, and the young family that he had acquired soon suffered from much the same type of economic hardship that beset the poorer classes from New York to California during the era of the Civil War. Experiencing poverty, George knew the way it warped men's minds, blunting their nobler impulses and driving them into wild schemes in efforts to retrieve lost prosperity.

Beyond the problem of poverty as a result of individual misfortune or improvidence lay the social sources of poverty. Here, George believed, the basic trouble lay in the ratio of population to land and in the system of taxes, which allowed vast tracts of land to be held for purposes of speculation. His solution — the taxation of the unearned increment in the price of land, or the taxation of unimproved land at the same rate as improved land in order to encourage its use — became famous with the publication in January 1880 of his *Progress and Poverty.* George's proposal, soon well known as the single tax, a term which he, however, disliked and which oversimplified his argument, had already been anticipated in some of his earlier writings.[16]

Back in 1868, in an interesting article in the *Overland Monthly,* entitled "What the Railroad Will Bring Us," George had speculated on the effect of the approaching completion of the Union Pacific and Central Pacific railroads. With the coming of the first transcontinental line there were signs in California of a prosperity reminiscent of the booming days of the first gold rush. While those of his neighbors who owned considerable property eagerly prepared to profit from the expected rise in land values, George lamented that the city had not been settled on the basis of free homesteads. "The locomotive," he warned, "is a great centralizer," which would kill small towns and small business and make possible large fortunes and also a poor class. "We need not look far from the palace to find the hovel. . . . Amid all our rejoicing and all our gratulation let us see clearly whither we are tending. Increase in population and in wealth past a certain point means simply an approximation to the condition of older countries — the Eastern states and Europe." High wage and interest rates, which, according to George, were tied to California's comparatively small population, would be lowered by the railroad. "The truth is, that the completion of the railroad and the consequent great increase of business and population, will not be a benefit to all of us, but only to a portion." Like the ancient Greeks to whom the future of their race had once seemed so bright, "Our modern civilization strikes broad and deep and looks high." But, George added, "So did the tower which men once built almost unto heaven." [17]

He continued his criticism of railroad land grants with the publication in 1871 of a pamphlet *Our Land and Land Policy.* Here he presented many of the ideas later elaborated in *Progress and Poverty*. Analyzing the different types of land grants made by the Federal government, he concentrated his attack on those given to the railroads. "Since the day when Esau sold his birthright for a mess of pottage we may search in vain for any parallel to such concessions." Especially reprehensible, George felt, was the national policy of building railroads before they were needed. This resulted in the diversion of funds from more productive enterprise, scattered population beyond the means of subsistence, helped to monopolize the land, and in general made the masses poorer and the few richer. If such policies were continued, the public domain would soon be exhausted and the people of the United States would find themselves in the situation of the populace of Europe. "We are monopolizing our land deliberately — *our* land, not the land of a conquered nation, and we are doing it while prating of the equal rights of the citizen and of the brotherhood of man." [18]

Despite the pessimistic implications of his writings, George actually embraced much of the optimistic tone of the eighteenth-century Enlightenment. Like Jefferson and other early American philosophers, he had a strong faith in the idealism of his fellow man and a great confidence in the educability of human nature. In his economic theory he united his own keen powers of observation with a serious study of John Stuart Mill and the other great English classical economists. Although his solution of the single tax led logically to the virtual confiscation of all rent and the socialization of the land, George was not a socialist in the nationalistic sense of the term. He had a Jeffersonian individualist's distrust of the power of the centralized state, and the core of his plan was the restoration of the economic rights of the individual to a share in the land. Attacking private property in land as of the same character as private property in men, George blamed increases in rent upon the growth in population, laborsaving machinery, and speculation. An agrarian in an industrial-capitalist economy, George distrusted the workings of technocracy and industry. His especial panacea, though hardly practical, attracted international attention. And his criticisms of the established order continued to inspire later generations of liberals.[19]

In more than anything else, George was significant because of his attempt to protect the individual from the joint collectivism being enforced by the national state and big business. As Hamlin Garland, one of George's early followers, pointed out in an exposition and defense of the single-tax position:

> We are individualists mainly. Let that be understood at the start. We stand unalterably opposed to the paternal idea in government. We believe in fewer laws and juster interpretation thereof. We believe in less interference with individual liberty, less protection of the rapacious demands of the few and more freedom of action on the part of the many.[20]

Garland felt that all of this was in strict accord with the philosophy of Jefferson and the Declaration of Independence, and with the theories of Herbert Spencer. But in the America of the eighties and nineties, doctrines of laissez faire and of the limited state were being twisted and distorted from their original meaning. Businessmen and judges took up the individualism of Jefferson and Spencer and converted it into a rationale for materialist exploitation. Resisting public intervention or government regulation when it confined or restrained special interests, the business community, however, could see no inconsistency in an acceptance of the stream of subsidies and tariffs, of which Henry George and other individualists complained. This contradiction in the businessman's thinking attracted the attention of James

Bryce, the celebrated English observer of American politics, who noted:

One-half of the capitalists are occupied in preaching *laissez faire* as regards railroad control, the other half in resisting it in railroad rate matters, in order to have their goods carried more cheaply, and in tariff matters, in order to protect industries threatened with foreign competition. Yet they manage to hold well together.[21]

In the eighties and nineties, the land monopoly that George had denounced in *Progress and Poverty* was almost being dwarfed in significance by the growth of large industrial combinations which in some ways were a direct result of the government's land policies. Also encouraged by the philosophy of government aid to business, which had taken such a strong hold in Washington after the Civil War, industrial trusts and combinations were still further aided and abetted by the Federal courts' all-inclusive interpretation of the Fourteenth Amendment. Whether or not it was originally intended only to protect the Negro freedman, there was little question that in practice the Fourteenth Amendment went far beyond the province of the Negro's rights. The famous provision that "No State shall make or enforce any law which shall abridge the privileges or immunities of citizens of the United States; nor shall any State deprive any person of life, liberty, or property, without due process of law . . ." was interpreted by the courts to include, within the legal meaning of the word "person," private corporations.

Thus the Fourteenth Amendment, with its due process clause protecting corporations as well as individuals, deprived the states of the effective exercise of their police powers and by implication vastly extended the domain of the Federal government. In effecting this transformation, the amendment helped to make possible the unrestrained rise of big business in the era following the Civil War. Later the techniques of exploitation and monopoly, thus encouraged, resulted in the progressives' call for Federal regulatory legislation. But overlooked in the whole development was the initial responsibility of the Federal government in helping to create what it was subsequently called upon to regulate. As Henry Steele Commager has pointed out in his discussion of what he calls "the watershed of the nineties,"

From the Interstate Commerce Act of 1887 and the Antitrust Act of 1890, we can conveniently date the beginnings of federal centralization; from Fuller's appointment to the Chief Justiceship in 1888, that revolutionary shift in the interpretation of the Fourteenth Amendment which did so much to nullify state action in the economic and social area. . . .[22]

The limited power of the states to regulate commerce gradually became apparent as railroad networks crisscrossed state lines. Although the Supreme Court in the Granger cases of 1877 at first approved state regulation of railroad rates involving interstate traffic, it soon reversed its position and in a long line of decisions severely restricted the authority of the states over all types of interstate commerce. These decisions paved the way for the passage by Congress in 1887 of the Interstate Commerce Act. Although subject to some opposition in Congress from state rights advocates who feared the growth of Federal power and the implications of the exercise of this power by a commission of five men, the bill was easily passed with the support of both political parties.[23]

Establishing a nonpartisan regulatory body with quasi-judicial authority over the railroads, the Interstate Commerce Act set a precedent for similar legislation in other areas. Of even greater importance was the fact that as soon as Congress began to legislate in any field, the Supreme Court was quick to rule that its jurisdiction became exclusive. In the case of the railroads, for example, the Supreme Court held that a state could not regulate intrastate rates if such regulation would affect interstate business. Most authorities have accepted the contention that the diversity of regulation, which would be the outcome of forty-eight differing state laws, made Federal legislation necessary and desirable, both as a means of effective regulation and also to prevent industrial chaos and to enable business to operate along national lines. The important point, however, was that Federal, as opposed to state, regulatory legislation was not necessarily a more effective control over business. If the destruction of big business were the sole aim, state regulation with all its diversity would have been more damaging. But, whatever the merits of this argument, there was no doubt that the Supreme Court's interpretation of the commerce clause became a powerful incentive to the expansion of the powers of the Federal government. As one authority has noted:

In all the efforts to attain greater national control, the commerce clause has been the great source of power. The rate cases were all upheld under the commerce clause. The anti-trust acts were upheld under the commerce clause. The encroachments of the States on each other and the Federal power, have been invalidated under the commerce clause.[24]

The entry of the Federal government into new spheres of economic regulation while it continued to pursue its lavish policy of grants and subsidies, provoked a mixed reaction from the citizenry. In general, of course, those who received its favors subscribed to the theory of governmental largess. Since the nation's resources were great, it was easy to equate exploitation with progress. And, considered in purely materialistic terms, the decades after the Civil War were undoubtedly years of progress. Even the immigrants, who made up the bulk of the country's unskilled labor and were crowded into urban slum areas, could usually look forward to a better standard of living for their children. Criticism of the policy which Parrington called Whiggery and likened to a great barbecue, therefore tended to confine itself to the demand for limited reforms of an administrative sort, such as the inauguration of a merit system in the civil service or the enforcement of more government aid and regulation.

The whole idea of government regulation in order to counterbalance the practice of subsidies and bounties to the business community was an attractive theory, popular in the great run of reform circles. By the nineties, when the distress of the farmer in the West and South was matched only by the bitter struggles of labor in conflict with employers, the Jeffersonian doctrine of the noninterventionist state, which confined itself to the preservation of free competition, seemed discredited with nearly all shades of liberal and radical opinion. Followers of Edward Bellamy, in line with the socialist utopia advocated in his best seller *Looking Backward,* organized a series of Nationalist clubs dedicated to the premise that the principle of competition was outmoded and needed to be supplanted by that of association. "The nationalization of industry and the promotion of the brotherhood of humanity" were the goals of the Bellamy Nationalists.[25] Like Bellamy's disciples, the Populists verged upon socialism in their platform calling for government ownership or regulation of the railroads and the trusts. James Baird Weaver, Populist candidate for president in 1892, appeared to state a truism of reform ideology when he declared: "We have tried to show that competition is largely a thing of the past. Every force of our industrial life is hurrying on the age of combination. It is useless to try and stop the current. What we must do is in some way make it work for the good of all."

Yet, with all their ideas, which seemed so radical at the time, the Populists basically believed in free enterprise, urging a program that sought to regulate the few in order to free the many and thus restore competition.[26]

Deriding the hostility of those who attempted to discredit it through their excited fears of socialism, Benjamin O. Flower, in his reform journal, the *Arena,* maintained that Populism was "a revolt of the millions against the *assumption of paternal authority on the part of the general government, and the prostitution of this authority or power for the enriching of a favored few."* Flower argued that Populism, like the ideas of Henry George and Thomas Jefferson, was essentially individualistic. Not socialist in the European sense of the term, it sought especially to combat the era of class legislation which had characterized the years since the Civil War. The "last full-throated attempt of the American dirt farmer to seize a government he had not wholly owned since Jackson's day, and had not owned at all since the Civil War had ended," was the way in which a later writer on the period characterized the Populist movement.[27]

Though its roots were deep in the American tradition, the direction of Populist doctrines in the nineties was nevertheless an indication that many of the discontented were beginning to think along illiberal lines in their demand for reform. Throughout the agrarian South and West, the laissez-faire liberalism of Grover Cleveland's second administration was much discredited by the time of Bryan's free silver campaign of 1896. "Cleveland might be honest," said Bryan, "but so were the mothers who threw their children into the Ganges." To many, liberalism seemed to have evolved into a pro-corporation doctrine, in which the Supreme Court used Herbert Spencer's laissez-faire precepts in order to protect railroads and other business enterprises from regulation by western state legislatures. Meanwhile liberals had followed the will-o'-the-wisp of civil service reform, an administrative measure popular with upper-class liberals but providing little solid attraction to Populists or other radical liberals. Except for a small minority of stanch individualists of a mixed liberal and conservative persuasion, the whole reform camp — from socialists and Populists to conservative exponents of a strong national state — stood ready to yield the values of traditional liberalism.[28]

The abandonment of liberalism was to be made explicit in the 1900's, when the reformers adopted the name Progressives and accepted much more than the liberals or Populists a frank nationalism and centralization under the aegis of the Federal government. But even before the turn of the century, old-fashioned liberals with a preference for limited government and a more simple economic order were becoming the voices of despair. Conservative in their desire to go back to older ways and in their pessimistic outlook on the future, these liberals or liberal-conservatives were above all else individualists. Their type of individualism, however, cut deeper than the so-called rugged individualism of the robber barons or business tycoons, who eagerly accepted protective tariffs and government subsidies and zealously enlisted courts and legislatures as their allies in the achievement of monopoly.

William Graham Sumner, for example, was admittedly a conservative in his bitter hostility to socialism and in his defense of laissez faire and the rights of property. But Sumner also fought many a liberal battle and devoted much of his time to denouncing the protective tariff, which he called "the greatest job of all." The crusade for government regulation in the United States, Sumner believed, was a counterpart of the German deification of the state and signified merely that all of us should take care of some of us. "The history of the human race is one long story of attempts by certain persons and classes to obtain control of the power of the State, so as to win earthly gratifications at the expense of others." The United States, he wrote, had started with the opportunity of choosing what it wanted from the European inheritance and, except for the Civil War, had on the whole adhered to the tradition of individualism. But by the eighties this individualism was again being badly compromised. "We have been borrowing old-world fashions and traditions all through our history, instead of standing firmly by the political and social philosophy of which we are the standard bearers." [29]

Sumner's complaints were echoed in the editorials of the *Nation* conducted by E. L. Godkin. To Godkin, government regulation spelled the beginnings of a policy of national socialism closely resembling the Bismarckian variety in Germany. For example, in reply to the arguments for Federal ownership of the railways, he asked what would happen when farmers wanted cheaper rates and labor higher pay? In the course of his editing, Godkin became progressively disillusioned with the prospects of democracy, not so much from fear of the uneducated masses as from the dangers of a corrupt plutocracy. In the comfortable shibboleths of the usual type of reformers, he saw no solution to the problems raised by the passing of the free lands of the frontier.[30] And so, by the decade of the 1890's, his earlier hopes for democracy gave way. He lost the idea that America would be different from Europe or that the great wealth gathered under American business would be well used. The disturbances of the decade, culminating above all in the Spanish-American War and imperialism, strengthened his feeling that America was following the European pattern of development. Of democracy, he wrote to his old friend Charles Eliot Norton:

I have pretty much given it up as a contributor to the world's moral progress. . . . I, too, tremble at the thought of having a huge navy and the war-making power lodged in the hands of such puerile and thoughtless people — a hundred million strong. Morals in this community, except sexual morals, are entirely gone. . . . We all expect far too much of the human race. What stuff we used to talk.[31]

While liberals' hopes for democracy degenerated into an interpretation of history that regarded politics as a constant struggle of the people against the predatory interests seeking to gain control of the state, the more sophisticated conservatives were ready to make their peace with the idea of the regulatory state. Instead of fighting such legislation as the Interstate Commerce Act and the Sherman Antitrust Act, the business community secured rulings from the courts that largely negated the purpose of those vaguely drawn measures. Asked in 1892 by a railroad official for his opinion of the wisdom of a projected effort to secure the abolition of the Interstate Commerce Commission, Richard Olney, a corporation lawyer destined to become in a few months attorney general of the United States, emphatically advised his correspondent against such a step. Pointing out that it might only result in strengthening the Commission by giving it additional powers, Olney added:

The Commission, as its functions have now been limited by the courts, is, or can be made, of great use to the railroads. It satisfies the popular clamor for a government supervision of railroads, at the same time that that supervision is almost entirely nominal. Further, the older such a commission gets to be, the more inclined it will be found to take the business and railroad view of things. It thus becomes a sort of barrier between the railroad corporations and the people and a sort of protection against hasty and crude legislation hostile to railroad interests. . . .

The part of wisdom is not to destroy the Commission, but to utilize it.[32]

Two years later, when Olney as attorney general encouraged Cleveland's use of Federal troops to break the Pullman strike of 1894, he gave further point to the way in which the power of government could be used in behalf of big business. Henry D. Lloyd, author of a famous early exposé of the Standard Oil Company's monopolistic business techniques, observed that Cleveland's intervention marked a shift in the traditions of the Democratic party. It sacrificed the long stand of the party against centralization "and surrendered both the rights of the States and the rights of man to the centralised corporate despotism to which the presidency of the United States was then abdicated." Lloyd, disillusioned with the sort of government regulation on which the special interests seemed to thrive, moved to a position of outright socialism. But government ownership, he insisted, must become a really popular democratic socialism, not just more "governmentalism." Government, he asserted, must be only a means to an end. "The least democratic countries in the world have state coal mines and state railroads, but they have no ownership by the people. The socialism of a kingly state is kingly still; of a plutocratic state, plutocratic. We mean to transform at the same moment we transfer." [33]

Much less cheerful than Lloyd at the prospects of living under a socialist utopia, Henry Adams nevertheless agreed with him that a new era was coming. "The reaction of fashionable society against our old-fashioned liberalism is extreme," he declared in 1897, "and wants only power to make it violent. I am waiting with curiosity to see whether the power will come — with the violence — in my time. As I view it, the collapse of our nineteenth century J. S. Mill, Manchester, Chicago formulas will be displayed — if at all

— by the collapse of Parliamentarianism, and the reversion
to centralised government." A year later, in the midst of a
stay in Hungary where he was able to observe at first hand
an example of state socialism, Henry wrote home to his
brother Brooks that this was a form of society that deserved
attention, especially in its possible connection with Russia.
"All monopolies will be assumed by the State; as a corollary
to the proposition that the common interest is supreme over
the individual." [34]

Whether in the direction of socialism, progressivism, or
semianarchist despair, the retreat of the liberals was well advanced by the turn of the century. The Spanish-American
War and ensuing adventure in imperialism, coming on top
of the hard times of the nineties, dashed even modest liberal
expectations for the future. To conservative William
Graham Sumner, the acquisition of the Philippines spelled
The Conquest of the United States by Spain. And to the
radical Tom Watson, the war doomed all reform hopes.
"The blare of the bugle drowned the voice of the Reformer." [35] Although the dismay of the anti-imperialist liberals was deepest, traditional liberals of whatever hue had
little reason for optimism. Under the leadership of Theodore Roosevelt and Woodrow Wilson, the trend toward big
government and big business was destined to continue. In
the midst of the popular enthusiasm for progressivism during the first decade of the twentieth century this was perhaps
not so clear. But from the perspective of a later age it is possible to see that the progressives were essentially nationalists,
moving to a state socialism along European lines and owing
relatively little to the American tradition of liberal individualism.

11

The Progressives as Nationalists

THE PROGRESSIVE movement, which dominated the American scene in the years from the turn of the century to United States entrance into World War I, was not primarily a liberal movement. It is true that the progressives fought for many a liberal cause and exposed many of the evils and inequities of post-Civil War industrial society. With the help of muckraking journalists and other idealists, the progressives were also able to put into practice a number of reform schemes — particularly in some of the old Populist strongholds in the West. But, in contrast to former American efforts at reform, progressivism was based on a new philosophy, partly borrowed from Europe, which emphasized collective action through the instrumentality of the government. In the progressive state of Wisconsin, for example, German influences were powerful, and many of the reformers who supported the La Follette program had a great admiration for the social legislation of the German states.[1] In the Federal government, and especially in the progressive philosophy of Theodore Roosevelt and his backers, this element of German nationalism and statism was equally strong. However liberal and idealistic such progressivism may have been in Wisconsin on a local grassroots level, on a national scale it came to have a quite different emphasis and ultimate purpose.

Progressivism, as it flourished in Washington at the turn of the century, was an outgrowth of post-Civil War trends in the direction of a greater concentration and centralization of political and economic power in the Federal government. Though the drive toward nationalism had been gathering momentum in the latter half of the nineteenth century, no satisfactory synthesis was achieved until after the War with Spain and Theodore Roosevelt's assumption of the presidency following McKinley's assassination. Roosevelt as president exemplified to a superlative degree the nationalistic side of progressivism. An enthusiastic believer in a strong centralized government, under firm executive leadership, Roosevelt was a patrician reformer who frankly preferred the principles of Alexander Hamilton to those of Thomas Jefferson. Concern over the welfare of the common man and an interest in clean government fitted in with his upper-class belief in the social responsibilities of the educated and wealthy citizen. At the same time he had only the greatest scorn for the kind of middle-class individualism and liberalism that emphasized minding one's own business both at home and abroad. In foreign affairs Roosevelt, despite a range of interest that was world-wide, was not fundamentally an internationalist in either thought or action. His major policies seldom rose above narrowly nationalistic considerations, and his venturesome diplomacy incited widespread animosity against the United States.

Following his death, soon after the Armistice of 1918, H. L. Mencken penned a savage "Autopsy" of the late President, in which he compared him to Frederick the Great and the Kaiser, in his love of armies and batteships, and to Nietzsche, in his distrust of the masses. An incessant advocate of "the duty of the citizen to the state, with the soft pedal upon the duty of the state to the citizen," Mencken depicted Roosevelt as an exemplar of the Bismarckian tradition of paternalistic reform from the top.

His instincts were always those of the property-owning Tory, not those of the romantic Liberal. All the fundamental objects of Liberalism — free speech, unhampered enterprise, the least possible governmental interference — were abhorrent to him. . . .

In all his career no one ever heard him make an argument for the rights of the citizen; his eloquence was always expended in expounding the duties of the citizen.[2]

Mencken's caustic appraisal has to some extent been reinforced in later studies of Roosevelt's career, but no one can question the Colonel's great influence on his times or his contemporary popularity. Though junior to most of his political associates, he gained the leadership of both progressive and imperialist forces in the United States, not only by virtue of being president but also by the possession of real abilities and a keen insight into the future. More than anyone else, he was responsible for Dewey's fleet being stationed at Hong Kong ready for its fateful dash to the Philippines — a voyage that did so much to launch the United States upon the course of imperialism. In domestic affairs, Roosevelt understood the radical temper of the nineties and the intensity of the public revolt against the monopolistic practices of big business. Determined therefore to avert the danger of an agrarian return to Jeffersonian liberalism or of a socialistic expropriation of private property, Roosevelt by a judicious mixture of trustbusting and benevolent regulation helped to safeguard American big business. The problem, as he saw it in 1905, was "to work out methods of controlling the big corporations without paralyzing the energies of the business community." [3]

Roosevelt's middle-of-the-road course of action in regard to the trusts, unforgettably characterized by Mr. Dooley — "On wan hand I wud stamp thim undher fut; on th' other hand not so fast" — was probably a popular compromise.

Although he disliked being cast in the role of a reformer, the rising rate of industrial combinations after the War with Spain forced Roosevelt into action. "Between 1898 and 1903 trusts were formed in rapid succession. The census of 1900 showed 185 industrial combinations, 73 of them capitalized at $10,000,000 or more, turning out 14% of the industrial products of the nation; 1901 witnessed the founding of the billion-dollar United States Steel corporation; and by 1904, 318 trusts controlled two fifths of the manufacturing capital of the country." [4]

In the technical sense of the term, trusts had been outlawed by the courts in the 1880's, but concentration of ownership continued apace. The Sherman Antitrust Act of 1890, though designed to prevent such an outcome, actually had the effect of encouraging monopoly in the new form of the holding company. By using this device, corporations were able to achieve the results of an outright merger, or of informal trade agreements, without incurring the charge of monopoly or of intercompany collusive action.

Meanwhile, the growth of big business was likewise encouraged by some of the government's more traditional policies. Thus, tariffs and government subsidies continued to be an important factor in preventing foreign competition with American business. President Henry O. Havemeyer of the American Sugar Refining Company claimed with some exaggeration that "The mother of all trusts is the customs tariff bill." Also vital to big business was United States patent law, with its provisions granting exclusive rights to an inventor for seventeen years; this enabled companies to buy up and hoard patents, using such control to maintain a monopoly. The United Shoe Company, for example, collected six thousand patents to protect its manufacturing process. It is not surprising therefore that an authority on the economic history of the progressive era, in noting the decline of laissez faire before the forces of reform, has pointed out the paradox that much of the regulatory legislation, which was passed with the idea of restoring free competition, had precisely the opposite effect.[5] In other words, government legislation was the greatest single factor in the decline of the very liberal economy that it sought to preserve and protect. Moreover, the progressive type of legislation, instead of encouraging democracy or competitive capitalism, in some ways perhaps, only made the whole economic system more difficult to operate.

Even when government withdrew its favors to business interests, as in the case of the decision to preserve as much of the national domain as possible from unregulated private exploitation, compensation was quickly forthcoming in substitute fields. In the Roosevelt administration, for example, business more than regained the advantages it lost through conservation by the new opportunities for industrial expansion that it received in connection with United States naval building and dollar diplomacy. Moreover, the conservation movement, sometimes pointed to as T.R.'s most lasting achievement, was in itself largely a nationalistic device popularized with much fanfare and publicity by Roosevelt and his friend Gifford Pinchot, chief of the United States Forest Service. After a century in which rapid exploitation of the resources of the West was encouraged in every way, the United States suddenly faced the prospect of potential exhaustion at a time when it was actively engaging in international rivalry with the other great powers of the world. Imperialism, with overseas markets and colonies, was one means of building up the nation's military might, but generally overlooked was the way in which conservation was also intimately related to economic preparedness in the event that the nation might be plunged into a major war.

The new nationalistic philosophy was clearly stated by

Charles R. Van Hise, president of the University of Wisconsin and one of the early leaders of the conservation movement. In a chapter of his standard work on the subject, entitled "Conservation and Patriotism," Van Hise noted that the era of free land was gone. In place of the individualism of the eighteenth and nineteenth centuries, "He who thinks not of himself primarily, but of his race, and of its future, is the new patriot." [6] Also a stanch advocate of governmental controls over the economy, Van Hise in his book *Concentration and Control,* published in 1912, suggested as a solution to the trust problem in the United States a frank recognition of the tendency toward concentration, and an equal acceptance of regulation through Federal commissions and administrative rulings. Critical of the policy of trying to enforce free competition by the antitrust laws, he declared:

It is to be noted that the development from pool to trust, from trust to holding company, and from holding company to complete consolidation, has been accelerated by the laws which exist in restraint of trade. The dissolution of pools by the courts led to the trust; the dissolution of the trust led to the holding corporation; the dissolution of the holding corporation at the present time is now leading to the consolidated company.

In contrast to the attitude in Western Europe, the American people were fearful of trusts and cartels; but Van Hise pointed out that, unless the United States was prepared to follow the European example, it would fall behind in the competition for world trade. If the Sherman Act continued to be enforced, American manufacturers would have to rely on the home market. "The United States," he concluded, "cannot successfully compete in the world's markets without large industrial units." [7]

Although President Roosevelt at first went along with the concept of trustbusting, any plans he may have had for the restoration of free competition soon yielded to the various contemporary pressures for a stronger economic nationalism. The growing twentieth-century rivalry for world trade indicated the need for such nationalism both at home and abroad. The net result of Roosevelt's policies in the instance of the trusts was not, therefore, a restoration of competition but a strengthening of the hand of the Federal government at the expense of the states. Although the borderline between state and Federal authority over the economy was often difficult to draw, the courts generally resolved any doubts in favor of Washington. This had been done in the case of the railroads, where the courts' interference with state regulation necessitated Federal action and resulted in the ineffective Interstate Commerce Act of 1887. The powers of the Commission were strengthened during the Roosevelt administration, but not to the point desired by western radicals, and the charge was made that the railroads actually pleaded for certain types of Federal legislation in order to avert the possibility of a new onslaught of state laws.[8]

This same story was repeated in regard to pure food and drug legislation. The Supreme Court, in a series of cases asserting exclusive Federal power over interstate commerce, denied to the states the right to interfere with the interstate shipment of goods in their original packages, thus making it difficult to enforce state liquor or pure food and drug laws. Undoubtedly, there was great abuse of the public by the patent medicine evil, by the use of dangerous adulterants and preservatives in food, and by false and misleading advertising. All these evils were much attacked by the medical associations and by the Bureau of Chemistry of the Department of Agriculture under Dr. Harvey M. Wiley. When it was finally passed by Congress in 1906 the Pure Food and Drug Act, together with a meat inspection law, represented a victory for the idea of government curbs on business. Yet, at the same time, these measures marked still another triumph of Federal power over the states. In pure food and drug legislation, the Federal government had the valuable aid of the courts as well as the advantages of the publicity aroused by Upton Sinclair's famous muckraking novel, *The Jungle,* and by Dr. Wiley's campaign for national action. But curiously, the pure food and drug law, as first enacted, failed to deal with the real crux of the problem — misleading and improper advertising — and it therefore had to be considerably amended five years later.[9]

The passage of the progressive legislation of the early 1900's, and the consequent enlargement of the scope of the Federal government, was accompanied by the development of a new ideology of reform. Obviously, the old Jeffersonian concepts would not do. Traditional liberalism, economic laissez faire, and the idea of the limited state were of little use in explaining the origins or significance of the progressives' program. Even Andrew Jackson, with all his thunder against banks and monopolies, and despite his nationalism and free use of the executive power, was not a suitable progenitor of progressivism. Such later-day agrarians as the Populists of the 1890's were also not fit predecessors of the progressive movement of the next decade. The Populists' primary concern, after all, was the interests of the dirt farmer, and their goal of an agrarian-type society could not help but repel the sophisticated urban reformers who took the lead in the progressive cause.

In contrast to the bleak despair of labor and farmers in the 1890's and the desperate class-conscious radicalism of the Populists, the progressives were on the hopeful side — at least in the beginnings of the movement. Coming into power on the high tide of prosperity after the successful War with Spain, they were confident of ushering in a new utopia. Unlike agrarian-dominated Populism, the reform of progressivism, as Eric Goldman points out, was to be "a product of the cities as much as of the farms, an amalgam of the Best People's liberalism and the nobody's Populism, a middle doctrine for a nation rapidly committing itself to middle-class ways of thinking. Progressivism accepted business America, even was enthusiastic about it, and aimed merely to correct abuses. . . . The restoration of opportunity by giving stronger powers to more democratized governments, a businesslike restoration with no disreputable caterwauling, . . . was a sweepingly appealing program, the most national one since the Republican platform that rode Lincoln into the White House. . . ." [10]

For a time during the depressed 1890's, large numbers of voters had seemed ready for almost any solution to their economic plight — whether Populism, socialism, or anarchism. But despite growing popular resentment over the favored position of big business, most Americans in the final analysis preferred to avoid a radical effort to solve their problems. Certainly, there were few who dared to propose what might have been the most drastic of reforms — the removal of all government aid to economic enterprise. Instead, the panacea for the hard times of the nineties, as it was again to be the attempted remedy in the 1930's, was a tightening of the bonds that tied politics to economic life. This type of program, in essence, was the same as that already being effected in many parts of Western Europe, notably in Germany and in England, where the industrial revolution had taken a strong hold. It was not without significance therefore that, as industrialism also gained pre-eminence in the United States of the post-Civil War era, American reformers and scholars should turn to Bismarck's Germany and to the Fabian Socialists in England as models for their political and economic theories. [11]

Industrial growth and combination, it was argued by progressives and reformers on both sides of the Atlantic, must be paralleled by a consolidation of regulatory powers in a centralized national government. Society in the future would have to be based more and more on an explicit subordination of the individual to a collectivist, or nationalized, political and social order. This change, generally explained as one of progress and reform, was of course also highly important in building up nationalistic sentiment. At the same time, the rising authority and prestige of the state served to weaken the vestiges of internationalism and cosmopolitanism and to intensify the growing imperialistic rivalries. With Roosevelt and his fellow progressives, the United States came of age as a great power, following England and Germany upon the world stage, and like them adopting the techniques of statism in the guise of reform. Carrying the confusion of terms to extremes, many of those who supported Bismarck's policies in Germany called themselves National Liberals, while the Liberal party in England under Lloyd George pushed through a Bismarckian program of nationalistic social legislation. In the United States, too, the progressives of both parties liked to think of their nationalistic measures as "liberal."

Underlying the example of practical, nationalistic reform in Germany, England, and the United States was a new ideology that placed heavy emphasis on the Darwinian theory of evolution and the economic interpretation of history. American intellectuals studying abroad were impressed with the new theories and, most important of all, returned home eager and ready to apply them to the reform cause. Darwinism, interpreted by Herbert Spencer as a justification of laissez faire, with government refraining from interference with the normal evolution of society, was redefined in terms of Darwinism as social control. According to reformers, evolution was not primarily a story of individuals in a "dog-eat-dog" competition with each other, but it indicated rather the success of individuals in a struggle with their environment. The lesson it taught was not laissez faire but social control. Instead of individuals being forced to adapt themselves to their environment, governments and reform agencies, the progressives believed, could help reshape the environment to meet the needs of individuals or of the species. Darwinian evolution, expressed in social terms, became reformism.

Also put to new use was the economic interpretation of history. Formerly the doctrine of conservative businessmen and statesmen, who from the time of Alexander Hamilton had adopted it as an argument for government protection of property interests, economic determinism was now called upon to justify government regulation of big business in the interests of the state. The economic motive was invoked to explain the rapacity of the plutocracy, and the thesis was advanced that reform could be accomplished only by opposing interest to interest. Thus, the national economic interest was deemed superior to that of the individual or group self-interest, and reform efforts were directed to furthering what was considered the welfare of the nation as a whole.

Both economic determinism and the theory of evolution were extremely important as weapons of social criticism. The contention that all ideas represented economic interests offered a medium through which abstract ideas, hitherto conceived as absolutes, could be tied to the motives of a single class, group, or individual. At the same time the evolutionary hypothesis posited a world in a state of constant change or development, in which ideas too were changing, and in which the truths of one generation might become the falsehoods of the next. "The eternal verities become, first, relative truths, then half-truths, or less than half-truths, even deliberate falsehoods. . . . Truth, in short, is a plan of action which is operationally successful." Such arguments, pointing to the relativist nature of truth and to its continual evolution under the impact of economic forces, were summed up in the philosophy of pragmatism and popularized in the writings and teachings of William James and John Dewey. Although the pragmatists were much concerned with the individual, they emphasized the importance of society and of the environment in effecting their goal of individual improvement. Inevitably, too, they stressed social and political reform, and pragmatism accordingly became the philosophy of the progressive movement, while pragmatists and progressives alike looked to the national state as the means of attaining their goals.[12]

Critics of pragmatism have lashed out at its doctrine of relativism for breeding "ideological eunuchs," and for leading to a philosophy of expediency. The association of evolution and economic interpretation, phrased as a union of Darwin and Marx, has been denounced as the source of the intellectual confusion of the modern age. Pragmatism, moreover, has been attacked not only for justifying the means by the end but for its undue emphasis upon means until they themselves became the end.[13] But pragmatism, and especially pragmatism in its relationship to the progressive movement, was perhaps most open to criticism from its own point of view, and for failing to live up to its own precepts. Whether or not such an outcome was an inevitable result of their teachings, it became increasingly evident that the pragmatists' and progressives' emphasis upon the state as a means of reform could easily lead to a situation in which the state appeared as the end or goal of all political and social change. The individual, in other words, would be dwarfed by the nationalism of the progressives.

In the same fashion, pragmatists and progressives, though

quick to criticize the past, were not always equally eager to apply the canons of relativism and economic interpretation of history to their own philosophy. Thus, progressives ignored the fact that their goals, too, were relative and subject not only to change but also to realistic, hardheaded economic and political criticism. As pragmatism sublimated its critical approach into a philosophy for the progressive movement, it began to lose its earlier liberal significance. From a philosophy of social criticism, it became an opportunistic program for political and social action. This shift from critical ideas to positive action entailed a change in eventual goals — from the emancipation of the individual to the aggrandizement of the powers of the national state.

A common substratum, underlying the whole progressive case, was the belief that the realities of modern economics and the theory of evolution made laissez-faire liberalism an old-fashioned and outmoded guide to political affairs. Traditional individualism was regarded as doomed, but the coming collectivism, it was felt, need not necessarily be socialism. For example, Charles W. Eliot, president of Harvard University, saw an American collectivism developing along the lines of the old New England community, instead of in the direction of a confiscatory socialism.[14]

In the progressives' battle against the laissez-faire concepts, which they viewed as still dominant in the political and economic order, every branch of the social sciences was enlisted. As early as 1884 a group of professional economists in forming a national organization drew up a platform which asserted:

We regard the state as an educational and ethical agency whose positive aid is an indispensable condition of human progress. While we recognize the necessity of individual initiative in industrial life, we hold that the doctrine of *laissez-faire* is unsafe in politics and unsound in morals; and that it suggests an inadequate explanation of the relations between the state and the citizens.[15]

A generation later, Simon N. Patten, a nationalist and optimist in his economic theories, which through his students had some influence upon the New Deal, published as a work in the American Social Progress Series his *New Basis of Civilization* (1907). According to Professor Patten, the old era of economic individualism had led to ruthless exploitation of the nation's resources. But these resources were still abundant enough to stamp out poverty and make possible further progress, if only they were subject to adequate social controls.

Along with economists and sociologists, other scholars called for the abolition of laissez faire and the institution of scientific social reform. At the same time jurists, political scientists, and historians united to show how the Constitution and courts had long supported laissez faire and conservative property interests in violation of popular democracy. J. Allen Smith's *Spirit of American Government*, a pioneer work in the economic interpretation of the Constitution, later much reinforced and documented by Charles Beard's famous volume, influenced among other progressives both Theodore Roosevelt and Robert M. La Follette. The book strengthened progressives' demand for constitutional changes and weakened the case for conservatives' devotion to the sanctity of the Constitution. Overlooked, however, by most progressives was Smith's insistence on the importance of reviving local government.[16] As another writer, the author of *An Essay on the Present Distribution of Wealth in the United States,* noted, "The smaller the area, the stronger the pressure of public opinion. As a rule, the middle classes can control the legislation enacted under their eyes by those whom they know, but only the wealthier classes can act unitedly and effectively upon legislation at the national capital." [17] Also important as a reform document, utilized by the progressive movement, was Charles Beard's *An Economic Interpretation of the Constitution,* but Beard did not write history with the needs of the progressives necessarily in mind.[18]

This task of formulating the ideology of progressivism into a systematic treatise was achieved most notably in Herbert Croly's *Promise of American Life.* Ten years in preparation, the Croly book was taken up by Theodore Roosevelt and applied in the Progressive party campaign in 1912. Croly reciprocated Roosevelt's enthusiasm by praising the President as the leading example of a constructive, nationalistic, and progressive reformer. When his book was published in 1909, Croly had just turned forty. Five years later he became editor of the *New Republic,* and during World War I, he supported Wilson and the New Freedom with all the same fervor that he had shown earlier in regard to Roosevelt's New Nationalism. It was not without significance that Croly, who was such an influential and enthusiastic adherent of the progressive movement in the United States, derived many of his ideas, as well as a good part of his early education, from abroad. One student of the period has called him an American follower of Comte, and there was certainly much of the positivist philosophy in his *Promise of American Life.*[19]

Croly began his long and detailed work with an attack on the theory of laissez faire and a plea that traditional Jeffersonian individualism be replaced by a more realistic philosophy. His basic hostility to Jefferson he illustrated in his reference to Alexander Hamilton, Jefferson's arch Federalist rival, as "much the finer man and much the sounder thinker and statesman." The Jeffersonian tradition, Croly believed, was inimical to a valid concept of nationalism, and he criticized the notion that opposition to national consolidation was the true mark of a democrat. The Jacksonians, he pointed out, had, by acting on this premise, destroyed such examples of nationalism as the Bank of the United States and the budding civil service bureaucracy. While Croly praised early Westerners as the first Americans to think in truly national terms, uniting democracy with nationalism, the abolitionists, no less than southern secessionists, earned his criticism for their weakening of national unity. Also the abolitionists made use of the natural rights argument, which Croly considered "one of the most perverted and dangerous . . . of all perverted conceptions of democracy. . . . Such a conception of democracy is in its effect inevitably revolutionary, and merely loosens the social and national bond." Abraham Lincoln, on the other hand, won Croly's approval because, although no abolitionist, he had refused to follow the old Clay-Webster policy of compromise on slavery. In Croly's eyes, abolitionism was too radical and Whig compromise too weak; only a vigorous middle-class, middle-of-the-road, nationalistic policy won his respect.[20]

The American philosophy of equal rights and of no government interference in private enterprise, Croly saw as leading inevitably to the conquest of the weak by the strong. The opportunities of a frontier society no longer existed in the United States, and government therefore must become a partner of the American people, while liberal followers of Jefferson would have to take over Hamilton's nationalistic methods. What was necessary, accordingly, was open government intervention in the economy and a redistribution of wealth.

The Promise of American Life is to be fulfilled — not merely by a maximum amount of economic freedom, but by a certain measure of discipline; not merely by the abundant satisfaction of individual desires, but by a large measure of individual subordination and self-denial. . . .

The automatic fulfillment of the American national Promise is to be abandoned, if at all, precisely because the traditional American confidence in individual freedom has resulted in a morally and socially undesirable distribution of wealth.

Urging democracy to exercise what he called "constructive discrimination," Croly explained:

Whatever the national interest may be, it is not to be asserted by the political practice of non-interference. The hope of automatic democratic fulfillment must be abandoned. The national government must step in and discriminate; but it must discriminate, not on behalf of liberty and the special individual, but on behalf of equality and the average man.

The practice of laissez faire and nonintervention, Croly maintained, was as dangerously selective as positive interference and selection by the state. "Impartiality," he concluded, "is the duty of the judge rather than the statesman, of the courts rather than the government." [21]

Croly realized that he was treading on dangerous ground in his onslaught upon traditional American ideals of freedom, and he frankly admitted that the corollary of the surrender of individualism was that "the American state will in effect be making itself responsible for a morally and socially desirable distribution of wealth." Like most of his fellow progressives, Croly believed that reform, to be effective, must be national in scope. Theodore Roosevelt accordingly won his warm praise as a reformer who was in the tradition of Hamiltonian nationalism. In contrast to a figure like Bryan, Roosevelt realized that reform could not be separated from nationalism. "He has, indeed," wrote Croly, "been even more of a nationalist than he has a reformer." Roosevelt, to

Croly, was a Hamiltonian with the difference that he accepted democracy and then emancipated it from its Jeffersonian heritage.[22]

In the latter half of his influential volume, Croly turned to a discussion of specific reform measures. Of some popular pieces of progressive legislation, particularly those looking toward a more direct democracy, Croly was openly cynical. Majority rule should not always be morally or nationally binding, he felt, while the secret ballot, direct government by the people, and more frequent elections might only damage democracy by making it less workable. In the same way, civil service reform hurt efficiency by enabling employees to become independent of their superiors. The political boss he condoned as necessary in an age of increasing specialization in order to overcome "a separation of actual political power from official political responsibility." [23]

Among constructive changes that Croly recommended was repeal of the Sherman Act and substitution of a national incorporation law with a Federal commission to regulate business. The government would also grant recognition to labor unions and, at the same time, control their operations. In all phases of his program Croly distinguished between nationalism and a European type of centralization. But Croly also felt that the United States, coming more and more to resemble the society and government of Europe, must copy European ways. In the realm of foreign affairs he accepted the need of a larger army and navy to go along with American interests abroad, and he defended war as a sometimes useful agent of civilization. While it would be inaccurate to apply the label "fascist" to Croly's ideas, there was no mistaking the extreme nationalistic tenor of his program or its similarities to a frankly collectivist and paternalistic type of corporate state.[24]

Although Herbert Croly accepted war as a possible resort, he was much less bellicose in his attitude toward foreign affairs than most progressives including, of course, Roosevelt himself and others like Senator Beveridge and Admiral Mahan, who were outspoken exponents of a policy of overseas imperialism. The progressive bloc in Congress generally followed Roosevelt and Beveridge in supporting a big navy and dollar diplomacy. The real political opposition to imperialism came from a small group of Democrats and Populists, although many of them, it was true, had originally supported the Spanish-American War as a fight for the liberation of Cuba. In foreign affairs therefore it was the anti-imperialists, rather than the progressives, who deserve the name "liberal." [25]

Historians, who make too rigid a distinction between foreign and domestic policy, have overlooked this intimate relationship between the aggressive foreign policy of the progressives and their emphasis on nationalism in home affairs. Likewise, many liberals themselves shared the historians' later confusion. So redoubtable an anti-imperialist as Carl Schurz, for example, nevertheless was enthusiastic over many of Roosevelt's domestic policies. But in such instances as the progressives' increasing acceptance of compulsory military training and of the white man's burden, there were obvious reminders of the paternalism of much of their economic reform legislation. Imperialism, according to a recent student of American foreign policy, was a revolt against many of the values of traditional liberalism. "The spirit of imperialism was an exaltation of duty above rights, of collective welfare above individual self-interest, the heroic values as opposed to materialism, action instead of logic, the natural impulse rather than the pallid intellect." [26] Such a description of imperialism also serves as a good evaluation of the temper of Theodore Roosevelt's nationalism, which achieved a new intensity in the election years 1910 and 1912.

In the two campaigns, Croly's book, touching the whole range of progressive policy, both foreign and domestic, was an especially pertinent document because its emphasis was on the nationalistic side of progressivism. It was this aspect, rather than any ideas of liberal reform, that won out in the formation of the Progressive party under Roosevelt's leadership. Earlier the former President had come home from his expedition to Africa, where he had hunted big game and lived the strenuous life. Returning by way of Europe, Roosevelt had reviewed troops with the German Kaiser, delivered several addresses, and talked seriously with the English Liberals, Herbert Asquith, Lloyd George, and Sir Edward Grey. While abroad Roosevelt had also managed to read *The Promise,* and he announced that the volume was "the most profound and illuminating study of our national conditions which has appeared in many years." [27]

Soon after Roosevelt's ship docked, author Croly received an invitation to lunch with the Colonel at Oyster Bay, and though the personal relationship waned, there was no lack of Croly's philosophy in the program of the New Nationalism, which Roosevelt announced in his famous speech at Osawatomie, Kansas, on August 31, 1910. Couched in demagogic terms, the address was filled with T.R.'s own peculiar mixture of moralism and nationalism. Equality of opportunity, he told his listeners, while essential to give every man a fair chance in life, also meant that "the commonwealth will get from every citizen the highest service of which he is capable. No man who carries the burden of the special privileges of another can give to the commonwealth that service to which it is fairly entitled." Reiterating his belief in an efficient army and navy, Roosevelt warned progressives "continually to remember Uncle Sam's interests abroad." [28]

Though the progressives' triumphs in the Congressional

elections of 1910 were not due to Roosevelt's campaigning, his speeches along with Croly's *Promise* marked another break in the traditional reform pattern of liberal individualism. In contrast to this, the New Nationalism, though not socialist in a Marxist sense, verged upon collectivism in its extreme statism. Croly, not running for public office, was unalarmed at the criticism of his book as socialistic, and actually the collectivism of both the *Promise* and the Progressive party was more nationalistic than socialist. Business leaders accordingly, instead of being fearful of the New Nationalism, rallied to Roosevelt as a possible Republican candidate in place of Taft. When Roosevelt criticized the President for his prosecution of the United States Steel Corporation under the antitrust laws, he won the even greater confidence of the business community and at the same time helped to counteract the effect of some of his own radical speeches.

By January 1912, representatives of business and finance were turning in force to Roosevelt as a presidential candidate. Daniel Willard, president of the Baltimore and Ohio Railroad, felt that the ex-President was the safest of the so-called progressives, while T.R.'s chief backer was George W. Perkins of J. P. Morgan and United States Steel. Publisher Frank A. Munsey, another important supporter, when asked for his advice on a vital speech, suggested that Roosevelt urge a frank statism. Even though the speech backfired because of Roosevelt's advocacy of the recall of state judicial decisions, the general tenor of the address was conservative and designed to appeal to the business world. Moreover, Roosevelt was careful to explain that his seemingly radical plan for the judiciary was necessary in order to push through his reforms and thus head off the dangerous ideas of Bryan and the socialists.[29]

The mixture of nationalism and paternalism continued

throughout the brief history of the Progressive party. George W. Perkins, in particular, strengthened his hold on its affairs, and he was responsible for the deletion of the antitrust plank from the 1912 platform. Perkins personally favored government regulation of the trusts through a commission empowered to set prices on industrial goods, and he, together with Frank Munsey, represented an element in the party and in the business community that especially admired German nationalism and the system of state reforms instituted by Bismarck. Roosevelt's own brand of progressivism was not unmarked by European parallels and had an obvious paternalism associated with its nationalism. Sensible regulation, Roosevelt had come to believe, was superior to trust-busting and a vain attempt at a return to an era of free competition. Appealing mostly to business groups and the urban voter, the New Nationalism was the antithesis of what the western farmer desired, and it has been suggested that Roosevelt's support in the West was a personal endorsement made in spite of his program. Though the seedbed of the progressive movement was in the Populist revolt of the nineties, the Progressive party was actually closer in its spirit and ideas to the later reforms of the New Deal than it was to Populism or to Wilson's New Freedom.[30]

Roosevelt himself, though disappointed by defeat in 1912, did not become completely embittered until he was forced to remain on the sidelines while Wilson led the country through World War I. More hopeful of democracy than some of his upper-class friends — Henry and Brooks Adams, for example — Roosevelt and his associates in the progressive movement nevertheless helped to turn reform further away from liberalism. Skeptical of either liberalism or T.R.'s progressivism, the Adamses were certain that the United States was following Europe toward state socialism. Increasing centralization and consolidation, leading to a revolutionary climax, was the theme that Brooks Adams had set forth as early as 1895 in *The Law of Civilization and Decay*. In this and in his later writings, Brooks swallowed the bitter pill and proceeded to carry to its logical conclusion the nationalism of Roosevelt and Croly. Imperialism, a greater militancy, a stronger national government, and a more effective public administration were the younger Adams's panaceas for staving off an impending social revolution.[31]

The Brooks Adams prescription of an imperialist state socialism was an extension of the Roosevelt-Croly version of nationalism. With so many progressives and reformers imbued with enthusiasm for the ideas of the New Nationalism, defense of liberalism was left in the hands of a dwindling minority of its traditional adherents, aided by a strange mixture of libertarians, which included radical socialists as well as old-fashioned conservatives. Socialists, though much divided among themselves, had no basic objection, of course, to the idea of government regulation of the economy. But socialists were not prepared to believe that the paternalistic nationalism of the progressives would ever lead to true socialism. Likening the trend toward economic and political monoply to a kind of benevolent feudalism, W. J. Ghent, the socialist writer, described the New Nationalism as the outline of a society in which "The State becomes stronger in its relation to the propertyless citizen, weaker in its relation to the man of capital." Conservatives complained of the usurpation of authority by the government and its executive branch. The danger of the growing powers of the president, and the extreme difficulty of interposing any constitutional check on such powers, was pointed out by William Howard Taft in airing his side of his well-known differences with Roosevelt. Also fearful of this tremendous centralization of authority, the New York *World*'s liberal editor asked: "Where will it all end? Despotism? Caesarism? . . ."[32]

To many of these critics of the Roosevelt variety of nationalistic progressivism, Woodrow Wilson's election seemed
to promise a return to older ways. The New Freedom as outlined by the former Princeton professor and such advisers as
Louis D. Brandeis, who believed that competition could be
made to work, was more hopefully liberal than the New
Nationalism. During the 1912 campaign, Wilson, who T.R.
complained was "not a Nationalist," attacked the bureaucratic statism and paternalism of Roosevelt's social welfare
program, offering in its stead a Jeffersonian view of society.
"The history of liberty," Wilson declared, "is the history of
the limitation of governmental power. . . . If America is
not to have free enterprise, then she can have freedom of no
sort whatever." [33] But the New Freedom was destined to
suffer its own contradictions, and it was also cut short perhaps by American entrance into World War I. By the conclusion of that crusade, the confusion and rout of the liberals
would be all but complete.

12

America Enters the Struggle for Power

THE YEARS of World War I brought the United States for the first time since the American Revolution into close political relationship with Europe. These years also climaxed a period in which American life and thought had increasingly begun to parallel that of Europe. Much of this contact, however, instead of bringing about a greater degree of international understanding, had acted merely to heighten nationalist feeling. The very entry of the United States into world affairs, somewhat ironically perhaps, seemed to intensify the official and popular desire to build up American military strength and power.

By the turn of the century, isolationism, fast vanishing in politics, was also breaking down in the realm of thought. The millions of immigrants who came to the New World, and the American scholars returning from the Continent, each helped to familiarize the American public with a broad variety of European ideas and ideologies. Many of the new currents of thought carried over from Europe were concerned with social changes that depended for their effectiveness upon the direct intervention of the government. This emphasis upon a kind of reform that was essentially nationalistic and socialistic in its approach came at a time when the older American individualism, continually weakened since

the Civil War, was rapidly disappearing. Although international socialism had never experienced in America the
relative success that it enjoyed in prewar Europe, much of
its program had been embraced indirectly in the progressive
movement of the early 1900's. Under progressivism, Americans had learned to accept a new centralization and concentration of political and economic powers in the hands of the
Federal government. Both European and American influences therefore helped to pave the way for the extensive role
that the government assumed after American entry into the
Great War. And it was also more than an interesting coincidence that America's involvement in the war followed immediately a decade in which its social and political contacts with
Europe had steadily mounted.

A few weeks before the Continent was plunged into the
horror of a general war, an outstanding American historian,
Frederick Jackson Turner, in a commencement address at
the University of Washington, pointed to the decline of
traditional American ideals before the onset of Old World
ideologies. Bearing in mind the disappearance of the unlimited resources of the United States, "we can understand,"
he said,

the reaction against individualism and in favor of drastic assertion of the powers of government. Legislation is taking the place
of the free lands as the means of preserving the ideal of democracy. But at the same time it is endangering the other pioneer
ideal of creative and competitive individualism. Both were essential and constituted what was best in America's contribution to
history and to progress. Both must be preserved if the nation is
to be true to its past, and would fulfil its highest destiny. It would
be a grave misfortune if these people so rich in experience, in
self-confidence and aspiration, in creative genius, should turn to
some Old World discipline of socialism or plutocracy, or despotic
rule, whether by class or by dictator.[1]

As Turner spoke to the graduating seniors, his thoughts may have strayed across the country to the White House, where his friend and old classmate at Johns Hopkins University was deep in the problems of his first term as president. Woodrow Wilson was chosen by the American electorate in 1912, in a campaign in which all the candidates — Wilson, Taft, Roosevelt, and Eugene Debs — had avowed in varying forms their loyalty to progressivism. Wilson, however, was in some ways an anachronism. A Southerner with a good deal of nostalgic sympathy for a Jeffersonian type of liberal society, he also had a deep admiration for the point of view of classic, nineteenth-century English political and economic liberalism. It was only in the later stages of his career, as he turned his attention from the academic world to the chance of success in politics, that he began to embrace the nationalistic and progressive currents of his time. These currents, however, he temporarily modified by his lingering affection for a Jeffersonian philosophy of limited government. And the legislation of his administration was characterized in large part by the effort to restore a regulated competition in contrast to the Roosevelt progressives' frank acceptance of a regulated monopoly. The Underwood Tariff, Federal Reserve Act, Clayton Antitrust Act, and Federal Trade Commission were major steps in this direction.

These substantial legislative achievements, together with the President's own administrative leadership and integrity, gained the general support of liberal groups. While previously many liberals had been almost equally antagonized by the aggressive nationalism of Roosevelt and conservatism of Taft, Wilson, perhaps more than any president since Jefferson, seemed destined to fulfill liberal hopes and ideals for the future. But, despite these fond expectations, there was evidence that Wilson's own enthusiasm for the New Freedom began to pale midway in his first administration. The impact of the European war and a severe business recession in the United States helped to drive the President into policies that seemed to vacillate between conservative business interests and the demands of the more nationalistic progressives. It was not surprising therefore that the attention of liberal admirers of the President soon shifted with the administration from domestic policies to an ever-increasing concern over foreign affairs. Here, liberal support helped Wilson to win re-election in 1916. And this same backing later enabled him to take the country into the raging European conflict on the high plane of idealism exemplified in the concept of a war for democracy and a war to end all wars.

In his first statements on the European war, the President expressed his fear of its possible effects upon American neutrality. Though anxious to keep the country at peace, Wilson also possessed qualities that made him peculiarly susceptible to the idea of the United States' assuming an active role in the great world conflict at arms. In the long run, this missionary note of militant leadership, under which America was to head a crusade for world peace and democracy, proved far more influential in Wilson's thinking than the concepts of a liberal pacifism or a traditional isolationism.

The notion of a crusade came naturally to Wilson, the son of a Presbyterian minister, imbued with a stern Calvinist sense of determinism and devotion to duty. The future President was to spend most of his adult life in academic halls as a teacher of political science, and when he resigned as head of Princeton University to become governor of New Jersey, he carried over into politics his belief in Christian moralism and his conviction of the duty of the scholar. These views, partly expressed in his domestic policy, emerged most clearly, however, in his conduct of foreign affairs. Here, despite the pacific and liberal implications set forth in his Mobile Address repudiating dollar diplomacy, Wilson was ready to play the role of apologist for the white man's burden and imperialism. He was convinced that isolation was outmoded and that the United States must assume its proper place in the world. Without yielding his horror of war, he inclined to an interventionist position that could lead to war. He seemed to feel that the United States had a mission to spread its institutions — which he conceived as liberal and democratic — to the more benighted areas of the world.

Though Wilson disavowed the language of dollar diplomacy, the ends of his policy were often much the same as those of his Republican predecessors. Indeed, according to his latest biographer, "The years from 1913 to 1921 witnessed intervention by the State Department and the navy on a scale that had never before been contemplated, even by such alleged imperialists as Theodore Roosevelt and William Howard Taft." [2] Believing an expansion of foreign trade vital, not only to the interests of the United States but also to world peace, the Wilson administration aggressively pursued American commercial interests in the Far East and in Latin America, expanded the foreign trade divisions of the Department of Commerce, and developed the American merchant marine. Wilson no doubt would have preferred the growth of United States foreign trade to come about as a result of free international competition, but he found it easy with his ideas of moralism and duty to rationalize direct American intervention as a means of safeguarding the national interest. In a sense therefore the use of American troops in Haiti, Nicaragua, and finally Mexico was the Wilsonian prelude to the most fateful of all his policies — the entrance of the United States into the European war.

Once the struggle against Germany was joined, Wilson accepted wholeheartedly the doctrine of an American mission for peace and democracy, but he nevertheless found it difficult to take the last, portentous steps along the road to war. His initial stern injunction to the American people to enforce a strict neutrality "in thought as well as in action" was not altered in the early months of the war as he perceived the selfish ambitions of the rival European powers. To the demand at home for expanded military preparedness he at first turned a deaf ear. In his annual message to Congress in December 1914 he made a strong answer to Theodore Roosevelt and those other critics of his neutrality policies who were urging a greater measure of rearmament by the United States. Preparedness, the President pointed out, was a relative term, and he recalled that the American tradition was one of peace and hostility to standing armies. Under his administration, he declared, we will prepare "to the utmost; and yet we shall not turn America into a military camp. We will not ask our young men to spend the best years of their lives making soldiers of themselves." [3]

Less than a year later, by the summer of 1915, however, Wilson was ready to change his views on preparedness. This decision, which has been explained in terms of domestic politics as well as by the threat of German submarine warfare, may also have been related to the President's desire to yield neutrality in favor of the concept of an enforced peace. Preparedness logically looked toward American intervention in the war, and it meant too that Wilson had joined forces with many of the big business and ultranationalistic groups which, for a mixture of patriotic and selfish reasons, were among the most enthusiastic backers of a larger army and navy.

By the spring of 1916, the question of preparedness dominated the thinking of the nation, and the presidential election that fall turned on the issue. Although both Wilson and his Republican opponent, Charles Evans Hughes, denied that the type of preparedness they advocated would lead to militarism, the country was whipped into a high state of excitement by the preparedness parades and patriotic motif of the campaign. The Wilson slogan, "He kept us out of war," though factually correct, gave a misleading impression with regard to the future. The President's own firm stand against the German methods of submarine warfare, coupled with increasing American sympathy for the Allied cause, had deprived his diplomacy of the flexibility and neutral point of view necessary to keep America at peace. As Wilson himself seems to have realized months before the election in November, if the European war did not come to an abrupt close, the United States would eventually be drawn into the conflict on the side of the Allies.

Peace therefore hung on the slender thread of Germany's averting the further loss of American lives by foregoing its use of the submarine. Moreover, although Americans had voted for peace in 1916, a considerable minority was urging American intervention in behalf of the Allies. To an increasing number of Americans, war, even to the point of militarism and illiberalism at home, seemed preferable to facing the consequences of a German victory in Europe. It was believed that United States entry into the war, if the President deemed it necessary, might become the means of extending the ideals of a progressive American democracy to a war-torn and reactionary Europe. Many apostles of the New Freedom at home were ready therefore to espouse the President's noble vision of an international crusade for peace and democracy.

Among the liberals who were helping the President in his struggle to convince himself and the American people of the justice of United States participation in the great European conflict, none was more important than the group of intellectuals associated together in writing for the *New Republic*. Born in the same year as the opening of the war, the *New Republic* under the editorship of Herbert Croly gradually shifted from a support of Theodore Roosevelt and the Progressives to a warm enthusiasm for the New Freedom of Woodrow Wilson. The magazine speedily achieved a reputation as the leading liberal reform journal in the United States, and its editors were widely supposed to have great influence in the White House. In its first two years, however, the magazine wavered in its foreign policy, uncertain as to whether it supported Theodore Roosevelt's militant preparedness or the President's pacific neutrality. But in the later stages of the debate over American foreign policy, the *New Republic* and its contributors accepted more and more the notion of American entry into the war via the Wilson formula of an enforced and democratic peace.

Of the *New Republic* group, no one was more forthright in arguing the case for preparedness and war than its editor. Croly, for example, believed that the preparedness program of 1916, though it violated America's historic traditions, was necessary because of President Wilson's decision in the summer of 1915 that there was a threat of war. Croly pointed out that the United States, following in the stream of European history, could hardly avoid adopting some of the features of European life, including a certain degree of militarization. "The American nation," he declared, "needs the tonic of a serious moral adventure." While he criticized the army legislation of 1916 as a militaristic measure, providing troops primarily for offensive action, he also expressed the hope that the new army, despite its danger to American traditions and institutions, might introduce a useful ferment into national life and give it a necessary "tonic effect." "The usual explanation that the United States is preparing only for defense, which is a policy on which all good citizens can agree, merely begs the question," Croly asserted, because, in the case of a large nation like the United States, "no sharp line can be drawn between defensive and aggressive armament." Thus the "dubious aspect" of preparedness lay not in its cost but "in the ambiguity of its underlying purpose." Croly frankly admitted that "there is a very real probability that the new Army and Navy will be used chiefly for positive and for aggressive as opposed to merely defensive purposes." [4]

Croly appealed to his liberal readers to be realistic about the war. But interspersed with his call to realism was Croly's emphasis on national ideals and morality. This same dualism also characterized the articles which America's leading pragmatist, John Dewey, published, mostly in the *New Republic,* during the war years. After the outbreak of hostilities in 1914, Dewey devoted considerable attention to a comparison of the national philosophies of the belligerents. He himself had early in his career rejected the absolutist philosophy of Hegel and the German idealists, imposed upon him while he was a graduate student. Now, in the process of the war, he saw this German idealist philosophy hardened into a rationalization of German war aims. According to Dewey, to the Germans the war was part of a ceaseless and agelong striving to realize the national will embodied in the German people. Such ideas of nationalism, he felt, were romantic, medieval, and rooted in a mysticism incomprehensible to other peoples. Thus, he saw the war as a conflict of ideas in which the German mind was quite incompatible with the American mind.[5]

Having made an interpretation of the war in intellectual terms, Dewey and his followers had to decide the important question of whether war and the use of force were justified. Historically, force and war could not be separated from the operation of the whole system of power politics in international relations. Here Dewey as a pragmatist and instrumentalist pointed out that a war could not be dissociated from the ends that it sought to achieve. Thus he found the customary pacifist objection to all use of force absurd and based on a lack of understanding of the function of a political state. What was objectionable was not the use of force itself, but the unwise or ineffective use of force. It "all depends," said Dewey, "upon the efficient adaptation of means to ends." While the use of force could be justified in terms of ends, Dewey did not believe that war, marked by "waste and loss," was "the most economical method of securing the results which are desirable with a minimum of the undesirable results." [6]

Dewey's rather theoretical analysis of the issues presented by the European war prepared him for the stand that he took on the practical problems facing America as a result of that conflict. Here he found American thinking too narrow and limited in its excessive preoccupation with the solely military aspects of preparedness — a larger army and navy and compulsory military training. The first means of preparedness that was needed, Dewey decided, was a truly national and compulsory educational system to counteract the provincialism and isolation of American life. American history, if it was taught to show American development as a reflection of European movements and problems, could be useful as a measure of national preparedness. Properly and uniformly taught throughout the United States, it could be a powerful factor in achieving a united America. "A generation educated in the facts of American history instead of in an American mythology would not be at a loss to find and express a unified mind in a crisis like the present, should one recur." Dewey's objection to a system of purely military training therefore was that it was not the best and most efficient means for achieving the Americanism and national unity which he believed should be the real goal of preparedness.[7]

Like President Wilson, Dewey moved steadily toward a position that favored American entrance into the war on the side of the Allies. Among the last of his essays prior to American participation in the world conflict was his fervent call to arms, "In a Time of National Hesitation." This emotional and pseudo-mystical ode to American nationalism was altogether a remarkable piece of writing for the realistic and pragmatic American philosopher who had two years before been so critical of the Germans' romantic and medieval notions concerning war. America, Dewey now asserted, was uncertain over entering the war because "we have not yet found a national mind, a will as to what to be." But that discovery was afoot and would apparently come with American entry into the war. This, then, would mark America's coming of age, and her independence culturally from Europe and England.[8]

In assessing the responsibility for America's hesitation in regard to the war, Dewey placed much of the blame upon the pacifists, who, he believed, had blinded themselves to the vital issues at stake. The peace movement thus seemed to Dewey to be a striking example of the lack of realism in American thinking in regard to war. Failing to recognize the "immense impetus to reorganization afforded by this war," American pacifists had wasted their power in trying to keep the United States out of a struggle "which was already all but universal." Instead of using all their energy "to form, at a plastic juncture, the conditions and objects of our entrance," pacifists had devoted themselves to the vain effort to preserve American neutrality. Thus the United States, entering the war without the conditions of American participation determined in advance, would have to use what means it could to see that its ideals were "forced upon our allies, however unwilling they may be, rather than [be] covered up by the débris of war." [9]

To counteract what he considered the pacifists' muddled thinking, and to help overcome American apathy regarding the war, Dewey called for more attention to the means of its prosecution. Opposed to creating a war motivation by appeals to patriotic hysteria, Dewey stressed the need for a practical "businesslike psychology" that would perceive the ends to be accomplished and make an "effective selection and orderly arrangement of means for their execution." Our national intelligence seemed to lie in the direction of the practical, and a realistic, businesslike attitude, he felt, should be emphasized along with the Wilsonian liberal note of "an underlying national idealism." Dewey's concentration on the practical did not mean that he ignored the emotional and irrational side of war. This, he realized, could easily get out of hand, spawning an insane mass hatred and intolerance. Accordingly, he made strong protest against the growing "conscription of thought" in America. But, though he warned against the excesses of war and nationalism, Dewey did not offer any solution as to how the good elements were to be separated from the bad, or as to how the emotional and irrational aspects were to be avoided.[10]

According to Randolph Bourne, Dewey's former disciple and most important wartime critic, illiberalism was a part of the very nature of war. "It is only 'liberal' naïveté that is shocked at arbitrary coercion and suppression. Willing war means willing all the evils that are organically bound up with it." On this thesis Bourne launched his biting attack upon Dewey and the *New Republic* group of progressive liberals who accepted the war.[11]

In the first years of the war, before American entrance, Bourne had agreed with Dewey's emphasis on the need for cultural nationalism and educational preparedness. In his article "A Moral Equivalent for Universal Military Service," Bourne recognized the American craving for service and unity of sentiment. "We want action," he wrote, "but we do not want military action." Noting that "Education is the only form of 'conscription' to which Americans have ever given consent," he suggested a plan of schooling until the age of sixteen, to be followed by two years of national service, primarily in the field of social work, but which might incidentally include some military training for a minority of the youths. This essay, largely a product of his great enthusiasm for Dewey's ideas on progressive education, had little in common, however, with the writing that Bourne did after the United States declared war.[12]

Following that decision, and as he perceived his old pacifist and liberal friends plunge with varying degrees of enthusiasm into war work — abandoning the "task of making our country detailedly fit for peace . . . in favor of a feverish concern for the management of the war . . . the coalescence of the intellectual classes in support of the military programme." Bourne complained of the feeling of being left in the lurch. Dewey's pragmatism, the philosophy that he relied on "almost as our American religion," no longer seemed to work. It "is inspiring enough," he wrote, "for a society at peace, prosperous and with a fund of progressive good-will. . . . It is a scientific method applied to 'uplift.' " But he emphasized: "What concerns us here is the relative ease with which the pragmatist intellectuals, with Professor Dewey at the head, have moved out their philosophy, bag and baggage, from education to war." [13]

Before his attack on Dewey, with its bitter title "Twilight of Idols," Bourne penned an even more savage satire upon the whole circle of his old liberal associates. "The War and the Intellectuals" was Bourne's answer to the liberals' pragmatic case for the war. "To those of us who still retain an irreconcilable animus against war," he began, "it has been a bitter experience to see the unanimity with which the American intellectuals have thrown their support to the use of war-technique in the crisis in which America found herself."

Not content with merely confirming the fact of war, the intellectuals "are now complacently asserting that it was they who effectively willed it . . . against the hesitation and dim perceptions of the American democratic masses. A war made deliberately by the intellectuals! A calm moral verdict, arrived at after a penetrating study of inexorable facts! . . . A war free from any taint of self-seeking, a war that will secure the triumph of democracy and internationalize the world!" [14]

While the intellectuals identified themselves with the least democratic elements in the United States, Bourne lamented: "No one is left to point out the undemocratic nature of this war-liberalism. In a time of faith skepticism is the most intolerable of all insults." In the idea of a League of Peace, which captured the imagination of so many of his former friends, Bourne saw only "a dogma to jump to." The real enemy, he concluded, was not Imperial Germany, but war, and he complained against the notion of a "world-order founded on military coalitions." Bourne also pointed out that a defeated Germany, forced to accept democracy, would become a constant menace to the peace of Europe. [15]

Gradually liberals who clung to their belief in an idealistic war were forced to admit, as in the case of the *New Republic,* their disappointment over the conduct of the struggle. But Bourne argued that the war did not need their enthusiasm — "Patriotism is really a superfluous quality in war." All that was necessary was "the cooperation of the men who direct the large financial and industrial enterprises." Adjusting to unpleasant inevitability, many of the liberals thereby preserved their pragmatism, but the "penalty the realist pays for accepting war is to see disappear one by one the justifications for accepting it." [16]

Bourne pushed his attack on the war to its ultimate con-

clusion in his unfinished book on the state, which was
published in 1919, a year after his death. In this work he
demonstrated how war, in its cultivation of the herd instinct,
made minority opinion a crime and unswerving loyalty the
sole test of citizenship. "The slack is taken up, the cross-
currents fade out, and the nation moves lumberingly and
slowly, but with ever accelerated speed and integration,
towards the great end, towards that 'peacefulness of being at
war. . . .' " The central ideas, which Bourne recurred to
throughout this last work, were that "War is the health of
the State" and "We cannot crusade against war without cru-
sading implicitly against the State." [17]

His impassioned opposition to the war cost Bourne most
of his friends and virtually all of his income. The better-
paying magazines were no longer interested in his articles,
and when the *Seven Arts,* which had printed his war essays,
suspended publication Bourne was deprived of his last medium of expression. After the war, it was true, the intellectuals' new-found admiration for Bourne's trenchant writings came to assume the nature of a literary cult, but in 1917
all except a small dissident minority accepted the war on
Wilson's terms.[18]

As the intellectuals helped prepare the country for war,
their leader in the White House, on the eve of delivering his
war message, was seized with some strange misgivings. Unlike the majority of the citizenry, Wilson cherished no hope
that America could fight a great war in a liberal or progressive atmosphere. Calling Frank Cobb, the editor of the New
York *World,* into a late meeting the night before he was to
deliver his war message to the assembled Congress, Wilson
poured out his anxiety. ". . . when a war got going," Cobb
reported the President as saying, "it was just war and there
weren't two kinds of it. It required illiberalism at home to

reinforce the men at the front. We couldn't fight Germany and maintain the ideals of Government that all thinking men shared. . . ."

"Once lead this people into war," he said, "and they'll forget there was ever such a thing as tolerance. To fight you must be brutal and ruthless, and the spirit of ruthless brutality will enter into every fibre of our national life, infecting Congress, the courts, the policeman on the beat, the man in the street." Conformity would be the only virtue, said the President, and every man who refused to conform would have to pay the penalty.

He thought the Constitution would not survive it; that free speech and the right of assembly would go. He said a nation couldn't put its strength into a war and keep its head level; it had never been done.[19]

Wilson's fears, privately confided to Cobb, had little echo as the country responded to his own eloquent plea for a declaration of war. The United States, the President emphasized in his war message, was entering a war of principle with "no selfish ends to serve." In contrast to Germany's use of the submarine to wage "a warfare against mankind," the United States proposed to fight to make the world "safe for democracy." Wilson obviously believed that a German victory posed a greater threat to American democracy than the illiberalism and militarism that he expected would accompany American belligerency.[20]

The President's anguished statement to Frank Cobb that it would require "illiberalism at home to reinforce the men at the front" did not wait long for fulfillment. In a little more than two months after the declaration of war Congress, in response to urgings from the President, approved legislation making possible conscription for military service, the establishment of an official propaganda agency, and a law for the suppression of any opposition or dissent. All these meas-

ures were justified by the administration as vital to winning
the war, and the alarmed protests of liberals were accordingly brushed aside.

Military conscription — or selective service, as it was
called to soften the blow — was the most obviously related
of all the war legislation to actual fighting needs. But the
American people had not expected that the war would entail
a vast American conscript army serving overseas. Despite
persistent agitation in military circles for some form of compulsory military training, the idea of conscription had never
been popular in the United States. Now, with American
entry into the war, the earlier military emphasis on training
or education was shifted to proposals for actual combat
service, and the President gave his backing to hitherto secret
army plans for a wartime selective service, or draft, law.

Conscription, whatever wartime needs, seemed to violate
all the tenets of traditional American liberalism. From a liberal point of view it was regimentation of the individual by
the state. As Frederick Palmer, the biographer of Secretary
of War Newton D. Baker, later wrote: "America for the first
time had regimentation on the European system, naïvely
unaware of its effects." Although Palmer saw the workings
of selective service as "an exhibition of democracy trium-
phant," he also noted that it was "our first great standardization of human material in mass production." [21] In peacetime, compulsory military service or training had always
been regarded by liberals as synonymous with the philosophy
and practice of militarism, and prior to 1917 it had been
considered a distinctive trait of Prussian militarism. As long
as American democracy was conceived of primarily in terms
of the free individual, conscription had been viewed as the
antithesis of democratic government. Only after the United
States began to borrow more and more from European concepts and practices was the argument seriously made that

conscription, in subjecting everyone to an enforced equality of sacrifice, was not incompatible with democracy.

This contention, plus the renewed emphasis on the duties instead of the rights of the citizen, fitted in very well with American progressives' urging of greater regulatory and administrative powers for the government. The relationship of conscription and statism was clearly pointed out by Oswald Garrison Villard, the liberal pacifist editor of the *Nation*. On the eve of the war, Villard reiterated his conviction that "there's a higher allegiance today than any one can owe to one's country," and he questioned the logic of the so-called practical capitalist who, in his advocacy of conscription and war, "never notices that militarism is the best friend of the Socialist, that where universal military service flourishes there are the largest armies of the advocates of the doctrines of Karl Marx." [22] While no measure was more abhorrent to such old-line believers in traditional liberalism as Villard, conscription in 1917 was being advocated almost as much by progressives as by conservative army officers and businessmen. In the Progressive party of Theodore Roosevelt these groups coalesced, and it was not without significance that in the 1916 election campaign only the Progressives' short-lived platform contained a plank calling for universal compulsory military training.[23]

Although the weight of opinion in the United States would probably have preferred to try the volunteer method of raising an army, most people in 1917 followed the President and acquiesced, however reluctantly, in the use of the draft as a purely wartime measure. June 5, the date set aside for the initial registration of some ten million men between the ages of twenty-one and thirty, passed with a surprisingly small show of disorder or protest. The editors of the *New Republic*, who were amazed to see "the success of selective service" despite the fact that it went beyond the original public understanding of a draft only for home defense, warned, however, that excessive coercion in the enforcement of the act might result in a reaction against the whole idea of conscription. Also among those who expressed surprise at the lack of opposition was Henry Adams, who was amused to see how Wilson leading the country into war had discomfited the Republicans and forced even Theodore Roosevelt and Henry Cabot Lodge to go at least part way with the President. "As far as I know," Adams wrote, "we have behaved like lambs and done everything we were told to do. Never could I have conceived that in a short three months we could have gone into a great war and adopted a conscription not unworthy of Germany, at the bidding of a President who was elected only a few months ago on the express ground that he had kept us at peace." [24]

While there was some truth in the *American Socialist*'s contention that the six million men claiming exemption constituted "an overwhelming vote against war, by those who must do the fighting," basically it was only a small minority of pacifists and conscientious objectors that attempted to resist the draft. The Selective Service Act provided noncombatant duty for religious objectors who were members of the Society of Friends or other sects traditionally opposed to war, but it failed to recognize the situation of those who might object as individuals to all wars, or to a particular war that they felt to be unjust. At Senate hearings on the draft bill, liberals had argued unsuccessfully for a more liberal exemption clause to include all sincere objectors, whether or not they were members of an historic peace church. However, neither the President nor Congress was disposed to deal sympathetically with the individual objector. While the draft bill was still pending, Wilson wrote that "it has seemed impossible to make the exemptions apply to individuals because it would open the door to so much that was unconscientious on the part of persons who wished to escape service." [25]

In all, about four thousand men refused to perform any type of service in the army. Some of these, however, eventually accepted noncombatant duties, while others were granted agricultural or industrial furloughs. A smaller group of some four hundred who continued to reject the uniform were court-martialed and sentenced to long terms in army prisons, chiefly at the disciplinary barracks at Fort Leavenworth. Still another group, including socialist, radical, or humanitarian objectors to war, were classified by the government as draft evaders because they refused to register or report for induction. Both of these small bodies of uncomprising objectors were forced to undergo harsh and barbaric treatment in army camps or in Federal penitentiaries, although some relief finally came after their plight was called to the attention of the President and Secretary of War Baker. The President, however, firmly rejected the suggestion that he grant a blanket pardon to those violators of the draft law who were not consciously disloyal or at all insincere in their stand.[26]

The extraordinary degree of conformity, illustrated by the lack of any real organized resistance to the draft, was backed up by an adroit mixture of propaganda and repression instituted by the administration. While the silencing of dissenting opinion was made possible through espionage and sedition legislation, the more positive task of indoctrination was placed in the hands of the Committee on Public Information, created by executive order of the President on April 13, 1917. George Creel, a progressive and rather liberal-minded journalist, was appointed as chairman of the committee, which has been termed by its unofficial historians "America's propaganda ministry during the World War." In their words, the committee was "charged with encouraging and then consolidating the revolution of opinion which changed the United States from anti-militaristic democracy to an organized war machine." [27]

To accomplish his formidable task, Creel assembled a large and talented group of writers and scholars who served as public relations counselors to the government and as press agents for transmitting propaganda and information to the people of the United States and their allies and enemies abroad. "It was a gargantuan advertising agency the like of which the country had never known, and the breathtaking scope of its activities was not to be equalled until the rise of totalitarian dictatorships after the war." [28] The Creel Committee, as it was popularly called, maintained in a highly complex and efficient way the war for men's minds. It carried to its logical conclusion the Wilsonian view, shared by John Dewey and many other progressives, that the war was a great ideological struggle, pitting the democrary of the United States and the Allies against German autocracy and militarism. The great tragedy, which Wilson had partially foreseen, was that such a crusade, however liberal in its intentions, could not be carried through without the sacrifice of many of the values that liberals especially prized. This meant not only propaganda and a partial twisting of the truth to meet military needs, but also outright suppression of freedom of speech and thought through prosecution of individuals and organizations under wartime espionage and sedition legislation.

The first of such measures, the Espionage Act of June 15, 1917, was thoroughly debated in Congress because the original bill contained a section providing for censorship of the press. However, once this provision had been removed, the formidable opposition of the newspaper publishers evaporated. Now popularly regarded as only a "spy bill," its implications as to civil liberties were ignored, and it passed through both houses of Congress largely unnoticed. In the actual enforcement of the act, the fears of liberals and pacifists that it would be used to muzzle dissenting opinions proved correct, as only a small minority of the defendants brought to trial could be fairly construed as the spies or enemy agents against whom the public thought the law was directed. Actually, it was one section of the act, that prohibiting any criticism of the armed forces or interference with recruiting, which provided the basis for the suppression of free speech and the attendant prosecution of a number of famous radicals on the grounds of antiwar or pro-German utterances. Although the newspapers were elated at the absence of an actual censorship clause, publications that incurred the displeasure of the Creel Committee could be punished in other ways. Thus radical journals, including the *Masses* and Victor Berger's Milwaukee *Leader,* were deprived of their second-class mailing privileges by order of the Postmaster General.[29]

In the cases that crowded the Federal courts as a result of the Espionage Act, judges almost without exception followed Justice Holmes's contention that the right of free speech was not an absolute right, but had to be considered in the context of the "clear and present danger" represented by the war. The American judiciary thus revived the old English practice of judging a statement in terms of its "bad tendency" and "presumptive intent." On the basis of this interpretation, socialist and pacifist statements critical of the war could be ruled to violate the Espionage Act because they might have the effect of encouraging disaffection in the armed forces. Any radical manifesto that directly incited its audience to violence, such as an appeal to commit murder, or arson, or treason could, of course, be dealt with by the customary criminal statutes. The great significance of the Espionage Act therefore was that it made the free expression of certain ideas, not hitherto subject to prosecution, a crime. In contrast to the clear-cut words of the First Amendment, the Espionage Act went back for its only precedent in American history to the Sedition Act of 1798, a measure which President Wilson in happier days had declared to have "cut perilously near the root of freedom of speech and of the press." [30]

The Espionage Act was followed eleven months later by a series of amendments in the form of a new and greatly expanded statute, the Sedition Act of May 16, 1918. This measure made virtually any criticism of the government or the war a criminal offense. In the hands of overzealous Federal attorneys, or by the stimulus that they offered to patriotic but misguided citizens who reported the least offense, the espionage and sedition laws made possible the arrest and imprisonment of a number of basically loyal but incautious individuals, guilty only of hasty or intemperate remarks. Men and women were arrested for criticizing the Red Cross or the methods of selling Liberty bonds, while Mrs. Rose Pastor Stokes was indicted and convicted for using, in an argument against war to a group of women, the words, "I am for the people, and the government is for the profiteers." Others were prosecuted for criticism of the Allies, and a movie producer received three years in prison for showing a film *The Spirit of '76,* which in depicting battle scenes of the American Revolution was deemed to be guilty of arousing antagonism to Great Britain. Even members of the Congress were not safe from war hysteria. In the Senate, for over a year, a bitter fight was waged to expel Robert M. La Follette from his seat because of an allegedly disloyal speech he had made in St. Paul, Minnesota, before a Conference of the Nonpartisan League. Not until after the Armistice was La Follette able to secure passage of a Senate resolution dismissing the disloyalty charges. [31]

The most famous of the World War free speech cases involved Eugene Debs, the socialist leader, who was arrested one month after the passage of the Sedition Act for his talk to a group of workers at Canton, Ohio. While Debs had made his usual attack on the war as a capitalist struggle, much of the speech was given over to an eloquent defense of the role that minority groups had played in history. Debs praised the radicals and young men who had had the courage to go to jail for their antiwar convictions, and he questioned the continual talk about patriotic duty by the capitalist leaders of the country. "It is not *their* but *your* duty that they are concerned about," he declared. "There is a decided difference. Their patriotic duty never takes them to the firing line or chucks them into the trenches." Brought to trial, Debs refused to call any witnesses and pleaded his own case. Denying that there was a word in his Canton speech to warrant the charge that he was an advocate of force and violence, Debs appealed to the precedents set by other rebels in American history: the founding fathers, the abolitionists, and the pacifists. All these had, at some time or another, urged a change in the American government or its policies. Aware nevertheless of his probable guilt under the terms of the espionage legislation, Debs made his defense on the basis of the First Amendment to the Constitution. "That is the right I exercised at Canton. . . . I believe in the right of free speech, in war as well as in peace." Although the war had come to an end before Debs's appeal reached the Supreme Court, his sentence of ten years' imprisonment was upheld on March 10, 1919, in a decision written by Justice Holmes.[32]

In general, he government concerned itself only with the more militant minority that spoke out in public against the war. But untold numbers suffered persecution of one sort or another as a consequence of their radical or pacifist views. People of German background especially were affected. Professional patriots were instrumental in having the teaching of German banned from a number of schools, and there soon developed "an hysteria marked by a passionate and unreasoning hatred of everything German — including German literature and music — a wild and fearful hatred of the Hun, the German beast, the murderous Kaiser." Ministers lost their pulpits or were forced to take leaves of absence. Teachers were subjected to various restraints, and many pacifist instructors, especially in public schools and colleges, were summarily dismissed. The way in which the government interpreted and administered the espionage and sedition laws effectively suppressed freedom of speech and press for all opponents of the war. But even if, as the government contended, the radicals and pacifists were wrong in their denunciation of the war, it was unwise for the administration to seal itself off from hostile criticism.[33]

In a democracy, how was the justice of a war, the advisability of its continuance, or the wisdom of the way in which it was fought to be determined if all unorthodox views were deemed subversive? Moreover, as one historian of the war years has pointed out, American democracy, deprived of the challenge of an effective minority, soon approached a state of mobbism, and invoked the rule of mob psychology against dissenting elements in the population.[34] In the midst of the war, Thomas Nixon Carver, consultant to the government and a past president of the American Economic Association, asked the question: "Are We in Danger of Becoming Prussianized?" Referring to the growing compulsion, mass hysteria, and concentration of powers in the hands of the government, Nixon wondered whether liberalism was being crucified in the name of a war for democracy. A democratic government, he noted, may indulge in absolutism of the worst sort, and he added the warning: "There are few things more democratic than a lynching bee, where everybody is satisfied except a small and insignificant minority of one." [35]

President Wilson, perhaps because of an inner fear of the illiberalism that he knew war would generate, was inordinately sensitive to any attack upon his thesis that the United States was fighting a "People's War." [36] Basically the problem went back to the President's concept of the war as a crusade and the difficulty of being a crusader for liberalism and still remaining a liberal. There was nothing more tragic therefore than the precipitous descent of liberalism during the war years, while the President, in his concentration on achieving victory, refused to consider any criticism of his policies. Wilson and his progressive and liberal supporters were themselves caught in the web of war, with all its inevitable pressures, but at the same time the responsibility of the President and others in high places could not easily be shrugged off. American liberalism, though much weakened by the sweep of economic forces in the nineteenth century and from time to time bitterly assailed by mob action, had never before been so systematically undermined or suppressed as it was through the official action of the United States government during the second Wilson administration. This unhappy heritage of the war was to prevail in the postwar years, vitiating all attempts to carve out a liberal peace. Thus the harsh reaction after the Armistice was in a sense only a continuation of the illiberal means used to gain what soon was regarded as a hollow victory.

13

Harsh Reaction and Bitter Disillusionment

THE NEWS of the signing of the Armistice, when it reached the United States, touched off what was perhaps the greatest public exhibition of joy and enthusiasm in American history. While it was true that the American people had gone to war with high hopes, much of this initial zeal was not over the war itself but over the popular rationalization that this was a "war to end war" and "make the world safe for democracy." For the American people, who had thus accepted the war on Wilson's idealistic terms, the victory on the Western front in 1918 meant more than just an armistice. It seemed to promise not only relief from fighting but also realization of the original ideals that had prompted "the great adventure."

The frenzied American celebration of November 1918 was again repeated abroad when Wilson, less than a month after the Armistice, arrived in Europe to help draft the final peace terms. Visiting the European capital cities, Wilson was everywhere greeted with touching demonstrations of mass adulation and idolatry. In his own person the American President seemed to symbolize not only the Allied victory but also popular longing for a just and lasting peace. And so, while American doughboys steamed home from war-torn Europe, Wilson carried the hopes of the world into the Paris Peace Conference.

Fastening their eyes upon the future, and beguiled by the eloquent promises of their wartime leaders, the generality of people could easily believe that they were upon the threshold of Utopia. But if the masses would seem to have been incredibly naïve, as judged from the standpoint of a later generation, what can one say for the liberal intellectuals who were persuaded by Wilson's visions of world peace to overlook his harsh management of the home front during the war months? For all their emphasis upon the pragmatic acceptance of the war, most liberals had not been very realistic about what the grim process of fighting would entail. Somehow they had appeared surprised by the administration's policies of censorship and suppression. It was this lack of realism—this unwillingness to see what was actually happening, instead of what it was hoped would eventuate—that helped explain the grave disillusionment that descended over the postwar years.

We now know that Wilson himself feared the effects of war upon liberalism and democracy, but at the time the only public protest against an acceptance of the war as a means of achieving liberal ends was sounded by a small minority of socialists or pacifists. Randolph Bourne, in his bitter denunciation of his fellow intellectuals for their espousal of the war, had pleaded: "There is work to be done to prevent this war of ours from passing into popular mythology as a holy crusade. . . . There must still be opposition to any contemplated 'liberal' world-order founded on military coalitions." Thorstein Veblen, the iconoclast economist, had warned that, if peace was to be anything more than a short armistice between wars, "it will have to come about irrespective of governmental management — in spite of the State rather than by its good offices. At the best," he concluded, "the State, or the government, is an instrumentality for making peace, not for perpetuating it." [1]

Unfortunately, the Wilson administration, in sealing itself off from wartime attacks, also discouraged the kind of realistic discussion of war aims that might have made possible a better peace. Instead, the pent-up feelings suppressed during the war broke out after 1918 in an angry tide of postwar antagonisms and disillusionment. Wilson's peace plans, revealed only in the seductive draperies of wartime appeals, were less alluring when stripped in the cruel light of 1919. Before the Armistice, Oswald Garrison Villard had warned Colonel House that "the President cannot put over his peace program even in this country unless he can rally behind him the liberal and radical opinion of the country that the Administration has been antagonizing by . . . prosecutions of newspapers and editors and anybody who dared to disagree." [2] But until the Treaty of Versailles was brought back to the United States by the President and thrown open for discussion in the Great Debate in the Senate, Wilson still seemed to command the bulk of liberal sentiment and support in the country. This liberal backing, formerly so unquestioning, was now predicated on a challenge, which Villard's skeptical and critical *Nation* had already put before the President while he was still on shipboard bound for Paris. "We are told that this was a war for democracy: very well, by its fruits we shall know it." In the *Nation's* words, the liberals were going to act as watchdogs to see whether the promised liberal war aims could be achieved. [3]

Particularly puzzling to liberals, in view of the apparently decisive victory of peace and democracy over militarism and autocracy, was the President's insistence on keeping up a large postwar army and expanding the navy, as well as his interest in the inauguration of some form of universal military training. At hearings before the House Committee on

Military Affairs in January 1919, Secretary of War Baker was asked if the establishment of the half-million man army recommended by the administration would not repudiate the President's declared intention of seeking disarmament after the war. Although Secretary Baker saw no inconsistency, Congress approved funds only for an establishment temporarily fixed at the prewar figure of 175,000 men, later increasing this number to 325,000. Many of the members of Congress believed that the size of any future army would depend in large part on what the country decided in regard to universal military training, and on August 3, 1919, Baker accordingly forwarded to Congress the administration's plan for the three months' compulsory service of all 18- and 19-year-old youths. This and other similar bills at once met with a widespread opposition, which was not confined to pacifist or liberal circles. In general, peacetime conscription was linked to the philosophy of the defeated Prussian militarists. Despite a letter of endorsement from President Wilson, Democrats in the House of Representatives resolved on February 9, 1920, by a vote of 106 to 17, that "it is the sense of this caucus that no measure should be passed by Congress providing for universal compulsory military service or training." [4]

The decisive defeat of administration plans for UMT and a larger standing army was paralleled by rejection of Wilson's recommendations for the navy. In December 1918, the President amazed the world by presenting to Congress a new three-year building program designed to be placed on top of the already huge and still uncompleted three-year plan of 1916. This vast American navy was envisaged not only as an answer to Japanese expansion in the Pacific but also as a means of strengthening Wilson's hand at the Paris Peace Conference. Armed with this threat, Wilson hoped to force the British and French to back up his plans for a peace based on the Fourteen Points and the League of Nations.[5]

Wilson's policies, however, not only antagonized the Congressional foes of a big navy, but they also gave opponents of the League and the Treaty of Versailles an opportunity to question the sincerity of his peace plans. To many observers it seemed as though the President was permitting himself to be placed in the contradictory position of espousing militarism and navalism at home in order to defeat it abroad. Thus the editor of the *Scientific American* objected that

in the very hour when the heavens are filled with the rejoicings of the people that the era of wars and armaments is over, at the very time when the enemy is handing over ten dreadnoughts and five battlecruisers as a pledge of his submission — comes this man of peace with the request that we hurry forward the building of a fleet even greater than the one that is being surrendered and that we put up yet another $600,000,000 to duplicate the addition.[6]

And Henry Cabot Lodge, a lifelong advocate of a big navy, nevertheless remarked on the floor of the Senate:

. . . it seems to me extraordinary that we should enter on a scheme for eternal peace throughout the world by proposing to build a Navy which in seven years is to be equal to that of England. . . . How it fits with the policy of reduction of naval and military forces or with the high objects of a league of nations I can not conceive.[7]

As a result of Congressional opposition, the three-year naval program was withdrawn late in May 1919, but Secretary of the Navy Josephus Daniels continued to urge greater naval preparedness. In the pages of a popular magazine he

told the American people that, if the United States did not
join the League,

we must become a super-Prussia. Militarism and navalism must
be interwoven with the warp and woof of our industrial life. It
must dominate our education and to some extent our religion.
We must be a national porcupine, so bristling with guns and so
trained to use them, that no other nation dares touch us. . . .

Better militarism for America than defeat.[8]

Trying to frighten the country into adopting the League,
which was one of the techniques also used by the President
in his speaking tour of 1919, had little effect upon a liberal
sentiment that was fast being hardened into disillusionment
over the work of the Paris Peace Conference. Oswald Garrison Villard wrote to Ramsay MacDonald, the English Labor party leader, complaining that "The Secretary of War
urges a large army and the League in the same breath and,
of course, there is no movement to decrease the Navy. Wilson has stated frankly that if he does not get the League, he
will recommend that the United States be placed on the German basis prior to the war as the only proper way to live.
This from the man who commanded us to destroy the
wicked old German order!" [9]

Although a variety of motives entered into the United
States' rejection of the Treaty of Versailles, the liberals'
primary basis for discontent revolved around the treaty's inconsistency with Wilson's own earlier peace proposals as outlined in the famous Fourteen Points. It was difficult to reconcile the Peace Conference's work with former high ideals.
Even the presence of the League of Nations in the treaty
could not overcome their conviction that it was a harsh
settlement imposed by the victor powers. Far from ensuring
a permanent world peace, the Treaty of Versailles, it was
felt, would lay the ground for future wars. Pacifist liberals

attacked the League for its proposed reliance on force as a means to peace, but most serious was the general unhappiness over the entire League and Treaty of Versailles that characterized so many progressives and liberals. "The more I study it, the more I am convinced," Villard wrote to Senator La Follette, "that it is the most iniquitous peace document ever drawn, that it dishonours America because it violates our solemn pledge given to the Germans at the time of the armistice and because it reeks with bad faith, revengefulness and inhumanity." Villard concluded that the treaty "seals the ruin of the modern capitalistic system and constitutes a veritable Pandora's box out of which will come evils of which we have not as yet any conception." [10]

Disillusionment over the war and the peace treaty was responsible for much of the political isolationism of the postwar liberals. Yet, in respect to cultural and intellectual life, this group was more attuned to world thought and more genuinely internationalist in its feelings than the statesmen who were supporting the League as a vehicle for continued American intervention in world affairs. In the Senate it was no doubt true that many opponents of the League were isolationist Republicans in whom partisan politics played an important role. But at least some of the "irreconcilables" who fought the League — Senators Norris, La Follette, and Borah, for example — were among the stanchest advocates of an international understanding based on disarmament and mutual cooperation. And certainly it was no narrow, isolationist nationalism that caused the *New Republic* and John Dewey, formerly two of Wilson's most loyal supporters, to break with him on the question of the League and ratification of the Versailles Treaty. The *New Republic,* as soon as the text of the treaty arrived in the United States, voiced its dismay. And on the cover of its next issue it proclaimed:

THIS IS NOT PEACE. Americans would be fools if they permitted themselves to be embroiled in a system of European alliances. America promised to underwrite a stable peace. Mr. Wilson has failed. The peace cannot last. America should withdraw from all commitments which would impair her freedom of action.[11]

Following its forthright announcement, the *New Republic* immediately became a vehicle for much of the early disillusionist writing. John Maynard Keynes's *Economic Consequences of the Peace,* with its criticism of Wilson and the economic provisions of the peace treaty, was serialized late in 1919. And in the October 8 issue John Dewey published his interpretation of the work at the Paris Peace Conference under the caption "The Discrediting of Idealism." Writing as one of those who, though "strongly opposed to war in general broke with the pacifists because they saw in this war a means of realizing pacific ideals," Dewey, however, admitted: "The defeat of idealistic aims has been, without exaggeration, enormous. The consistent pacifist has much to urge now in his own justification; he is entitled to his flourish of private triumphings." For those who, like himself, had counseled war for idealistic reasons, there was little now to urge "except the scant though true plea that things would have been much worse if Germany had won, as she would have done without the participation of the United States." The defeat of American aims, Dewey argued, was due to the failure to back them up by the intelligent use of force. In practice, he thought, the United States should have insisted on the terms of its entry before going into war on the side of the Allies. But just how this could have been done, or how force was to be directed by intelligence, Dewey did not say.[12]

A young liberal who went much further in his disillusionment than Dewey, and who in a sense continued Randolph

Bourne's attack upon the pragmatists for their justification of American entry into the war, was Harold Stearns. Stearns in many ways fulfilled the popular American notion of a literary radical. The son of a widowed mother, he managed to go through Harvard on slender financial resources and gravitated to New York, where in Greenwich Village he mixed a career of writing and editing with the gayer side of life. Then, in the twenties, he joined the group of young American intellectuals who became expatriates in Paris.

In the Preface to his *Liberalism in America,* which he published in 1919, Stearns pointed out that decentralization and individualism were qualities that were more marked in Europe than in the United States — at least as intellectual attitudes. In Europe, for example, people were less sentimental about the political state, regarding conscription and taxes as unmitigated evils, in contrast to the Americans' naïve willingness to think of them as somehow patriotic. This judgment set the tone for Stearn's definition of liberalism as a respect for the dignity and worth of the individual. Liberalism was thus the complete antithesis of the militarism and statism coming out of the war.[13]

Stearns believed that the war had failed in its liberal ends, partly because the statesmen themselves were not liberal, but also because the intellectuals flocking to Washington easily became the dupes of the military and readily condoned the conscription of men and thought. In a chapter that he bitingly called "Timidity and the Seductions of Office or Career," Stearns noted the charm of being "a big-shot" and of being on the inside. Thus Washington in 1917 and 1918 was filled with such a tremendous flood of energy that "The war itself was forgotten in the intensity of waging it." While the war also encouraged the herd instinct and mob violence, releasing all normal inhibitions, it was the intellectuals more than the masses who became hysterical, allowing themselves to be captivated by the President's fine phrases. Stearns bitterly criticized Wilson for what he termed "The Technique of Liberal Failure," and he argued that if the President had had to fight for men and to make his ideals popular he would have negotiated a better peace. Exploring the wide gulf between Wilson's pretensions and his policy — his suppression of free speech in the midst of extolling it — Stearns quoted Amos Pinchot's famous remark: "He puts his enemies in office and his friends in jail." Stearns wrote that Wilson showed "to what extremes of cruelty and intolerance and injustice the idealist in politics can go," and he concluded sadly:

The plain truth of our war to make the world safe for democracy is that today there is less freedom of speech and right of assemblage, less tolerance, more governmental control over political and economic opinion, less liberty for teachers and college professors, more reaction and militarism than was the case the day we declared war on Germany.[14]

The dissatisfaction of the liberal and progressive forces over the Treaty of Versailles because it did not fulfill Wilson's Fourteen Points might, as Eric Goldman has suggested, in time have become even greater if the treaty had lived up to Wilson's ideals. The root of the trouble was not that Wilson's policies were rejected at Paris, but that those policies were already hopelessly out of date. The President, in other words, was trying to recast the world in a nineteenth-century liberal mold which, if realized, would have been anathema to many of his old progressive supporters in the United States.[15]

This is an interesting thesis which enables one equally to defend Wilson's program as sincere, though old-fashioned and misguided, and to justify the presumably more realistic and progressive attempts to create a new world order in our

own time. It was true that the laissez-faire liberalism envisioned in the Fourteen Points was hardly compatible with
the stronger nationalism advocated by progressives in the
United States and by state socialists in Europe. Such former
supporters of Wilson as the progressive Herbert Croly, who
broke with him over the Versailles Treaty, might therefore
have been much more disappointed if a Wilsonian type of
League had actually come into being to preside over a world
made up of a congeries of nineteenth-century liberal states.
But, actually, how much credence should be given to the
Fourteen Points in view of their obvious conflict with the
Allies' secret treaties, spelling out a postwar division of the
spoils among the victor powers? The Fourteen Points were
not only incompatible with the realistic aspirations of such
American progressives as Herbert Croly, but they were also
at odds with the Allies' war aims. While Wilson's idealistic
wartime speeches concealed this fact, as well as his own
knowledge of the secret treaties, from the American people,
they raised questions as to the sincerity of his whole war
program. The truth was that, once America went to war,
such liberals as Bourne and Stearns and Villard no longer
trusted the sincerity of the President or believed his statements that he was working to establish a liberal peace.

From a liberal point of view, the action of the United
States in entering the war sealed the doom of an idealistic
peace through American influence. For example, the *Nation*
in the fall of 1920, taking note of the distress of Herbert
Croly and the *New Republic* over the demise of liberalism
since 1912, observed: "The temporary knell of American
liberalism was sounded the minute its false leader put it into
war." The great figures in the history of liberalism, the
Nation believed, were those who opposed the war instead of
the contrary cases of Lloyd George and Woodrow Wilson.
"For war and liberalism to lie down together anywhere, at

any time, with any excuse, means only one thing — disaster to liberalism. When war is declared on a foreign foe it is also declared on every forward-looking cause, every liberal, every reformer at home." [16] In reply to this criticism, Croly defended his thesis that it was lack of realism on the part of liberals, rather than the war, that was primarily responsible for the death of liberalism. Admitting, however, his own disappointment with the results of the war and also the growing popularity of the *Nation*'s pacifist position, Croly added: "Considering the nature of the Treaty of Versailles . . . pro-war liberals have much to explain." [17]

Croly unconsciously pointed to the differences that divided progressives and liberals by praising Theodore Roosevelt as a liberal and invoking his role in the Spanish-American War and his later career as proofs of the compatibility of war and liberalism. The *Nation*, on the other hand, was unrealistic in its liberalism or, in other words, not progressive. The great miscalculation, both his own and Wilson's, Croly asserted, was the failure to anticipate the way in which the American people were to become unrestrained militarists in the course of the fighting, intoxicated by the government's propaganda and losing sight of all other objects in their desire for military victory. How this result, partially foreseen by Wilson, could have been avoided, Croly left unsaid, although a contributor to a later issue of his magazine pointed out that no liberal movement, without a stronger popular and labor base than that of 1917, could have resisted the conservative reaction of the war years. "No President could have put this country into war in 1917 without enlisting the voluntary cooperation of the business community, and of that articulate, conscious, purposeful part of the business community that has no use for liberalism." [18]

Although many liberals after 1918 heeded Randolph

Bourne's injunction "to prevent this war of ours from passing into popular mythology as a holy crusade," later generations have tried to revive the notion of Wilson's being hood-
winked by the vindictive European politicians at Paris and
then being thwarted by the isolationist Republicans in the
the United States Senate. This picture of Wilson, the lonely
liberal idealist, going down to defeat at home and abroad is,
however, persuasive only if one ignores, first, the extent to
which contemporary liberals repudiated Wilson's leadership and, second, and most important, the reactionary policies that Wilson permitted to be continued on the home
front after all fighting had ceased. Whatever may be said
for the liberalism of his first administration or of his idealistic internationalism before the American declaration of
war, there was precious little liberalism left in the United
States after April 1917 and less after November 1918.

In many ways the illiberalism that followed the Armistice
was worse than that of the war period. Though this reaction
repeated a phenomenon also characteristic of other postwar
periods in American history, the President could not be ab-
solved of responsibility. In his authority over the executive
departments of the government, and by his use of the pardon-
ing power, the President could have done much to lessen
the hysteria and intolerance of the last years of his administration. But even before he was struck down by illness, the
President had set his face against any leniency to radical or
pacifist opponents of the war. Thus conscientious objectors,
socialist and IWW radicals, political prisoners, and others
who had violated the wartime Espionage and Sedition Acts
were kept in jail. Toward Eugene Debs, the most famous of
these war prisoners, Wilson was especially vindictive. Although Debs was not brought to trial until after the Armistice, Wilson refused all pleas for a pardon, which came only

after Harding had entered the White House. The campaign for a general amnesty made little headway. The League for the Amnesty of Political Prisoners, in urging the prompt release of Emma Goldman, Debs, and others, argued fruitlessly that, even if it was granted "that their imprisonment was necessary to preserve wartime morale, how can it be justified now that peace is declared?" Of all nations in the World War the United States alone, as Zechariah Chafee has pointed out, "still refused in 1920 a general amnesty to political prisoners." [19]

Instead of pardons for wartime offenders, the postwar period witnessed a new surge of repressive laws directed against individual freedom. Justification for these measures and for the increasingly harsh methods used in their enforcement was found in the popular and official fears of a "Red Menace," striking at America. The seeming success of the Bolshevik Revolution in Russia, despite the abortive attempts at intervention on the part of the United States and the Allies, plus the renewed outbreak of radicalism at home, led to a demand for action against the American "Reds." The war itself had heightened class antagonisms and aroused the bitterness of labor. Strikes, especially in such key industries as steel, coal, and textiles, as well as by the Boston police force, aroused the anxiety of conservative interests. At the same time there occurred a succession of bomb scares, in which a large number of missiles addressed to Federal officials and other prominent persons were seized in the mails. Before their discovery, however, bombs wrecked several homes including Attorney General Palmer's, one person was killed, and an atmosphere of public hysteria was created from which high officials were not exempt. Though the labor troubles were rooted in postwar cutbacks in wages and employment, and although the bomb outrages were never solved nor pinned to any radical group, any strike or threat of violence immediately became identified in the popular mind with radicals and Reds.

Conveniently at hand in this crisis was a variety of wartime legislation, ostensibly directed against espionage and sedition, but also capable of use in stamping out so-called radical activities. Not only were the Federal laws still in existence, but in addition there was a tremendous volume of state legislation that had been added to the statutes during the war. Extending the old common law against conspiracy, the states added new and far-reaching measures dealing with opposition to war, display of the Red flag, sedition, unlawful assembly, and criminal syndicalism. The most important of these laws in terms of the postwar scene were the criminal syndicalist statutes, making it a crime to advocate and teach, or to aid and abet the commission of, sabotage or unlawful acts of force and violence with the aim of accomplishing a change in industrial ownership or control, or of effecting any governmental change. Laws of such a broad nature obviously provided a basis upon which state authorities could move to suppress strikes as well as the expression of any kind of radical opinions. However, except in California, most of the state criminal syndicalist laws became dead letters until revived again after World War II.[20]

In the immediate postwar period, the most conspicuous instance of state illiberalism occurred in New York, where on March 26, 1919, the legislature set up a joint committee of six, under the chairmanship of Senator Clayton R. Lusk, to investigate radical and seditious activities and report back to the legislature. Although only an investigating, and not a prosecuting, body, the Lusk Committee in its search for materials proceeded to stage a series of spectacular and illegal raids upon radical organizations. On the basis of its activities and charges, five Socialist assemblymen, duly elected by the people to represent their districts in the state legislature, were denied their seats and expelled from the Assembly chamber.

The Lusk Committee also instigated the prosecution of various radical leaders and was responsible for two new school laws. The first of these laws required a loyalty oath of all teachers and directed the expulsion of any teachers deemed guilty of advocating "a form of government other than the government of the United States or of this state." The second law required all private schools to be licensed by the state and stipulated that no license would be granted to a school "where it shall appear that the instruction proposed to be given includes the teaching of the doctrine that organized governments shall be overthrown by force, violence or unlawful means." On the basis of this second law, the Rand School of Social Science, a socialist and labor college in New York City, which had already been raided by the Lusk Committee, was brought before the courts for refusing to take out a state license. Before the case could be decided — either on the basis of the school's refusal to apply for a license or, if licensed, on the question of whether or not the school was guilty of revolutionary teachings — Governor Alfred E. Smith approved two acts of the state legislature canceling both of the Lusk school laws. These laws, he declared, were repugnant to American democracy and a violation of freedom of opinion and freedom of speech for teachers and schools, both of which could be compelled to defer to what a state officer deemed loyalty. In signing the repeal measure, Governor Smith asserted: "I firmly believe that I am vindicating the principle that, within the limits of the penal law, every citizen may speak and teach what he believes." [21]

Meanwhile throughout the nation the Federal government continued to enforce the censorious policies of the war period. A year after the Armistice, the Attorney General raided and closed the office of the Seattle *Union-Record,* while Postmaster General Burleson kept the socialist New York *Call* and Milwaukee *Leader* from the mails. During this time Victor Berger, editor of the *Leader,* and next to Debs the most prominent of the individuals imprisoned under the Espionage Act, was denied the seat in the House of Representatives to which he was twice re-elected by the people of Milwaukee. Though each house of Congress traditionally acted as sole judge in the seating of its members, the stand in expelling Berger for his words opposing the war was unprecedented.

Most active of all Federal officials in the postwar assault on liberalism was Attorney General A. Mitchell Palmer. Not satisfied with the wartime sedition law, Palmer urged Congress to pass a peacetime act along the lines of those already adopted in many of the states. Although no such measure was passed, Congress during the winter of 1919–20 had some seventy sedition bills under consideration. The refusal of Congress to enact a peacetime sedition law did not mean, of course, as was often imagined, that the country was defenseless against genuinely treasonable or revolutionary activities. But the intent of a sedition law was to go beyond actions and to prosecute thoughts and opinions. When this became less possible of accomplishment after the war, at least in so far as American citizens were concerned, the government then turned to the alien population of the United States and instituted what became known as the "deportations delirium of nineteen-twenty."

The alien as far back as the time of the French Revolution, when Congress passed the Alien and Sedition Acts, had been suspected of harboring radical designs upon American institutions. By the close of the nineteenth century, this general American suspicion of alien radicals was intensified as a result of the activities of a small group of European anarchists who had not hesitated to resort to such violent techniques as bomb throwing and assassination. Acting to meet public fears, Congress in its various measures dealing with immigration, beginning with the law of March 3, 1903, provided for the exclusion and deportation of anarchists and other dangerous radicals from the United States. The question immediately arose as to what constituted an anarchist, but exclusion cases were rare until public hysteria during World War I created a new wave of anti-alien feeling. Alien legislation was thereupon broadened to include not only anarchists but also any alien guilty of violating the Espionage Act or of holding radical beliefs or associations.[22]

Not only was the authority of the Federal government supreme in all matters concerning immigration, but alien legislation also made deportation a subject to be decided by administrative discretion without the necessity of resort to the courts for enforcement. As a practical matter therefore, if an alien was deemed to be a radical within the meaning of the law, deportation could automatically follow his apprehension and arrest. The only question affording any possibility of court review was the decision as to what radical organizations were illegal and whether the suspected radical alien was in fact a member of a proscribed group.[23]

The postwar campaign against alien radicals got under way just before Christmas 1919 when the United States transport vessel *Buford,* nicknamed "the Soviet Ark," sailed under sealed orders with two hundred forty-nine aliens in the process of deportation. The deportees, who were bound for Russia, had been expelled by executive orders in accordance with the law of Congress. Contrary to wild newspaper stories that excited the public imagination, most of the passengers on the *Buford* were an obscure lot who had had the misfortune at one time or another to have been anarchists or members of inconsequential Russian organizations later deemed subversive. Only the celebrated anarchists Emma Goldman and her friend Alexander Berkman, who had been conspicuous radical agitators for several decades, could conceivably be thought of as dangerous to the existing order and institutions of the United States. In the case of Emma Goldman, though she was already in prison for counseling resistance to the wartime draft law, deportation was accomplished only by the devious method of revoking her husband's citizenship, on which her own depended.

The departure of the *Buford* and its unfortunate passengers, some of whom had left families behind and almost all of whom were going back to a Russia much different than the czarist land of their birth, was followed in January 1920 by carefully prepared raids in a number of cities, in which over four thousand persons were rounded up and held under deportation charges. The work of carrying out these raids was in the hands of the General Intelligence Division of the Federal Bureau of Investigation in the Department of Justice. This newly created division of the Bureau placed its chief emphasis on radical literature as decisive evidence of subversive beliefs or intent. Disregarding private rights, the GID, usually without the use of warrants, ransacked the personal possessions of suspected anarchists or "Reds" and conducted raids on publishing houses and radical clubs. Especially sought out as radicals were members of the IWW, Communists, radical intellectuals and writers, and Negro radicals. Accepting the doctrine of guilt by association, the Department of Justice agents justified their raids on the assumption that radical membership or purported membership was in itself a crime.[24]

The public at first gave its approval to the raids because it was convinced that those arrested were dangerous foreigners bent on acts of violence. But the raids, unprecedented except for the similar and bitterly resented "slacker" raids during the war, eventually resulted in a reaction against such extreme and manifestly unjust methods of accomplishing alien deportations. Many of those arrested and subjected to various indignities, while their families were consumed with worry and fear, were subsequently found to be law-abiding citizens. Others were released because of lack of any evidence of radical actions or associations. "At no place," as Louis F. Post wrote, "in all that nation-wide raiding of January, 1920, were any weapons or explosive materials or destructive mechanisms discovered from which an inference of projected crime, private or political, could be reasonably drawn. Even as to criminal thoughts the proof was flimsy — absurdly so in contrast with the severity of the raiding." [25]

Post, as Assistant Secretary of Labor in charge of immigration, was able to prevent further injustice by canceling the warrants for the arrest of all those who could not definitely be tied to membership in a radical organization. In practice, the test of subversive radical beliefs came to depend on membership in the IWW or in the Communist party, which the law, the courts, and the Departments of Justice and Labor agreed were proscribed organizations according to the meaning of the language in the alien and deportation statutes. For his humane and intelligent administration of these laws, Post, however, was bitterly criticized and even threatened with impeachment by some members of Congress. In all, over seven hundred alien radicals were deported in the two years 1920 and 1921; after that the number dropped off sharply, although deportations for other reasons mounted during the twenties.[26]

January 1920, the month of the alien raids and of the expulsion of the five Socialist assemblymen from the New York legislature, represented the climax of the post-Armistice campaign against radicalism. Though sanity gradually returned, the intolerance of the war and postwar era was not easily eradicated. Two unpleasant mementos of the period that lingered on into the twenties to become *causes célèbres* were the Sacco-Vanzetti and Mooney-Billings cases. Tom Mooney and Warren Billings were radical unionists convicted of responsibility for a bomb outrage that killed eight persons in a San Francisco Preparedness Day parade in 1916. Although they escaped the death penalty, their continued imprisonment on a conviction secured by flimsy evidence, and perhaps by perjured testimony, bolstered the belief of liberals that their penalty was due more to their radical opinions than to any actual complicity in the bombing of 1916. A similar feeling of injustice stirred the protests against the execution of Nicola Sacco and Bartolomeo Vanzetti, two Italian anarchists accused of a payroll robbery and murder at South Braintree, Massachusetts, in April 1920. Brought to trial in the midst of the antialien and antiradical atmosphere of the early twenties, the anarchist philosophy of the defendants seemed to many liberals to be an important factor in their conviction. This highly controversial case, which touched off demonstrations of protest abroad, continued to trouble the American conscience long after the defendants themselves had been executed in 1927.[27]

Ultimately, the antiradical hysteria subsided, if only because it had so largely accomplished its intent. The organizations capable of providing leadership for any sort of mass radical or labor movement had been broken up or hopelessly weakened. Thus the IWW, the Nonpartisan League, and the various Socialist and Communist parties were all depleted in membership and influence. Although much of the radical movement was liberal in neither its methods nor its goals, the toleration of dissenting minorities and the free expression of dissenting opinion had always been cardinal liberal tenets. Radical minority views, it was true, had previously been subject to restraint in American history, but never until World War I did the suppression of freedom enjoy the almost unanimous support of the various agencies of the government — national, state, and local.

The official attack on all evidence of postwar radicalism paved the way for the emphasis of the 1920's on conformity and "one hundred per cent Americanism." In attempting to carry out his policies by suppressing liberal and radical criticism, President Wilson had helped to ensure his own defeat. Though Wilson had departed widely from idealistic internationalism, inviting still further liberal disaffection and discord, there was tragedy none the less in the complete American nationalist revulsion of the twenties. Perhaps, as some of Wilson's critics argued, the fault lay in the fact of the war itself and in American participation. But in any case there was little doubt that the war and postwar years carried further the decline of liberalism and bequeathed to the future an atmosphere in no way compatible with the high hopes that many liberals and progressives had entertained in 1917. For his own part, following his return from Paris in 1919, the President had warned that failure of the world to agree on a method to prevent war would result in another vast struggle within a generation, destroying mankind's vision of permanent peace. And he added: "When I think of the homes upon which dull despair would settle if this great hope is disappointed, I should wish for my part never to have had America play any part whatever in this attempt to emancipate the world." [28]

14

The Cult of Conformity
and Prosperity

THE AMERICAN people found it difficult to stamp out the embers of World War I. Despite a growing disillusionment, much of the wartime spirit of intolerance and repression lingered on, while the examples of self-sacrifice and idealism were lost in an engulfing wave of postwar hysteria. Yet there was undoubtedly a great nostalgia on the part of the American people for the ways of a peaceful society. The Harding 1920 campaign slogan of "back to normalcy" was an apt summary of the popular mood, and the verdict of the elections, if not necessarily a repudiation of the League of Nations and the Treaty of Versailles, certainly expressed a revolt against almost everything connected with the late war. The problem of the twenties therefore resolved itself into a struggle to disavow the heritage of the war while, at the same time, its effects continued to exert a subtle but powerful influence on almost all aspects of American life and thought.

In the transition from war mood to the disillusionment of the 1920's, the philosophy and practice of liberalism was the chief victim. Assaying the prospects as they appeared in the 1920 presidential election, liberals felt that they were faced with a "Hobson's choice." To the argument that they should vote for Cox and the Democrats in order to avoid the danger of repudiating Wilson's ideals through the election of Harding and the Republicans, the *New Republic* replied that the Democratic party was liberal only in the sense that it stood in greater need of the independent voter. Once in office it flouted the liberals' will and ignored their influence. "Liberals have nothing to gain by being courted before election only to be betrayed after election. They will not persuade the Democratic party to be more liberal by supporting it after it has proved false to its promises of liberalism. Defeat rather than victory," the *New Republic* concluded, "will teach the Democrats to take liberalism seriously." If liberals voted Democratic, it meant that they accepted Wilson's Russian policy, the Treaty of Versailles, and the work of Postmaster General Burleson and Attorney General Palmer. On the other hand, liberals did not have to vote for Harding; instead they could best make known their protest by merely abstaining.[1]

Echoing this view, the *Nation* in a post-mortem on the election results observed that the people had seen through Wilson's falseness and pseudo-liberalism. Now, at least, Burleson and Palmer could no longer claim approval for their policies. Liberals, the *Nation* felt, could deal more frankly, and with less danger of disillusionment, with the openly reactionary Harding — although admittedly there was little basis for confidence in the incoming President. "He receives the greatest office in the world with the slightest record of achievement," the *Nation* pointed out.[2] In a personal letter Villard, commented that Harding "is more to be pitied than any man who ever took high office in America, he is so utterly inadequate by culture and training and experience and, of course, so absolutely ignorant about everything abroad. His viewpoint is entirely that of Marion, Ohio." [3]

A necessary condition of any return to a semblance of

normality was the ending of wartime militarism. Here liberalism, though its triumph was only partial and temporary, won its greatest success. The defeat of postwar plans for some form of universal compulsory military training and the demobilization of four million men from the army, trimming it back to almost its prewar size of around one hundred thousand, slowed the trend toward militarism. Yet the insistence of liberals and pacifists on a more complete disarmament was hardly met. Much of the liberal case against the Treaty of Versailles was based on the belief that it was incompatible with future world peace, and this conviction was steadily strengthened as liberals perceived the way in which the victor powers maintained their large armaments and continued to prepare for war. Liberal spokesmen accordingly urged the American government to take the leadership in a world crusade for disarmament and, as evidence of good faith, begin to reduce its own naval and land forces.[4]

This postwar campaign for disarmament enlisted the backing of a number of groups not usually associated with a pacifist or liberal position. Alarmed at the mounting costs of preparedness, and particularly of naval building, many conservative businessmen, for example, supported the call for the Washington Disarmament Conference. Although limited in its achievement, the Conference temporarily averted a full-scale naval race and gave the world a chance to recover from the economic ravages of World War I. It was this widespread desire for economy and lower taxes, plus the intense popular aversion to another war, that had forced the Conference and was responsible for its modest accomplishments.[5]

A reduction in the tools of war, while encouraging to liberals, did not blind them to other evidences of militaristic ways. The continent of Europe remained an armed camp. In

the United States, military training in the colleges under the
Reserve Officers' Training Corps program was expanded
after the war, and behind-the-scenes plans were being
readied for the total mobilization of American resources and
manpower in the event of future hostilities. Also the United
States continued to practice military intervention in Latin
America.

But more threatening to American liberalism in the
twenties than these seeds of future wars was the immediate
challenge offered by the continuance of wartime modes of
thinking. The demobilizing of the armies, closing of government agencies, and restoration of railroads and shipping
lines to private ownership were not accompanied by a similar
demobilization of the official control of thought. Instead,
the aftermath of the war, fought supposedly in the interests
of an idealistic internationalism, was an intolerant and chauvinistic insistence on nationalism.

Disillusioned over the venture in internationalism represented by the League, and accustomed to resounding wartime appeals for patriotic unity, the American people enlisted eagerly in the enforcement of a program of one hundred per cent Americanism. This meant not only turning
away from Europe in the political sense of rejecting the
League, but also a revulsion against all things foreign. American tourists returning from abroad repeated the criticisms
of the Old World and its customs voiced earlier by some of
the homesick American soldiers. Europe was regarded as
bankrupt and decadent in contrast to a United States enjoying the surge of postwar prosperity that followed the
brief slump of 1920. To help preserve this prosperity, and
to further isolate the United States from the contaminating
influence of Europe, Congress raised tariff rates and acted to
stop the tide of immigrants waiting to enter the United
States after the war. In a series of measures culminating in

the National Origins Act of 1924, the United States reversed its traditional liberal immigration policy of more than a century.

Part of the appeal of the new immigration acts rested on the fact that they made possible drastic cuts in the number of immigrants arriving from Southern and Eastern Europe, or from Italy and the Slavic countries. Thus, in addition to the understandable American desire to prevent, for economic reasons, the continued large-scale immigration of the poverty-stricken masses of war-torn Europe, the new legislation also had a racialist base. United with old fears of radicalism or labor competition from the immigrant was a strong prejudice against many of the foreigners on the grounds of their national origins. A distinction was therefore drawn in favor of the immigrants from Northern and Western Europe, with Great Britain alone receiving almost half the total yearly allowed quota of 150,000 persons.[6] This postwar resurgence of Anglo-Saxon racism was similarly illustrated by the popularity of such works as Madison Grant's *The Passing of the Great Race* and Lothrop Stoddard's *The Rising Tide of Color Against White World Supremacy*. Mourning the decline of the Anglo-Saxon race, which they saw as the inevitable result of the intermingling of European immigrants with the older American stock, these writers also warned of a future dominated by Asiatic and African nonwhites.

Paradoxically, all the emphasis during the war and after upon Americanism and Americanization seemed oftentimes to have precisely the opposite effect from that intended. Under the insistent demand for a one hundred per cent Americanism, the old idea of America as a melting pot was subverted. The belief that the immigrant's dissimilarities would gradually be transformed or modified until a new man, having all the advantages of a mixture of races, would emerge gave way to the idea of an enforced assimilation.

Also rejected was the concept of a mixed culture, in which the immigrant's different customs would lend a pleasing variety to American life and thought. But while the immigrant was thus being urged into a standardized pattern of conformity to American national values, he was more than ever associating himself with a number of the so-called hyphenated societies and organizations.[7]

Not only had the melting-pot idea become illiberal in its emphasis, but it no longer seemed to work effectively or smoothly. This same failure was illustrated in the case of religious groups that had formerly been reluctant to allow themselves to be singled out from the general population. Catholics, for example, began to emphasize the segregation of their membership, popularizing Catholic Boy Scouts, Catholic Daughters of America, and even a Catholic Mother of the Year. Jews and Negroes, the two domestic groups hit hardest by the intolerance of the twenties, turned to nationalistic movements of their own. Among Jews, Zionism took on a new popular appeal, while Negroes by the thousands supported the "Back to Africa" movement of Marcus A. Garvey, an adventurer and promoter who attempted to appeal to Negro racial pride.[8]

But of all the postwar hostility toward foreigners and other minority groups, probably the most extreme manifestations came from the Ku-Klux Klan. Using the name and many of the methods of the organization that had flourished in the South after the Civil War, and taking advantage of the fondness of many Americans for joining secret societies or fraternal clubs, the revived Klan united in its program all the most intolerant and illiberal features of the cult of postwar nationalism. Popularly thought of as merely an anti-Negro society, the Klan was against all alien forces in American life. Representing a recrudescence of American nativism, the society derived strength from the antiforeign feeling that followed the war. Its slogan of "native, white, Protestant" supremacy was aimed quite as much against the Catholic, the Jew, and the alien white immigrant as against the colored man.

Although first organized in 1915 by three members of the original post-Civil War Klan, the new society did not become important until about 1920. Five years later, at the height of its powers, there were perhaps four or five million members on its rolls, and its influence extended beyond the South into almost every part of the United States. In Indiana, for example, David Curtis Stephenson, a leading Klansman, established a virtual dictatorship through his control of the Republican state machine. In the Democratic party, the Klan fought the nomination of Alfred E. Smith for president because of his religion. Wherever it reached, the Klan fostered intolerance and hate. Setting itself up as a law-enforcement agency, it championed Prohibition and censored sexual morals, "sending warning notes and even flogging expeditions to punish men and women who had violated the seventh commandment." Its religious outlook was favorable to the extreme conservative views of the Fundamentalists, and like them it warred against the teaching of evolution. In all matters pertaining to foreign affairs, the Klan preached a chauvinistic nationalism, denouncing internationalism and pacifism and insisting on a more militantly patriotic tone in school history texts.[9]

In its interference in the school system, the Klan reinforced similar attempts at censorship exercised by a variety of superpatriotic groups such as the American Legion. The Legion was especially active in the effort to indoctrinate American youth in the military virtues, subsidizing their various leisure activities along these lines and coming to the aid of the ROTC whenever it was criticized by pacifists and educators.[10]

Though an undoubted power in the early 1920's, the Klan, owing to its resort to violence and intimidation, was soon disgraced even in the eyes of its own membership. During its sway, however, the Klan was an unpleasant reminder of the postwar wave of illiberalism, providing a vehicle for unscrupulous demagogues who traded on the vague fears and prejudices of great numbers of their fellow citizens. Yet, despite its excesses, the Klan was not as lasting a factor in the decline of American liberalism as the contempt for the individual that continued to characterize official thinking and action. Nowhere was the insistence on conformity carried further than in the realm of social and morals legislation. Although most of this legislation was not instigated in the postwar period, the decade of the twenties was the scene of the most drastic example of such legislation, the enactment and enforcement of Prohibition.

Although Prohibition as a local or state measure went far back in American history, its real success as a national movement came in the progressive era of the early 1900's and then, finally, during World War I when it was imposed as an emergency device to save grain for food. Prohibition was thus an interesting example both of wartime controls over the citizen and of the progressive reformers' belief that the state knows what is best for the individual. Prohibition was also an excellent illustration of the split in liberal and reform circles between those who emphasized the traditional liberalism of individual freedom and those who favored the progressives' creed of state intervention and regulation for the general welfare. To the former group the good intentions of the Prohibitionists were no justification for their arbitrary means. As Harold Stearns pointed out in 1919, "Coercion for the sake of virtue is as repugnant as coercion for the sake of vice. If American liberals are unwilling to fight the principle of coercion in the case of the Prohibition

Amendment simply because they are not much interested in whether the country is dry or not, then they are discredited the moment they fight coercion in those cases where they *are* interested." [11]

The contrast on the Prohibition issue between nonconformist individuals and social-reforming progressives was still apparent as late as 1930, when a mixed group of liberals, united largely by their opposition to Prohibition, blue laws, and other state interference with individual freedom, attempted to form what they called a Liberal party. Their abortive effort, soon forgotten in the rise of the New Deal, made one practical political gesture, however, by campaigning in an unsuccessful attempt to defeat Gifford Pinchot for governor of Pennsylvania. Pinchot, an old Theodore Roosevelt progressive and Bull Mooser, was anathema to them because he advocated Prohibition and sundry other restrictive blue laws.[12]

Prohibition, with the great temptation to break the law that it invited, soon resulted in a nation-wide wave of bootlegging and racketeering that made any thorough effort at enforcement virtually impossible. The growing unpopularity of national Prohibition also seemed to indicate that the overwhelming approval originally registered for the Eighteenth Amendment had been the result of a mixture of wartime hysteria and the lobbying efforts of fanatical pressure groups. The latter, deriving their main strength from some of the more Fundamentalist churches and from women's organizations, still were able to exert a potent political influence, even after it became apparent that Prohibition on a national scale was unworkable.

The repeal in 1933 of the Eighteenth Amendment marked, however, no general retreat from governmental interference with private morals. Important Federal legislation still remained on the statute books. The Mann Act, or

White Slave Traffic Act, passed in 1910 with the purpose of preventing the importation or interstate transportation of women for purposes of prostitution or commercialized vice, gave the Federal Bureau of Investigation, created two years earlier, its first big assignment. But, instead of smashing any widespread organized white-slave traffic across national or state borders, the Mann Act soon lent itself to legalized snooping and to censure of the private morals of couples who happened to stray across state lines.[13]

The Mann Act was part of a pattern of what many jurists felt were archaic American laws dealing with sex. Despite all the postwar talk of freedom of sex expression and the flouting of older conventions by the flappers and "flaming youth" of the twenties, the laws on the subject remained severe. Liberals made little headway with the plea that prosecution be confined to offenses against children and common decency or to the use of violence, as in rape, while other sexual conduct between adults in private be left alone. Summing up the laws on the subject of sex, one judge concluded: "Only in marriage is sex expression socially and legally acceptable." [14]

The other important area of morals legislation, into which the Federal government entered, concerned narcotic drugs. The Harrison Narcotic Drug Act of 1914 provided that such products could be sold only under certain specified conditions by registered dealers, who were required to pay an excise tax of one dollar a year. Although accepted by the Supreme Court as a revenue-raising measure, the purpose of the law obviously was "to control the drug evil by prohibiting the indiscriminate and clandestine sale of narcotics." This measure seemed therefore to approach the limits of Congress's ability to enact police regulations or morals legislation through the taxing power, but the interesting point of the narcotics law was its curious reverse effect. By outlawing the use of all drugs except by prescription, an entire new criminal class was created. Illegal drugs henceforth commanded prices that almost inevitably led the habitual user into crime and also encouraged a whole new apparatus of graft and corruption comparable to that surrounding the illicit liquor traffic. As Federal agents became successful by the end of the 1920's in stamping out the trade in the more powerful drugs, such as morphine and cocaine, the use of marijuana spread and for the first time became current among high school youths. Largely ignored was the opinion of some experts that the drug addict, like the alcoholic, was basically a sick person and not a criminal. Also escaping attention was the fact that, in some civilizations and by some individuals, drugs were used much as alcohol as a part of man's search for escapes and dreams. But the contention that use or misuse should depend on the individual and not on the state attracted little support.[15]

Some observers viewed this growing interference of the government with personal habits, by means of social and morals legislation, as an example of the Puritanism of democracy. With the rise of modern democracy, they saw a tendency for government to become more aggressive in the passage of such legislation, while the mass of the people came to cherish the reputed middle-class virtues of chastity, temperance, and thrift. The theory that the average citizen must be protected by his government from the temptations of vice was also invoked as justification for the growing number of state and local statutes authorizing the censorship of books and motion pictures. Despite the tremendous difficulty of drawing a line between art and obscenity, complete control over what the public could lawfully read or see was frequently entrusted to narrow-minded officials or private pressure groups. The main defense urged for such censorship was the need of keeping youthful eyes and ears from contact with books or motion pictures fit only for adults. Gradually films became classified as to suitability for various age groups, but few authorities seemed to agree with the suggestion that "we might even go back to *laissez-faire,* and trust sensible parents to keep their children at home from mature films." [16]

Morals legislation, as in the case of Prohibition, might result in a radical interference with personal liberty, and it might also, like Prohibition, set standards beyond reasonable power of enforcement. The ensuing confusion was bound to result in lawlessness and in a weakening of the very standards sought by the legislation. In any case, the old paternalistic attitude of indulgence toward a common human weakness seemed to be in the process of abandonment — at least in so far as the law was concerned — as liquor, narcotics, vice, and gambling became the subjects of increasingly restrictive Federal legislation. According to one scholar in the field of law and public administration, the American people living under free institutions "submit to public regulation and control in ways that would appear inconceivable to the spirit of oriental despotism." [17] Another student of the subject pointed out that much of the Federal social and morals legislation could be handled through the police power of the states. "Regulations of this kind certainly have not been due to commercial necessity," he concluded.[18]

In revolt over Prohibition and other censorious restraints on the individual, many liberals, especially of the younger generation, responded enthusiastically during the twenties to the caustic criticisms that H. L. Mencken directed at his fellow citizens from the pages of the *American Mercury.* Although the "sage of Baltimore" also alienated many liberals by his antipathy toward democracy and idealistic reform, much of his criticism was motivated by a genuine concern over what he felt was a decline in traditional liberal values. For example, the emphasis on one's duty to the race or state, an ever-popular theme of the privileged classes, had become more than ever a symbol for docile obedience.[19]

In his *Notes on Democracy,* published in 1926, Mencken argued that fear and envy were the two main characteristics of democracy and "of its twin, Puritanism." Evidence of fear he saw in the American tendency to chase monsters, from the time of the British Redcoats during the American Revolution to the Bolshevists in the Red scare of 1919. In a democracy motivated by such hysteria, "The statesman becomes, in the last analysis, a mere witch-hunter, a glorified smeller and snooper." The Department of Justice he attacked as misnamed and as the chief violater of the Bill of Rights it was supposed to defend. Nine-tenths of American presidents, he pointed out, had reached office by making promises that were basically immoral. Yet, after election day, the President was criticized, not for making the promises but for his failure to keep them. "No man," he wrote, "would want to be President of the United States in strict accordance with the Constitution. There is no sense of power in merely executing the laws; it comes from evading or augmenting them." [20]

Waging a continual personal fight against censorship and "Comstockery," Mencken attacked as vulgar publicity seekers the professional reformers who were upset over alleged obscenity in literature. The "Clean Books bill" they sought, he declared, would put the Bible out of print; but he doubted that such a law would achieve its purpose any more than the Volstead Act had stopped drinking in the United States. And in an essay entitled "Memoirs of a Subject," Mencken lamented that, though Americans prided themselves on their liberalism and liberty, "Yet it must be obvious that their hold upon it is always precarious, and that their government tries to take it away from them whenever possible — not completely, perhaps but always substantially." [21]

Mencken's varied writings touched, not too lightly, upon some of the illiberal aspects of American democracy in the twenties. But his pleas for greater personal freedom, though welcomed in liberal and intellectual circles, had little effect in reversing the nation-wide tendency toward restraint and conformity. Thus, when the restrictive legislation, of which Mencken and other liberals complained, contributed to an increase of crime and racketeering, the popular solution was not repeal of the laws but the passage of more laws with stricter enforcement and harsher penalties and treatment for those guilty of infractions. As Rudyard Kipling had once pointed out, the American seemed under a twofold compulsion "to flout the law he makes" and again "to make the law he flouts." [22]

In its treatment of the criminal, who bore the full force of American indignation over the various "rackets" that sprang up in the twenties, American practice departed widely from the recommendations of contemporary students of criminology and penology. Official investigations of American prisons reported inadequate institutions and barbaric treatment of the inmates. Brutal police methods, popularly known by the term "third degree," only tended to confirm criminals in their bitterness toward society and in their desire for revenge. Despite the rejection by criminologists of harsh punishment as a deterrent to crime, and their repudiation of the objective of making the punishment fit the crime, law-enforcement officers continued to emphasize this approach. By the close of the decade, however, there were signs of improvement in some of the better American prisons. Also encouraging was the steady decrease in the number, though not in the individual brutality, of lynchings. But still off in the future was an acceptance of the liberal point of view that the criminal was a sick person in need of rehabilitation. Also not generally accepted was the thesis that the only real question that should be involved in the use of imprisonment was "whether or not the individual accused is a fit person to be at large before or after adequate treatment." [23]

Government interference in the realm of private morals and conduct was matched by its growing solicitude for the welfare of business enterprise. Paralleling the cult of nationalism and Americanism after World War I was the cult of prosperity and the worship of business methods and business values. Contrary to the often-held view that this business prosperity of the twenties was due to the workings of free competition under a philosophy of laissez faire, the decade actually witnessed a decline of competition in favor of a system of paternalistic government benefits to private enterprise. As early as 1923, Thorstein Veblen showed how the old Victorian spirit of competition had been succeeded after the war by a new era in which statesmen zealously pushed forward the business interests of their respective nations. "So the propagation of special interests under the shelter of national policy has come into the case . . ." The outcome of the war fought, as Veblen believed, for commercial domination was a kind of democratic imperialism compounded of national inflation and "business enterprise bent on getting something for nothing at any cost." [24]

In the United States, the administrative control of business, already proposed by Theodore Roosevelt and others, had actually come into being through the various World War I emergency agencies headed by the War Industries Board under Bernard Baruch. Though these agencies were for the most part speedily dissolved after the Armistice, many of the techniques of consolidation that they had fostered as wartime conservation measures remained in existence. Standardized products to eliminate duplication of facilities, trade associationism among competitors, and agreements to share the market and fix prices were all means of reducing competition which continued beyond the war, and which by now enjoyed the benevolent protection of the government. The so-called regulatory bodies such as the Interstate Commerce Commission, created originally to encourage competition, became in many cases large bureaucracies working in close conjunction with big business. A scholar not unsympathetic with the government regulatory agencies has nevertheless concluded, on the basis of a group of detailed case studies, that regulation "has done little more than outlaw practices that are frowned upon by the majority of businessmen. It has brought order into fields where the industrialists themselves recognized the need for control. The self-interest of politically effective groups has been identified with such departures from laissez faire." The new philosophy of the regulatory agencies was also pointed out by William E. Humphrey, himself a member of the Federal Trade Commission. The commissions, he reported, had reversed their stand to become "the bulwark instead of the oppressor" of industry.[25]

Meanwhile Herbert Hoover as secretary of commerce sought to bring business and engineering principles into government. Seeing no conflict with the rugged individualism he prized, and which his own career had in a considerable measure exemplified, he proceeded to make the Department of Commerce into a vast agency for the promotion of business interests both at home and abroad. In this process he specifically encouraged business to organize itself into trade associations and to develop its own codes of fair competition. "We are passing," Hoover said, "from a period of extremely individualistic action into a period of associational activities." [26] And by the time he left the White House after twelve years of government service, more than two thousand of these trade associations were in existence, compared with the dozen or so that had been functioning in 1920. Though the United States sealed itself off in this period from many foreign products through its return to the Republican policy of higher protective tariffs, markets for American exports were still carefully cultivated. Political isolation at any rate implied no accompanying economic indifference to Europe or Asia, while in Latin America the United States continued as of old to be active in both spheres.

By the twentieth century, the growth of the complicated apparatus of the modern administrative state was being closely paralleled by the development of the large-scale corporation. Big business under the various corporate devices of holding companies or cartels was able to compete on equal terms with the national state. Often, however, instead of competition being maintained, an informal bargain was struck, and big business became the partner of big government. In the United States, the antitrust laws therefore seemed to have only the curious effect of encouraging large combinations. Any attempt to enforce these laws had necessarily been suspended during the war, and in the twenties there was no disposition on the part of the Republican administrations to resume prosecutions. Also after the war, the Supreme Court discouraged rigid enforcement of the antitrust laws. Holding that mere size was not an offense, it refused to dissolve the United States Steel Corporation as an unlawful combination in restraint of trade. On the other hand, the Court continued to maintain that labor unions were subject to the antitrust laws and liable for damages caused by labor disputes. Thus the antitrust laws remained on the books mostly as monuments of economic self-righteousness and as a curb on labor union activity. According to Thurman Arnold's subsequent analysis, they were part of the folklore of American capitalism, "the answer of a society which unconsciously felt the need of great organizations, and at the same time had to deny them a place in the moral and logical ideology of the social structure. They were part of the struggle of a creed of rugged individualism to adapt itself to what was becoming a highly organized society." [27]

Large corporations also challenged economic individualism by fostering a transformation in the character of private property and business enterprise in the United States. Under the impetus of what James Burnham was later to call "the managerial revolution," ownership was becoming more and more divorced from control of its property, yielding authority to the executive management. At the same time, a decline in the ownership of real property in favor of a type of liquid wealth in the form of stocks and bonds enhanced the role of the managers and also encouraged an increase in the amount of money devoted to administration and overhead as compared with production. While the long-range effect of the large corporation in conjunction with the managerial revolution was a complex one, the immediate effect seemed to point clearly enough to a further weakening of economic individualism.[28]

The gravest danger, perhaps, in the alliance of government and business was in the rigidity and opportunities for favoritism that it imparted to the economy. Thus, in the twenties, the farmer seemed neglected, sharing no government benefits comparable to the largess received by business. Organized labor also declined in strength, and its strikes again became subject to active government interference and to judicial attack by injunction. Curiously and significantly, however, while many of the unions lost their wartime gains, the ones that "best maintained their membership strength were those which had received no, or only incidental, aid from the government during the war." Although labor and farmers were bitter over what they felt to be the deflationary policies pursued by the government, industry, protected by the semimonopolistic character of big business and by the high tariff wall, did not suffer a corresponding decline in prices. Also helpful in keeping up the domestic price level of all but farm goods, which had to sell at world market prices, was the easy money policy of the Federal Reserve Board. The Board's practices were later much criticized for encouraging the exaggerated stock market speculation that preceded the crash of 1929.[29]

In government, as in business, the trend was toward a growing concentration and centralization of functions. In place of the direct democracy emphasized in the progressive era, or the local government long prized by Jeffersonians, there was the development of the Federal bureaucracy and the administrative state. By the twenties, the idea of putting government into the hands of the individual citizen through the operation of the initiative, referendum, and recall was either infrequently used or falling under the control of political bosses and selfish pressure groups. Women's suffrage, made nation-wide by the Nineteenth Amendment, also failed to achieve any noteworthy political reform or change in voting patterns. The one serious attempt to form a new national party, the La Follette Progressive movement of 1924, attracted considerable liberal backing, but it was not able to secure any widespread mass support from farmers or labor. Meanwhile, state and local governments were constantly finding their responsibilities taken over by Washington.[30]

To old-line liberals these changes were the cause of much dismay and protest. A case in point was Frederic C. Howe, a long-time reformer with his roots in progressivism, who had attempted as Wilson's commissioner of immigration to resist the alien deportations. The collapse of idealism in the war and postwar hysteria embittered Howe, and he wrote in his *Confessions of a Reformer:*

My attitude toward the state was changed as a result of these experiences. I have never been able to bring it back. I became distrustful of the state. It seemed to want to hurt people; it showed no concern for innocence; it aggrandized itself and protected its power by unscrupulous means. It was not my America, it was something else.[31]

As a young man Howe had done some investigating in New York City for the vice-crusading Dr. Parkhurst's Vigilance League. But a talk with a local bartender gave him a lesson in political realism, and Howe's resulting report to Parkhurst ended their association. "By taxation and regulation we made the saloon an evil," Howe recalled, "involved it in politics, associated it with graft. We tried with it, as with almost every problem of its kind, every solution except letting it alone." The goal that Howe had worked for under Tom Johnson, the reforming mayor of Cleveland, was getting government closer to the people by decentralizing its functions. But this seemed an increasingly forlorn hope after the war. Civil service reform, the other great shibboleth of the prewar reformers, had turned into a leviathan bureaucracy.

This was the administrative state — the state that often shapes political action, that conspires with congressmen. In a generation's time, largely through the Civil Service reform movement, America has created an official bureaucracy moved largely by fear, hating initiative, and organized as a solid block to protect itself and its petty unimaginative, salary-hunting instincts.[32]

That Howe's disillusionment was not confined to a small minority of liberals and reformers was suggested by the relative decline in the number of voters in postwar elections. For his own part, Howe could only argue fruitlessly his thesis that "Profits are created and protected by law," and "Exploitation is born of the political state." [33]

On the Supreme Court bench, Justices Brandeis and Holmes wrestled with the problem of big business and big government. Both men were widely known for their decisions in favor of government regulation of business, but the public was less familiar with their concern over growing centralization, which they discerned as a feature of both government and business. In his private correspondence Brandeis complained of the tendency of state rights to succumb to the rights of nations, with a resulting atrophy of state duties and functions. "The extremes of concentration are proving its failure to the common man. . . . The new Progressivism requires local development — quality not quantity." Holmes supported his colleague's fears, and in one of his famous dissenting opinions he remarked:

I have not yet adequately expressed the more than anxiety I feel at the ever increasing scope given to the Fourteenth Amendment in cutting down what I believe to be the constitutional rights of the States. As the decisions now stand, I see hardly any limit but the sky to the invalidating of these rights if they happen to strike a majority of this Court as for any reason undesirable.[34]

Much of the liberals' disillusionment over the way in which the old goals of Populism and Progressivism had been perverted during and after the war was summed up in a now almost forgotten work by J. Allen Smith, entitled *The Growth and Decadence of Constitutional Government*. Smith had attracted considerable attention in an earlier book in which he anticipated some of Charles Beard's stress on the economic origins of the Constitution, but his second work, published posthumously in 1930 with an Introduction by Vernon L. Parrington, his colleague at the University of Washington, was virtually ignored. Pointing out the wide discrepancy between the theory and practice of democracy, Smith noted that the principle of majority rule was no guarantee of individual liberty, while natural rights in the United States were being more and more repudiated in favor of governmental supremacy. This centralization of government, accompanied by a steady growth of militarism and imperialism, he believed, was a direct threat to popular rule through local control.[35]

What Smith saw in current developments, his long-time friend Parrington traced historically in his celebrated *Main Currents in American Thought*. Both authors had been Populists in their youth, and their political philosophies continued to be strongly Jeffersonian. But in contrast to Smith's *Growth and Decadence,* Parrington's *Main Currents,* with all its rich historical detail on American literature and thought, was an instantaneous success. Reread today for the insight it provides into Parrington's own beliefs, the work stands as an impressive monument to his lamentations over a declining liberalism. The essential problem or dilemma facing liberals by the 1920's, Parrington summed up in a letter to a friend, which he wrote a few months before his own death in 1929:

Wherever power is lodged a great struggle for control and use of that power follows. When one controls the political state, whatever one wants can be done under cover of the law and with the sanction of the courts. Have you been able to convince yourself that the corporative wealth of America will permit the centralized political state to pass out of its control and become an agent to regulate or thwart its plans? . . .

You see the dilemma in which I find myself. We must have a political state powerful enough to deal with corporative wealth, but how are we going to keep that state with its augmenting power from being captured by the force we want it to control? [36]

The unhappiness of political liberals during the 1920's was matched by the dismay of many sensitive observers, conservatives as well as liberals, who saw a decline in all the more humane values as a result of the materialism and nationalism of the postwar era. Irving Babbitt, the celebrated apostle of New Humanism, attacked democracy as "likely to be idealistic in its feelings about itself, but imperialistic in its practice." Joseph Wood Krutch, drama critic for the *Nation*, ventured the hypothesis that modern civilization might be in the process of becoming decadent and destined for rejuvenation along more simple lines by a new society of barbarians. Others predicted a rising of the masses in primitive revolt against all liberal and individualist thinking. And still others saw the same results coming from military dictatorship or from the mechanistic materialism of a predominantly industrial and business-type society.[37]

European commentators upon the American scene shared, or in some cases encouraged, the strictures of native American critics. The hostility of the foreign authors was a reaction to the extreme nationalism of the American temper after the war. This nationalism was reflected not only in chauvinistic attitudes but also in American economic and trade policies. Much earlier, at the turn of the century, Henry Cabot Lodge, one of the chief progenitors of this nationalist feeling, in a letter to his friend Theodore Roosevelt had urged American military preparedness because, he wrote, "there is a fundamental danger which arises from our rapid growth economically. We are putting a terrible pressure on Europe, and this situation may produce war at any time." [38] In the midst of World War I, Lodge's analysis was realized as America exchanged the status of a debtor for that of a creditor nation. The new role, however, was not calculated to enhance the average European's love of the American government. Thus a British philosopher, on the basis of anecdotes of the United States, which he had never himself visited, attacked American civilization as *The Babbitt Warren*. A French writer, in the Preface to his book *America the Menace,* pointed out that the Continent was being conquered by America and that "Before twenty years have passed we shall be able to find all the stigmata of this devouring civilization on all the members of Europe." [39]

Professor André Siegfried, a more serious French critic, summed up much of European feeling in his well-known book *America Comes of Age.* Amazed at what he called "Puritan Resistance to Freedom of Thought," Siegfried argued that a truly individual existence was available to only a few in the United States. In the midst of the forces of Puritanism and business conservatism, he wrote: "It is essential to realize that the liberalism of the eighteenth century philosophers counts for little . . ." Turning to economic questions, Siegfried noted that despite American efforts, the United States exported a comparatively small percentage of its manufactured goods. The American investment abroad was based less on the expectation of profits than on the hope of saving tottering governments or of picking up bargains. Because Europe could offer the United States nothing in return, the old equality between borrower and lender was lost. Europe was humiliated, while America could be as arbitrary as it pleased, and from this, he concluded, "may arise a new and subtle imperialism unlike anything we have known before." [40]

Siegfried also felt that the tyranny of public opinion, manifested in pressure groups of all kinds, was greater in the United States than in Europe. In the eyes of both its European and American critics, the decline of liberalism in the United States was associated with the excessive nationalism and materialism of the twenties. The twin cults of Americanism and prosperity, coming on top of the intolerance and hysteria of the war and postwar years, served to undermine many of the traditional liberal values of freedom and individualism. Criticism and dissent, though tolerated, were still much resented. Not until the depression of the thirties did radical social criticism again gain respect. But the reformers' goal of a planned society bore little resemblance to American liberalism.

15

The Cult of Planning
and Reform

THE PROSPERITY of the twenties was suddenly foreclosed by
the collapse of the stock market in the fall of 1929. Speculators and investors, many of whom had purchased shares
on credit or margin, were sold out, and in the precipitous
decline of prices thousands saw their life savings swept away.
As the first days of panic subsided into the numbing business
stagnation of the early thirties, an ugly pessimism settled
over American life and thought. The complacency of the
cult of prosperity gradually yielded to a growing alarm and
self-criticism.

For the man in the White House, the collapse of prosperity was a personal tragedy almost equal to the disaster that
overtook Woodrow Wilson in the last years of his administration. Less than a year before the crash, the American people
had elected Herbert Hoover as the great engineer and businessman who would be able to sustain the prosperity of the
twenties on a permanently high level. Now, in the midst of
the wreckage of the depression, the Republican slogans and
promises of the twenties had a hollow sound, and Hoover
seemed an anachronism. Neither his rugged individualism
nor the new business philosophy he had espoused as secretary of commerce appeared suited to the all-prevailing hard
times. Deterred by individualist leanings from calling for

stronger government action to cope with the depression, and suspected in what economic measures he did recommend of favoring big business, he was doomed to failure. As one historian of American politics has well pointed out, Hoover, the "victim of his faith in the power of capitalism to survive and prosper without gigantic governmental props . . . was the last presidential spokesman of the hallowed doctrines of laissez-faire liberalism, and his departure from Washington marked the decline of a great tradition." [1]

In the elections of 1932, whatever Hoover might have argued would probably have been unavailing. His attempt to explain the depression as a world-wide phenomenon caused by the late war therefore carried little conviction with voters looking for immediate changes and drastic reforms. In contrast to Hoover, Franklin D. Roosevelt, the Democratic nominee, and his advisers proved themselves master politicians capable of a sympathetic understanding of the popular psychology. Exuding an air of jaunty confidence, Roosevelt, though never too clear or explicit in the details of his program, did manage to convey the hope of positive government action. This nationalistic, collectivist note was accompanied by incongruous avowals of faith in the traditional, limited-government ideal of the Democratic party of Jefferson and his successors. But in 1932 a linkage of essentially contradictory ideas did not bother either Roosevelt or the mass of the electorate. Rendered desperate by the depression and the alternative of four more years of the Hoover administration, the American public was not inclined to inquire extensively into the logic of the Democrats' case. Among liberals and progressives there was perhaps even less disposition to criticize the Democratic nominee. The dwindling ranks of traditional liberals could accept Roosevelt's quasi-Jeffersonian principles better than Hoover's business philosophy, while all shades of progressive reformers, except a scattering of doctrinaire Socialists or Communists, could wax enthusiastic over Roosevelt's promise of national economic planning.

By the early 1930's, the concept of a planned economy was achieving widespread support. Economists and experts in government, business, and the universities were suggesting possible blueprints for comprehensive reform, while spokesmen for industry, labor, and the church were giving their almost unqualified approval to the idea of planning along collectivist lines. College professors formed the nucleus of Roosevelt's original group of advisers, the so-called "brain trust," and many academic people gravitated to Washington to become government administrators. Other groups of teachers and professors, anxious to see the schools assume an active role in preparing American children for an impending cooperative, collectivist society, urged a shift from an individual-centered to a community, social-type education. "These educators defined education far more broadly than mere school training. They sought an alliance with organized labor and other progressive forces in the American community in order to lay the basis for recovery and reconstruction along collectivist democratic lines." [2] Reflecting this view, the Committee on Social Studies of the American Historical Association reported: "The age of individualism and laissez faire in economy and government is closing and a new age of collectivism is emerging." [3]

Education for democracy implied an explicit indoctrination—a position accepted by a wide range of opinion, including Catholic as well as Communist spokesmen. Though much of what was popularly called progressive education was bitterly contested by those who continued to think of education in terms of discipline and the study of the classics,[4] there was little doubt that the progressive point of view was in line with the demands of the thirties.

Indicative of the temper of the times and of the wide-spread advocacy of planning were such statements as Nicholas Murray Butler's address in 1931 before the American Club of Paris. Butler, the generally conservative president of Columbia University, and a lifelong Republican, told his listeners that the disastrous effects of poverty and unemployment were threatening the whole fabric of Western civilization. Believing that the statesmen and other leaders of the country could no longer delay the imposition of bold schemes, he explained to his audience that "if we wait too long somebody will come forward with a solution we may not like." Butler also ventured the opinion that "the characteristic feature of the experiment in Russia . . . is not that it is communist, but that it is being carried on with a plan in the face of a planless opposition. The man with a plan," he added, "however much we may dislike it, has a vast advantage over the group sauntering down the road of life complaining of the economic weather and wondering when the rain is going to stop." [5] Echoing President Butler, Stuart Chase rushed into print late in 1932 with a popular work on economics entitled *A New Deal*. "Why," Chase asked with real envy at the close of his book, "should Russians have all the fun of remaking a world?" [6]

In the midst of repeated insistence on planning and action, Roosevelt's evident willingness to experiment and his receptivity to all kinds of suggestions endeared him to the voters. Although he may have lacked a consistent over-all political philosophy, Roosevelt's approach to the problem of the depression had the popular merit of being more dynamic and less rigid or doctrinaire than Hoover's. Likening himself to the quarterback of the team, who called the plays in response to the situation, with the future sequence depending on the varying fortunes of the game, Roosevelt gave an apt picture of New Deal methods. In the eyes of Hoover and other critics, the New Deal pointed toward state socialism or fascism. But this charge, to which later developments gave considerable point, overlooked the grave crisis at the time of Roosevelt's inauguration in March 1933. At that juncture of history there were few who caviled at either Roosevelt's opportunism or his readiness to attempt some sort of planned economy along collectivist lines. As Walter Lippmann pointed out in delivering the Godkin Lectures at Harvard University the following year, "After the collapse of 1932–1933 a New Deal of some sort was imperative." [7]

In his speech accepting the nomination for president, Roosevelt had pledged himself "to a new deal for the American people." This phrase, singled out, became the slogan of the campaign and the descriptive tag applied to the whole Roosevelt era. As a term and promise of a program, it invited comparison with the earlier Square Deal of Theodore Roosevelt and New Freedom of Woodrow Wilson. Though the New Deal in office was to carry out some of the ideas of its progressive predecessors, F.D.R. had only a remote interest in Wilson's old hope of a restoration of free competition. At the same time, he went much further than Theodore Roosevelt had ever found possible in the direction of paternalistic government intervention and planning. Despite the conventional and polite homage paid by the Democrats to Wilson's New Freedom, Franklin Roosevelt was actually much closer in his philosophy of government to the Square Deal of his distant relative. Like Theodore, Franklin Roosevelt was essentially a strong nationalist. His emphasis on the solidarity of the nation and the ability of the people, working through their government, to solve the depression was a dominant theme of his political thinking. [8]

Much of the political philosophy of the New Deal, as it pointed toward long-range social reconstruction as well as immediate economic recovery, was forecast in a major campaign address which Roosevelt had delivered before the Commonwealth Club of San Francisco in September 1932. Tracing the rise of the modern political state, Roosevelt noted that the concept of limited government had developed as a protest against the centralized power of absolute monarchs. Monarchies, in turn, had arisen from the semianarchy of the feudal period. While American tradition had long favored limited government, in the past half century the growing consolidation of economic power in large industrial units had forced the government to assume the task of modifying or controlling big business. As America built up the West and reached its last frontiers, individual freedom and economic competition no longer operated automatically. The government as an enlightened administrator had to step in to preserve both liberty and prosperity. Seeing it as the task of government to assist business in formulating "an economic constitutional order," Roosevelt added: "Happily, the times indicate that to create such an order not only is the proper policy of Government, but is the only line of safety for our economic structure as well." [9]

Roosevelt's analysis depicted the United States as a mature economy in which the major problem was no longer one of production but of the proper distribution of consumer goods. The concentration of wealth in the hands of a few had resulted in underconsumption by the many. Accordingly, the revival of business without far-reaching social and economic reforms would be fruitless. And reform to be effective would require new regulatory and taxing policies as well as a greater degree of centralized planning. A resultant redistribution of wealth on a more equal basis would, it was hoped, make it possible to reverse the cycle of overproduction and underconsumption. The United States, then, without sacrificing capitalism, would be able to achieve a balanced economy, and at the same time free itself from dependence on world export markets.

Roosevelt was convinced that American freedom stood in greater danger from vast aggregations of private wealth than from any government abuse of individual rights. Accordingly, the New Deal philosophy denied the older American assumption that the people themselves could preserve their liberties from any type of interference except that which might come from a centralized government. The emphasis of the New Deal was on a type of liberty that minimized individual freedom in favor of a greater social security and economic equality of the whole. "The vision of liberty, then, commensurate with this change, is one in which the new positive power of government is to be employed for each against each to achieve a larger sum total of liberties for all. This is libertarian, but simultaneously it is egalitarian." [10] In its consideration of liberties in the collective sense of the general welfare, the New Deal was more concerned with strengthening and increasing the power of such organized groups as labor and the farmer than with protecting the civil liberties of the individual. The latter tended more or less to be assumed. Liberalism from the standpoint of the New Dealers meant economic reform and not the emancipation of individuals or minority groups from the restraints of social or political conformity. As Eric Goldman has written, "Talk of liberty in reform circles now was likely to produce a yawn, if not a scowl; opportunity, at least opportunity for the millions to have jobs, was the point." [11]

The relative indifference of the early New Deal to civil liberties continued an attitude that had characterized certain types of business and conservative thinking in the twenties. In the same way, many of the planning techniques of the New Deal also had their antecedents in the business associational activities of the preceding decades. During World War I, for example, businessmen under the leadership of Bernard Baruch and his War Industries Board were able to accomplish the regimentation of the American economy for war purposes. Later, in the twenties, business, with the encouragement of Hoover's Department of Commerce, transformed many of the wartime controls into a system of voluntary cooperation operating through its own trade associations. Both these associations and the War Industries Board were useful precedents for the New Deal's most characteristic and controversial experiment in planning, the National Recovery Administration. This conservative heritage, plus the role that the Chamber of Commerce and other business groups played in the organization of the NRA, might have aroused more suspicion among liberals had it not been for their widespread confidence in the broad nature and humanitarian goals of the New Deal's planning. Although Roosevelt, it was true, proposed to use the methods of big business and of wartime regimentation, his purpose included more jobs and better working conditions along with business recovery.

The National Recovery Act, which was hailed by the President as "the most important and far-reaching legislation ever enacted by the American Congress," [12] was placed under the direction of General Hugh Johnson, an old associate of Baruch on the War Industries Board. Johnson, described as combining "a limited amount of homely wisdom with the irritating methods of a drill sergeant," was soon alternately whipping and cajoling the country into accepting the codes of fair competition being drawn up for each industry. To the tune of blaring bands and the noise of crowds cheering the monster parades held in larger cities, the NRA and its emblem of compliance, the Blue Eagle, were popularized and publicized across the country. In the national effort to break the force of the depression via the NRA codes, little attention was paid to the fact that it was industry itself that had largely prepared the regulations governing prices and production. Also ignored was the fact that the NRA meant the suspension of the antitrust laws along with the whole theory of free competition and free enterprise. "Within a year, more than four hundred codes were completed and put into effect, covering about ninety per cent of American business enterprise and approximately twenty-two million wage and salary workers." This achievement vied with the World War I efforts to direct the American economy, and like the various wartime measures, but without the excuse of war, the NRA soon presented features that posed a dilemma for many liberals.[13]

As far back as the year of the Declaration of Independence, Adam Smith, the celebrated English expositor of economic liberalism, had written in his *Wealth of Nations:*

> People of the same trade seldom meet together, even for merriment and diversion, but the conversation ends in a conspiracy against the public, or in some contrivance to raise prices. It is impossible indeed to prevent such meetings, by any law which either could be executed, or would be consistent with liberty and justice. But though the law cannot hinder people of the same trade from sometimes assembling together, it ought to do nothing to facilitate such assemblies; much less to render them necessary.[14]

Giving some examples to illustrate his point, Smith noted that a government regulation requiring those of the same trade to enter their names on a public register would bring together individuals who might otherwise remain unknown to each other. A regulation calling upon businessmen to tax themselves for some charitable purpose would have the same effect.

Smith's argument of 1776 was similar to the charges with

which critics confronted the NRA less than a year after it became law. The accusation most frequently made was that the NRA was dominated by big business at the expense of the small producer, labor, and the consumer. In response to this criticism, Roosevelt set up the National Recovery Review Board to investigate the operations of the NRA. The Review Board, under the chairmanship of the celebrated criminal lawyer Clarence Darrow, but composed largely of businessmen, was able to substantiate a good part of its attack on the big-business slant of Hugh Johnson's codes, but it was unable to agree on a remedy. Darrow lamented before a Senate committee investigating the NRA that the concentration of wealth in the country was constantly accelerating, but he was uncertain whether this indicated a return to enforcing the antitrust laws or to the adoption of "something like a socialist system." [15]

In Darrow's main report to the President, he asserted that "fair competition is merely a resounding and illusory phrase. . . . *All competition is savage, wolfish, and relentless; and can be nothing else. One may as well dream of making war lady-like as of making competition fair.*" But Darrow also maintained that the powers granted the NRA boards were too drastic. *"We believe that such powers, if given at all, should be conferred only on an organization having governmental character."* Johnson and his assistant, Donald Richberg, bitterly pointed out the contradictory nature of Darrow's recommendations, but the Supreme Court a year later resolved the immediate issue by unanimously declaring the NRA unconstitutional.[16]

That many liberals were reluctant to yield the NRA ideal was illustrated by the action of a group of over two hundred editors and publicists, led by Oswald Garrison Villard, who signed a plea to the President calling for a stronger NRA with more government action in the economic field to spread out income, relieve unemployment, and avoid a default of the economy to big business.[17] What the liberals got instead, however, bore little resemblance to their petition. Although the NRA was at an end, the same philosophy that had called it into being was continued in the state and Federal fair trade and price-fixing laws. These measures were designed to eliminate unfair competition by permitting manufacturers to bind retailers not to sell their products at less than a prescribed minimum price.

By the middle of Roosevelt's first term, and after the abortive NRA experiment, the New Deal seemed to point in various directions, many of which were liberal only in the sense that they continued to command the general support of progressive and reform groups. Left-wing elements meanwhile attacked the New Deal on the ground that it was not revolutionary, while conservatives, on the other hand, denounced Roosevelt's policies as socialistic and prolabor. In actual practice, however, all the major economic pressure groups in the country derived some benefits from the New Deal and, in general, accepted many of the postulates of the positive state and a planned economy. Though business became hostile, it had been enthusiastic at first over the NRA and was later to welcome New Deal defense spending. The farmer was eager for the government aid and subsidies of the Agricultural Adjustment Administration, even though as an individualist he might resent Federal controls.[18] Labor, though not wishing the government to interfere in internal labor matters, was the most enthusiastic of all groups in backing the New Deal. Government protection of the right of collective bargaining was the basis for the great gains made by organized labor in the thirties, and John L. Lewis, head of the United Mine Workers, was quite atypical among his fellow labor leaders in fearing that what government could give it could also take away.

The most socialist of all the New Deal experiments, and thus logically the ones most open to objection from the standpoint of a traditional liberalism, were, rather surprisingly, often the ones least attacked. This was true in the case of both the Tennessee Valley Authority Act of 1933 and the Social Security Act of 1935. Social security legislation in the form of old-age pensions, sickness and accident benefits, and unemployment insurance had become commonplace in Europe by the time of World War I. Put forward as a state enterprise by Bismarck in the 1870's in order to head off the demands of German socialist and labor groups, similar legislation had also been resorted to in England early in the twentieth century when Fabian socialism and the new Labor party began to threaten the Liberals' position.

In the United States there had been little sentiment for Federal social security laws until the onset of the depression and accompanying loss of individual and family security. Roosevelt at first was reluctant to give his full support to measures that in the American Federal system belonged logically in the hands of the state governments, and which were also out of harmony with past American traditions. But the mass formation of local clubs agitating for the share-the-wealth schemes and old-age pension plans, variously advocated by Huey Long, Dr. Francis Townsend, and Father Charles Coughlin, forced Roosevelt's hand and helped bring about the passage of the Social Security Act. The law of 1935, subsequently expanded, forestalled much possible objection by not including such controversial features as medical insurance and by inviting the states to participate in the administration and financing of the measure. Also, the social security idea soon won wide acceptance because it brought the benefits of the welfare state down to the level of the average individual.

Of even greater moment in its departure from past American practice than social security legislation was the establishment, in one of the first New Deal measures, of the Tennessee Valley Authority. The original Wilson dam along the Muscle Shoals section of the Tennessee River had been built in World War I to furnish hydroelectric power for the manufacture of explosives and fertilizers. Not completed, however, until the end of Woodrow Wilson's second term, Muscle Shoals lay idle during the twenties as Presidents Coolidge and Hoover were rebuffed in their efforts to sell the facilities to private business. During this same period presidential vetoes killed Senator George Norris's bills providing for government operation, and Norris, a lifelong exponent of public-run power, had to wait until 1933 before he saw his vision realized. Then the Muscle Shoals project was quickly expanded, far beyond Norris's original expectations, by the New Deal administration. As first set up, the Tennessee Valley Authority was designed not only to furnish hydroelectric power but also to establish cooperatives, subsidize homesteads, enforce rural zoning, and encourage general regional planning. Coming into conflict with industrial and agricultural interests, whose main concern was cheap power and fertilizers, the TVA gave up its social and collectivist ideals.

With some of these initial difficulties of the TVA resolved, David Lilienthal, one of the original commissioners and later the chairman, assumed the task of defending the TVA as an example of democracy at work. Lilienthal believed that democratic government was impossible without popular control, and this in turn was not possible under centralized administration. Centralization, however, was not primarily a matter of size but of the degree to which power was delegated by Washington to administrators in the field and of how closely the latter worked with local people and their organizations. According to Lilienthal's view, the TVA showed the possibilities of collectivism without the sacrifice of democracy.[19] Later in World War II, the TVA's vast facilities were used for the manufacture of atomic bombs — an ironic achievement "of turning to destruction the energies of a region that had been entered for the express purpose of conservation and development." [20]

Some observers of the whole planned experiment in the Tennessee Valley, who were less lyrical in their attitude than Lilienthal, questioned how well his grass-roots approach to the TVA worked in practice. The democratic tie-in with local sentiment could easily be used to cover concessions to special interest groups. Thus the original collectivist and cooperative goals of the TVA had been shelved in response to local charges of socialism. Rexford Tugwell, an early New Deal braintruster, who believed that it was precisely these original TVA ideals that justified the venture in planning, summed up his criticism with the assertion that "TVA is more an example of democracy in retreat than democracy on the march." [21] Also dubious of the merits of the TVA were many of the New Englanders who saw their section receiving a disproportionately small share of Federal benefits in comparison with the taxes they paid into the United States Treasury. While New England mills were shut down, southern industry, enjoying its traditional advantage of cheap labor costs, now also reaped the additional reward of cheap and partly subsidized government electric power.[22]

The unhappy position of New England, America's first old section, not only in point of settlement but in the maturity of its manufacturing and industry as well, found an interesting counterpart in the growing dissatisfaction of older liberals with the program of the New Deal. While many of the more extreme attacks on the New Deal came from conservative businessmen, worried largely over economic freedom, there was also much criticism on broader liberal grounds. Of particular concern to all liberals was the preservation of individual freedom, and the question of whether the New Deal might not lead toward the same kind of state socialism already exemplified in most European nations.

One of the first to speak out in criticism of the New Deal from the standpoint of traditional liberalism was Herbert Hoover. Hoover's bitter opposition in detail to specific parts of the Roosevelt program was well known and to be expected, but the general liberal position, which he outlined in his *Challenge to Liberty,* provoked much surprise, especially among liberals. Albert Jay Nock, a libertarian follower of the agrarian ideals of Thomas Jefferson and Henry George, was amazed at Hoover's volume. "Think of a book on such a subject, by such a man!" he exclaimed. Nock also warned of the danger that anyone who might write on liberty in the next few years would automatically be considered a Republican.[23]

Defining liberty as freedom of the individual both intellectually and economically, Hoover viewed the world-wide attack on this liberty as the fundamental issue facing the American people. In its haste to control the forces loosed by modern war and technology, he believed that mankind was in danger of sacrificing liberty to the exigencies of security. This, he felt, was the case with the New Deal program of governmental planning and regimentation of the economy. Such experiments as the NRA, which he labeled "sheer fascism," invited the descent on Washington of a host of businessmen and lobbyists who were accomplishing the corruption and decay of representative government. "Congress," he pointed out, "cannot run business but business can run Congress — to the bankruptcy of Liberty." In international relations, a government-controlled economy held out the danger of economic warfare. "Men can higgle with each other in the markets of the world and there is no ripple in international good-will, but when governments do the higgling, then the spirit of antagonism between peoples is thrice inflamed." [24]

Hoover in his attack on the New Deal made little reference to his own policies of the twenties, policies not always in harmony with the position he now outlined. Like other presidents before him, from the time of John Adams and Thomas Jefferson, Hoover out of office was more liberal than when he was burdened with the responsibilities of power. It was left therefore for other critics of the New Deal, who were in sympathy with Hoover's outlook, to answer the charge that the debacle of 1929 was proof of the unworkability of a free economy. Temporarily pessimistic over the future, William Allen White, the newspaper sage of Emporia, Kansas, asked an assembly of college students in 1934: "Can freedom live in the machine age?" Under business control, competition became ruthless; with the politicians, there was the danger of regimentation. Despite his admiration for President Roosevelt, White was troubled by the trend toward centralization of power and authority in Washington, and he expressed the opinion that politicians were as bad potentially as the leaders of Wall Street.[25] In more thorough fashion, such thoughtful critics as Lewis W. Douglas and Walter Lippmann, both of whom had supported Roosevelt initially, turned back to a defense of a free enterprise economy and society.

Douglas, briefly Roosevelt's director of the budget, until he broke with the administration over its devaluation of the currency, argued that the depression was not a result of the operations of free capitalism but of the undermining of capitalism by the economic policies of the twenties. The high tariffs, price fixing, cheap money, and government subsidies of all sorts tended to keep prices artificially high, while the Federal Reserve Bank's low discount rates made money cheap and encouraged inflation. Also dangerous was the rigidity of the national economy in the twenties, which prevented reductions in the cost of production. This same lack of flexibility was again being encouraged through the New Deal's planned economy. It was not free enterprise or rugged individualism that was at fault in 1929, Douglas maintained, but rather a degenerate form of capitalism which utilized government support of the marginal and inefficient producer and relied on an inflation made wilder by political means. "This was the system, if it can be called a system, which failed," he concluded bitterly.[26]

Walter Lippmann, in his *Inquiry into the Principles of the Good Society* published in 1937, admitted growing disillusionment over his pre-World War I optimistic faith in collectivism. Now searching for a workable, meaningful philosophy, he defended a modified liberalism as the basis of the good society. Lippmann was dubious of the often-held assumption that the advance of technology and the complex modern economy required a collectivist system of control. Pointing out that the industrial revolution and rise of modern capitalism had occurred in the midst of a revolt against a multitude of commercial and political regulations, Lippmann suggested that the responsibility for the concentration of industrial power lay not in technology but in the modern limited liability corporation and its tendency toward monopoly. This invited the collectivists, either socialists or businessmen, to turn to an authoritarian concept of society. At the same time, democracy was changing from a government of negative limitations upon the state, in the form of a bill of rights, to the enfranchisement of the masses and the dictatorship of the majority. Pessimistically, Lippmann argued that the new political and economic forms tended inevitably toward war. All collectivism was basically militarist, although it might be masked as social reform. In the United States, for example, there was the curious contradiction of the American publicists of a planned economy who, though they were in most cases confirmed pacifists, nevertheless looked back with admiration upon the American war experience of 1917 and 1918 as a tentative sketch of a rationally ordered society.[27]

Lippmann's identification of a collectivist form of society with preparation for war was to underlie much of the liberal criticism of the New Deal by the close of the 1930's. Other problems that might have achieved greater attention from liberals were overshadowed by the specter of war, in Europe after the rise of Hitler and in the Pacific as a result of the Sino-Japanese War. Thus the Supreme Court fight, which contributed to liberal disaffection with the New Deal, soon lost its intensity and importance as an issue. Also responsible for this outcome was the fact that the Roosevelt plan for revamping the Court failed of approval by Congress, while the Court itself in the meantime, helped by an infusion of new justices, moved toward a liberal position.

This shift in the thinking of the Supreme Court during the second Roosevelt administration was not without its elements of paradox. The new Roosevelt Court, though zealous in invoking the Constitution to defend civil liberties and free speech, proceeded to modify or eliminate some of the constitutional barriers to Federal or state regulation of the economy. In other words, the Court reversed in part the traditional liberal position, long exemplified by Justice Holmes, that the judicial function was a limited one. Like the conservatives before them, the new justices seemed to have a double standard for judicial review. While not interfering with government regulation of the individual in economic cases, the Court interpreted the Constitution broadly to prohibit government restraints on civil liberties. This was the opposite of earlier Court procedure, when conservative justices had defended economic freedoms but not personal liberties. This constitutional dilemma also illustrated the plight of liberals in their relation to the Court and the folly of their placing undue reliance on the courts for the protection of essential freedoms.[28]

A last-minute major transformation in the thinking of the New Deal on domestic policy, more in accord with a liberal point of view, was the brief return to a program of encouraging competition and enforcing the antitrust laws. In 1938 the President appointed as assistant attorney general, in charge of the Antitrust Division, Thurman W. Arnold, professor in the Yale Law School, and a leading critic of business practices in restraint of competition. At the same time, the Temporary National Economic Committee, or TNEC, established by Congress upon the President's recommendation, began an extensive investigation of the concentration of economic power under American capitalism. Though Arnold instituted a number of prosecutions for alleged monopolistic practices, the outbreak of the European war and the accompanying American preparedness effort precluded any real possibility for a vigorous enforcement of an antitrust policy.

What the TNEC submitted in its final report to the President in 1941 was already unreal, though still historically significant. Arguing that democracy must extend to "all the organizations through which man operates," the report set forth the thesis that "Political freedom cannot survive if economic freedom is lost." To restore free enterprise and at the same time safeguard efficiency, it urged as a government policy the decentralization of industry, stimulation of competition, an end to the basing-point system of determining prices, the repeal of fair trade laws, centralized government purchasing, a national corporation law, enforcement of the antitrust laws, limits on the restricted sale of patents, and registration of trade associations. Criticized, in turn, for its dogmatic quest of a panacea and its tendency to lay all blame upon monopolies, the TNEC report nevertheless raised questions that again would become a matter of pressing concern to liberals after the war.[29]

Possible changes in the philosophy and direction of the New Deal, illustrated by the TNEC investigation, were never realized, as the administration began to concentrate its attention on the scene abroad. In retrospect, it would seem that the New Deal, despite the high tide of liberal enthusiasm on which it was launched, marked no deep or lasting shift in the ebbing fortunes of a declining American liberalism. Originating in the black despair of the depression, the New Deal as an active philosophy and program came to a standstill somewhere within the period of World War II. In the brief interval between those two dates, the American people under the leadership of President Roosevelt absorbed an unprecedented volume and variety of reform ideas and laws, touching virtually every aspect of American life. In contrast to the dark days of 1933, a measure of returning prosperity and a more hopeful popular psychology had been achieved. But the New Deal was unable to solve the problem of the depression or accomplish any considerable economic recovery, except as expenditures for preparedness and war brought on the new boom of the 1940's. This turn from peace to war, whether forced from the outside or accepted as a conscious national policy, could hardly be regarded as an answer to the problems of mankind or the ills of society. In the United States, war had never been the friend of liberalism, and American liberals, looking ahead into the 1940's, could not expect the future to be more encouraging than the past.

16

From New Deal to New War

THE THREAT of a second world war, never wholly absent in the post-Versailles world, showed new signs of becoming a reality by the middle of the 1930's. After the onset of the depression, the halting efforts to achieve a stable, peaceful world order crumbled rapidly. Although nationalism was rampant in all countries, it reached extremes of chauvinism and militarism in Italy, Germany, and Japan. Each of these nations was dissatisfied with the work of the Paris Peace Conference and was thus all the more ready to resort to war as an instrument of change. Even though World War I had hardly accomplished a victory for the liberal ideals of peace and democracy, these ideals were unfavorably linked with the peace settlement. And as the feeling toward the Versailles Treaty grew more bitter, much of Europe turned against the liberal values that it unfairly associated with the verdict of the war.

In the United States disillusionment took the somewhat different form of a reaction, not only against the World War I experience but also against possible American participation in any future war. The traditional pacifism of liberal thinking was reinforced by the widespread development of strong isolationist sentiments, which were further deepened in the 1930's by the Nye Committee's investigation of the role of the munitions industry in connection with American entrance into World War I. Revelations of business unneutrality and profiteering uncovered by this committee of the United States Senate were paralleled by the publication of critical historical works on the origins of the war. To many Americans, therefore, World War I became an object lesson in the economic interpretation of history, a lesson which they attempted to apply in the neutrality legislation from 1935 to 1937.

Coming into power in the midst of this swelling antiwar and isolationist feeling, the Roosevelt administration shared the general public attitude. In the 1932 elections, foreign affairs had not been a major issue although Roosevelt, despite his earlier identification with the Wilson administration and the League of Nations, tended to be regarded as the isolationist candidate. It was true that a few liberals, including Oswald Garrison Villard, called attention to Roosevelt's lifelong interest in the navy and the danger that in office he might pursue a militarist course.[1] But such fears seemed to lose their point as the depression compelled the New Deal to concentrate on domestic affairs. With adequate natural resources and no apparent need for more territory, the American people did not envisage war or the abandonment of isolationism as a possible solution to the grave economic problems facing them at home. The early thinking of the New Deal, instead, emphasized the necessity of positive planning to achieve a balance between domestic production and demand. Foreign trade, which had declined to the vanishing point, was largely ignored in favor of developing a stronger consumer economy.

For many liberals the New Deal's program of a balanced economy served as a guarantee that the United States would be able to avoid the dangers of overseas imperialism and foreign wars. Thus Secretary of Agriculture Henry Wallace, in his widely read pamphlet *America Must Choose,* offered planning "to build up consumption per capita at home, as a substitute for the continual search for new consumers abroad." Stressing intelligent planning as a middle ground between nationalism and internationalism, and as a step toward "new dealing with the world," Wallace wrote: "Our New Deal seeks to promote consumption more soundly. It directs purchasing power to those in need, by wage advances and alleviations of debt. It lessens the need to force exports. It looks toward balancing production with consumption at home." [2]

Planning as a substitute for war was also the thesis advanced by Charles Beard in his realistic studies of the economic mainsprings of American foreign policy. Beard, a supporter of the early New Deal, believed that national interest in the twentieth century had come to mean an increasingly intensified struggle on the part of industrial nations for world markets. Swelling armaments and resort to war had become concomitant features of modern industrial statecraft. Glorious little wars, however, were not always available, and any war once started was not easy to control or bring to a close. While force and war had hitherto been powerful factors in world history, in themselves they had not provided solutions to world economic problems or to maintaining "any culture save that of the barracks." Historically, Beard found that "in cruel truth, internationalism may be a covering ideology for the aggressive nationalism of one or more countries," and he turned therefore to an advocacy of what he called "the open door at home." This Beard hoped to see achieved under the planned economy of the New Deal. "Offering to the world the strange sight of a national garden well tended, the United States," he wrote, "would teach the most effective lesson — a lesson without words." [3]

Beard's vision was reminiscent of the old American dream, looking to the peaceful advance of democracy through adoption by the rest of the world of America's beneficent example of orderly self-government. What most liberals overlooked, however, in their initial enthusiasm for the New Deal's economic planning was the ease with which such planning could be diverted from peace to war. Also forgotten in the popular concentration upon the New Deal's efforts to fight the depression, was the fact that the dividing line between domestic economic recovery and military preparedness was never too clearly drawn. Despite the prevailing pacifist isolationism of the early thirties, with which the Roosevelt administration went along, there was never any reason to doubt the President's own personal sympathy for a big army and navy program. At first, however, campaign promises of economy, and the political dangers inherent in a too sudden adoption of a larger military budget, resulted in a program of rearmament by indirection.

As early as June 1933, the President allocated over two hundred million dollars from the NRA appropriation to the construction of new battleships. Funds intended for the Public Works Agency also were used to bolster up the army and navy, and aircraft carriers, military airplanes, airports, highways, wind tunnels, and hospitals were constructed from PWA money. In 1935 public opposition to this policy persuaded Congress to state the specific purpose for which appropriations were made. But in the case of some agencies of the New Deal little change resulted. As the biographer of Harry Hopkins has noted, "despite the prohibitions against any military activities which had been written into the Work Relief Bill, W. P. A. accomplished a great deal of construction — airports, highways, bridges, etc. — that had deliberately strategic importance." [4]

As the public became conditioned to large-scale New Deal expenditures, economy and indirection in the military budget was less necessary. For example, conservative businessmen, though hostile to outlays for domestic reform, were willing to accept government spending for military purposes. But the major factor behind increasing New Deal appropriations for the army and navy was the administration's growing concern over world affairs and the diversion of its primary interest from domestic to foreign policy. By late 1936 the President, according to Under Secretary of State Sumner Welles, was already "obsessed" with the dangers to the United States stemming from the threat of war in Europe and Asia.[5]

The most dramatic expression of the New Deal's changed emphasis came in Roosevelt's famous "quarantine" speech attacking aggressor nations, which he delivered at Chicago in October 1937. Although the President's words were general in nature, the address implied the possibility of some sort of collective action to deter the ambitions of Germany and Japan. Supporters of the President's abandonment of isolation argued that the best pathway to peace lay in United States encouragement of a strong collective security stand by the nonfascist nations of the world. On the other hand, widespread fears that such a policy, if carried beyond mere words, might presently involve the United States in another world war were probably responsible for the generally unfavorable public reaction to the Chicago speech. The popular neutrality laws, designed to keep America out of war, rather than to try to prevent war from breaking out overseas, were obviously not in harmony with the President's now evident desire to use American power and influence to curb the expansionist aims of Germany and Japan. While the President and the State Department wanted a flexible law that would enable the United States to withhold war supplies from any belligerent deemed an aggressor nation, Congress and the country were determined that the neutrality legislation should apply equally to all warring nations.

Although President Roosevelt, aware of the extent of

isolationist sentiment, and with an eye to his own re-election in 1940, continued to maintain a precarious balance between peace and war, such administration measures as repeal of the embargo and enactment of lend lease pointed clearly to eventual American involvement. Even though America was not a belligerent in the first two years of the war, Roosevelt did not believe that the country could be neutral or indifferent to Nazi war aims. On the other hand, former President Hoover was convinced that his successor was leading the United States into a foreign war despite the desire of the majority of the people for peace. Modern war, Hoover warned, "means that our country must be mobilized into practically a Fascist state. It would be so organized. It went some distance in the last great war, although we did not use that term at the time." [6]

Echoing Hoover's gloomy prediction, Senator Arthur H. Vandenberg, Republican of Michigan, in the midst of the Congressional debate over repeal of the embargo, charged that sending munitions to the Allies would be the prelude to further intervention in their behalf, until ultimately the United States would enter the war as an avowed cobelligerent. If this came true, the senator warned, "we would get such a regimentation of our own lives and livelihoods, 20 minutes after we entered the war, that the Bill of Rights would need a gas mask, and individual liberty of action would soon become a mocking memory." [7]

To many American liberals the now-changing situation at home was almost as disheartening as the menace of totalitarianism and war from abroad. An aggressive United States foreign policy, they realized, spelled the end of domestic reform. Already the New Deal had lost much of its initial allure. Its evident failure to achieve any real prosperity was highlighted by estimates of ten million workers still unemployed at the close of the thirties. With the road to recovery via planning and reform seemingly at a dead end, some critics wondered whether the administration's growing attention to foreign affairs was entirely a result of the worsened international situation. Viewed in such a light, much of the New Deal's nationalism and centralization, and its vast expenditures, could be reconsidered as steps in preparedness for an impending war.[8]

Among the first to argue such a thesis was Albert Jay Nock, an intransigent and uncompromising individualist who had no doubt about the eventual direction of the New Deal's planned economy. "What we and our more nearly immediate descendants shall see," he wrote in 1935, "is a steady progress in collectivism running off into a military despotism of a severe type. Closer centralization; a steadily growing bureaucracy; State power and faith in State power increasing, social power and faith in social power diminishing." Three years later, Nock confided to a correspondent: "I see that Franklin is playing what is usually the jobholder's last card — 'National defence.' " And after America entered the war, Nock, as unreconciled as ever, observed publicly: "At any time after 1936 it was evident that a European war would not be unwelcome to the Administration at Washington, largely as a means of diverting public attention from its flock of uncouth economic chickens on their way home to roost, but chiefly as a means of strengthening its malign grasp upon the country's political and economic machinery." [9]

Particularly among those liberals who resisted the administration's foreign policy, war was feared as a prelude to totalitarianism. The answer to the problem of fascism, they believed, depended on more than the defeat of Italy, Germany, or Japan. Like communism, fascism was viewed as part of a world revolt against many of the values of liberalism and democracy. And the United States, by concentrating its attention on the danger of a fascist or nazi aggression from abroad, overlooked the more real threat of an approaching totalitarianism at home. This threat, however, did not come primarily from some of the more blatant, radical demagogues of the right who encouraged such profascist organizations as the German-American Bund. Rather, as Huey Long, one of the first and most able of their number, explained, if fascism ever took hold in America it would arrive in the guise of antifascism.

Lawrence Dennis, the leading American exponent of intellectual fascism, underlined Long's point with his thesis that a purely American fascism would not have to include all the undesirable features of Hitler's nazi state. In his *Coming American Fascism,* published in 1937, Dennis maintained that neither economic planning nor the use of force was un-American. Liberal capitalism, he argued, was doomed and could no longer be made to work short of the economic incentives supplied by war. The latter, in turn, would automatically, and of necessity, result in the imposition of some kind of fascist state and economy.

Although most Americans had little sympathy with avowed fascist-type organizations or leaders, there was a growing fear, especially in liberal circles, that fascism and the totalitarian collectivist state were symptomatic of a deeply rooted malaise striking at the heart of Western civilization. Fascism, according to this view, was part of a Machiavellian or managerial revolution that sought to overthrow the remnants of an already declining liberal society. It fed on the craving of the masses, not only for economic security but also for the type of psychological security found in authoritarian institutions. The so-called revolt of the masses was thus actually more an apathetic resistance to the initiative that a free liberal society entrusted to the individual — a "flight from freedom," or a retreat from reason. Catering to the psychological and social needs of the people by offering them all sorts of nationalistic and militaristic flourishes, the fascist states were able to stir the patriotism of the masses. In this way, too, the state gained acceptance for the cutting back of consumers' goods and could devote the savings to war preparations. In Karl Mannheim's dire words, "The less bread, the more circuses." [10]

The role of fascist ways of thinking in American life provoked continued commentary in the months before American entrance into World War II. Noting that many of those who had formerly deplored the fascist tendencies of the domestic program of the New Deal now "accepted the inevitability of the Fascist impact in a period of preparedness," Edgar Kemler, a young journalist, chronicled what he called *The Deflation of American Ideals*. "We have reduced a rich heritage of hopes and dreams to the bare endeavor to make the system work," Kemler wrote, but he added: "I, for one, am willing to pay this price." Others also noted that the multiplicity of New Deal laws, even though they had promised some social good, in no way changed the fact that they were often gained at the price of individual liberty. [11]

Most cynical, perhaps, was James Burnham, who argued in his well-known book *The Managerial Revolution* that United States hostility to totalitarianism was merely resentment of its foreign aspects — "a 100% American totalitarianism would not be objectionable." While the United States was the most primitive of the managerial states, it tended in the same direction as its European counterparts. American liberals were naturally confused by the mixture of aims and purposes put forth under the New Deal banner. Such old-fashioned liberal individualists as Oswald Garrison Villard, for example, whom both Kemler and Burnham regarded as typical, were especially bewildered because "the New Deal's liberalism and progressivism are *not* liberalism and progressivism in the historical meaning of these terms." [12] Villard, despite his admiration for much of the early New Deal and his approval of Roosevelt's stand against fascist aggression, could not reconcile growing American militarization or Roosevelt's Supreme Court plan and third-term ambitions with his own liberal philosophy. Believing that New Deal liberalism was being slain by preparations for war, Villard unhappily continued to protest that he was still a New Dealer as well as a stanch pacifist.[13]

As the United States moved ever closer to war, American liberals, already at odds over the issues at stake, were still further divided by charges that the scholars and writers among them had been notably indifferent to the totalitarian advance threatening the free world. In an earlier view of this question, the so-called treason of the intellectuals was regarded as not to the state but to their responsibilities as intellectuals. Their treason therefore was not a lack of patriotism but their renunciation of the philosophy of liberalism for the favors and dictates of the state. It followed from this that "One of the gravest responsibilities of the modern State is that it has not maintained (but could it do so?) a class of men exempt from civic duties, men whose sole function is to maintain non-practical values." [14] The New Deal, with all its emergency WPA aid to art and letters, had been able to avoid political censorship because the criterion was the individual's need for relief and not the content of his work. But now, with the approach of war, the old conservative refrain of "rights without duties" was revived as a whip to lash the hesitant, nonconformist liberal intellectuals into line.

After the fall of France in the late spring of 1940, Archibald MacLeish led a group of American intellectuals in accusing their fellows of a "failure to understand what it is that is happening to their world," and of failing to oppose soon enough the fascist destruction of scholarship and humane values. Having seen "the crisis of our time" in France, Mac-

Leish charged that American intellectuals continued to think and write of it in a detached way as a purely European phenomenon. This criticism, as it was later developed and enlarged in the course of the war, was basically a charge that many American liberals and intellectuals, imbued with the disillusionist and critical viewpoint of the twenties and early thirties, had not responded with sufficient enthusiasm to the stimulus of American nationalism and patriotism. Presumably guilty of this charge of having been overly critical in their writings were such authors as Sinclair Lewis, H. L. Mencken, and Charles Beard. According to the MacLeish school of thought, these writers, "The Irresponsibles," had undermined the confidence of American youths in American institutions and had thus weakened their will to fight the battle of democracy against fascism.[15]

This indictment was a natural outgrowth of the new spirit of nationalism that had begun to develop in the thirties. In part, a result of the support that the New Deal gave to various intellectual and cultural projects, this cultural nationalism was also related to the search for positive values in the midst of a deteriorating world order. In such a time of stress, the kind of liberalism that indulged in a critical view of accepted institutions and beliefs was likely to be subordinated to a philosophy of emotional affirmation and uncritical faith. Accordingly, two days after Pearl Harbor, the Writers' War Board was organized to meet the need for a wartime propaganda agency. This Board had as its "basic function . . . the fulfillment of requests from governmental agencies for all kinds of writing required to win the war." [16]

The very virulence of the MacLeish attack on the writers and intellectuals of the interwar period, in a sense, provided its own explanation for much of their pessimistic and critical spirit. But, as a later defender of the accused authors was to point out, it never occurred to their wartime detractors that the bitterness of the writings they attacked was rooted in the fact of one world war and was in the process of being justified by another even greater global conflict.[17]

In the midst of these final intellectual preparations for possible war, important changes were overtaking American democracy. Almost unnoticed, Congress passed what was in effect the first peacetime sedition law in the United States since the unhappy Federalist Act of 1798. Serious interest in such a law had its origins in the period immediately after World War I, when Wilson's attorney general, A. Mitchell Palmer, tried unsuccessfully to persuade Congress to transpose the wartime sedition legislation into a permanent statute. In the twenties most of the illiberal war legislation, except in some of the states, became a dead letter, and then in the 1930's the Supreme Court began to bolster liberals' confidence in the matter of civil liberties. The Court, under Chief Justice Charles Evans Hughes, became a zealous defender of the right of free speech, and Justices Holmes and Brandeis, formerly in a minority on such cases, now found their views accepted by a majority of their colleagues.

But, while the Court was thus giving the country more liberty, toward the end of the decade Congress and state legislatures began giving it less. Fears of communism revived and soon resulted in state laws interfering with freedom of speech, press, and teaching. In 1935 Congress called for hearings on a peacetime sedition law, and three years later the Dies Committee began its investigation of un-American activities. Concerned with ferreting out subversive nazi and communist activity in the United States, the Dies Committee also had the effect of intimidating left-wing and radical sentiment within the New Deal administration and in the labor movement.[18] The drive for a peacetime sedition law, accordingly, seemed based on more than a foreign threat to America.

A month before Hitler moved his army into Poland, the House of Representatives after weeks of thorough discussion passed a sedition bill by an overwhelming majority. Less than a year later, in June 1940, the bill became law, but the brief final debate made no reference to the collapse of France that spring or to the danger of a nazi attack on the United States. Indeed, the chief connection of the bill with events in Europe seemed to rest in its misleading title of Alien Registration Act. The impression that most Americans had of the act was that it was a statute for the registration and fingerprinting of foreigners. Zechariah Chafee, an authority on the history of legislation pertaining to freedom of speech, has admitted: "Not until months later did I for one realize that this statute contains the most drastic restrictions on freedom of speech ever enacted in the United States during peace." Chafee added that the law commonly called the Smith Act "is no more limited to the registration of aliens than the Espionage Act of 1917 was limited to spying." The comparative liberal silence regarding the Smith Act at the time of its passage, he felt, was probably a result of the rush of legislation that spring, the lessened critical feeling of the country in the face of impending war, and finally the false stress on the bill as a measure dealing chiefly with aliens.[19]

This latter emphasis was true of the bill as originally drawn up, when Congress, in a mood of bitter and vindictive antiforeign feeling almost akin to nazism in Germany, was ready to pass any kind of restrictive measure dealing with aliens. Justified at first on the grounds that it applied only to the alien deemed guilty of subversive activities, the bill was then, in turn, criticized because it did not apply equally well to suspect citizens. Congress suddenly seemed panic-stricken by the realization that the country had existed for almost one hundred fifty years with no law governing sedition in time of peace. Accordingly, the bill was amended so that citizens as well as aliens were prohibited from such activities as interfering with the loyalty of the armed forces. This antisubversive section put into effect again the terms of the World War I Espionage Act. Finally, the whole bill was broadened not only to include activity involving the army or navy but to forbid anyone from teaching or advocating the "overthrow or destruction of any government in the United States by force or violence; or to be or become a member of, or affiliate with, any such society, group, or assembly of persons . . ." [20]

This last provision contained the "guilt by association" clause that provided a foundation for the antiradical campaign following World War II. Thus it was evident that the Alien Registration Act included far more than its title indicated and that it carried sedition legislation beyond the World War I example. The only precedent in all American history for its insistence that guilt was not necessarily personal but could be determined by membership or association was in the alien deportations of 1919. "Neither the Sedition Act of 1798 nor the Espionage Acts of 1917 and 1918 included such a conception. We got safely through the Civil War and the World War without finding it necessary to create group guilt outside the limits of an actual conspiracy." [21]

The general aim of the 1940 sedition legislation, like that of the more limited laws of 1798 and 1918, was, of course, to suppress the dissemination of opinions and beliefs deemed subversive, but which nevertheless could not be prosecuted as treasonable within the meaning of the Constitution and the courts' interpretation of treason as dependent on some overt activity. The danger in all such legislation was not its actual provisions dealing with subversion of the armed forces or overthrow of the government — practices which almost all would accept as undesirable — but the way the law could be used to threaten free speech and nonconformist activity. "The truth," as Chafee has pointed out, "is that the precise language of a sedition law is like the inscription on a sword. What matters is the existence of the weapon. Once the sword is placed in the hands of the people in power, then, whatever it says, they will be able to reach and slash at almost any unpopular person who is speaking or writing anything that they consider objectionable criticism of their policies." [22]

Although at least one congressman warned that the Smith Act could also be used to prevent conservatives from agitating against a type of government they deemed radical and un-American, in practice, legislation of this type was more liable to operate "as a device to keep down the agitation of discontented workmen." [23] Thus the Smith Act was largely unworkable in World War II when it was invoked in the mass sedition trial of a group of alleged nazi sympathizers, but it was used effectively in 1941 against a number of Trotskyist labor leaders. Eighteen men and women members of the Socialist Workers party and the Minneapolis Motor Transport Workers Union, a CIO local, were the first to be convicted under the Smith Act's provisions against any conspiracy to overthrow the government by force or violence. Wartime liberals who ignored the Minneapolis case and were willing to enforce the doctrine of guilt by association against members of the pro-nazi German-American Bund, were later to reap a heavy harvest of retribution when the Smith Act was found to be susceptible of use against left-wing and radical groups in the period after the war.[24]

In the same month in which Congress passed the Alien Registration, or Smith, Act, it began serious consideration of another measure also unprecedented in American peacetime history — military conscription. Some form of military training in peace as a preparation for universal service in war had long been desired in military circles. This enthusiasm, however, was not shared by the American people or the Congress, and all such plans looking toward compulsory training or drill were rejected after World War I. Although such a New Deal measure as the Civilian Conservation Corps of the 1930's provided a degree of military training and preparedness, there had been no real opportunity to revive the draft issue until after the coming of the war in Europe.

Presented to the people as legislation for the better defense and protection of the United States by a system of peacetime military training, the Selective Service Act of 1940 was in reality a war measure. Despite the emphasis on training for defense, the law forecast the sending of an American army to Europe or Asia as soon as the United States might become an actual belligerent. Conscription, widely denounced as the sure path to war, held out far-reaching implications for American foreign policy. And, at the same time, as Senator Norris pointed out in the debate over the measure, a permanent system of compulsory military training would go far to transform the domestic pattern of life in the United States as he and his colleagues had known it.[25]

With its potentiality for heightening nationalist and militarist sentiment, conscription was obviously inimical to the ideals of peace and individual liberty long prized by all liberals. In conflict with traditional liberalism, conscription was also at odds with democracy, except in an interpretation of the latter from an extreme equalitarian or collectivist point of view. This conflict between conscription and democratic ideals was immediately pointed out in a statement signed by some three hundred prominent educators, authors, clergymen, business and professional leaders, who denounced the impending draft as totalitarian and unworthy of the spirit of American democracy.[26]

Liberals, with a respect for the historic tenets of their principles, could justify conscription only to the extent that they viewed United States entrance into the war as necessary and desirable. It was again the old World War I confusion over ends and means. The dilemma of the prowar liberals lay in the fact that they could not logically refrain from acceding to the militarism that might be needed to back up the President's interventionist foreign policy. Thus Freda Kirchwey, editor of the *Nation,* wrote somewhat reluctantly "There Is No Alternative." And the *New Republic,* which at first believed that the United States should limit its efforts to continuing as the arsenal of democracy, announced in September 1940: "It is with heavy hearts that the editors of the *New Republic* endorse the principle of compulsory service at this time." [27]

In contrast to the tortured consciences of the editors of the liberal journals, some conservative spokesmen, who did not join in the general military and business enthusiasm for conscription, were able to suggest that the draft was basically a New Deal totalitarian measure. For example, the *Commercial and Financial Chronicle,* which had greeted the Burke-Wadsworth selective service bill with the caption "Involuntary servitude must not be restored," asked: "Does not this defense program in some of its aspects take on the appearance of another New Deal project tainted with the philosophy of totalitarianism and heavy with risk of further infringement of individual liberty?" [28]

After the passage of the Selective Service Act, the problem of the conscientious objector to military service thrust itself upon all those liberals who were not completely captivated by the war spirit. While the small number of actual CO's was to prove disappointing to the many liberals who had taken seriously the antiwar pledges of college youths in the 1930's,

the prospect of even a few thousand objectors was disquiet-
ing to the government. Although Selective Service procedures in regard to the CO came to represent a considerable
advance over World War I legislation and practice, Congress
in 1940 refused to follow Britain's liberal example and accept as sincere those objectors who were motivated by other
than religious beliefs. Liberal and pacifist spokesmen at the
first draft hearings therefore warned the congressmen that
they were enacting a measure which, in providing insuffi-
cient protection for the cause of conscience, would again fill
Federal jails with objectors to war. This prediction was in
part realized as many CO's were either denied such a classification on technical grounds or themselves refused to comply
with the strict provisions of the act.[29]

In the course of the war, some six thousand CO's, including four thousand Jehovah's Witnesses denied classification
as ministers, were convicted of Draft Act violations and sentenced to prison terms of as much as five years. Twice this
number, or some twelve thousand men, were assigned to the
civilian work camps or to special units on farms or in mental
hospitals. A much larger number of CO's, variously estimated at from twenty-five to one hundred thousand men,
were granted noncombatant status in the army. For the CO
in general there had been a significant change since World
War I. Although not in agreement with his views, most
people seemed to feel that the sincere objector had a right to
his convictions. Many of the churches, for example, though
they again followed the populace in giving their sanction to
war, coupled this stand with resolutions affirming support of
the individual whose conscience compelled him to stand
aside.[30]

In the light of the comparative toleration extended at least
to the religious objector, the most serious victims of wartime

hate and hysteria were the Japanese Americans living along the Pacific coast and in the Hawaiian Islands. Although there was no case of espionage or sabotage by a single Japanese, citizen or noncitizen, all Americans of Japanese descent were evacuated from the Pacific coast, and military government was imposed upon the Hawaiian Islands, where Japanese Americans formed the largest single element in the population. Later, after the close of the war, the Supreme Court declared the army rule of Hawaii to have been an illegal invasion of the rights of the inhabitants. But, in the case of the removal of the West Coast Japanese Americans, the Court refused to intervene.

On the authority of a presidential order allowing the commanding general on the Pacific coast to designate military areas from which any or all civilians could be excluded, General John L. DeWitt gave more than one hundred thousand Japanese Americans, two-thirds of whom were citizens of the United States, five days in which to leave their homes and be transferred to government relocation or detention centers. As a stanch advocate of evacuation, General DeWitt played the key role in the affair, but his decision enjoyed the approval of both President Roosevelt and Secretary of War Stimson. In the post-Pearl Harbor mood of anti-Japanese feeling, no attempt was made to distinguish between citizen and alien or between the loyal and disloyal. The protests emanating from such organizations as the Fellowship of Reconciliation and the American Civil Liberties Union were ignored, and even the latter organization at first approved, or at least condoned, the evacuation.[31]

Gradually, however, liberals perceived the falsity of the blanket charges of disloyalty directed against the Japanese Americans, and the harsh injustice of depriving them of their homes, property, and means of future livelihood. In 1943 the Supreme Court, although refusing to rule against the army decision, nevertheless expressed its grave suspicion of the necessity of the evacuation. And after the war the Court decided that the evacuees must be permitted to return to their Pacific coast homes. Still another judicial criticism of the army's procedure was handed down by the Circuit Court of Appeals in 1949. Affirming the restoration of citizenship to those Japanese Americans who had renounced it during their incarceration in the wartime relocation centers, Judge William Dunham wrote a decision which the *New York Times* described as "a blistering denunciation of Lieut. Gen. John L. DeWitt." The judge likened the relocation centers to German concentration camps and denounced the general's doctrine of enemy racism as similar to the Nazi philosophy.[32]

Except for the glaring instance of the treatment of the West Coast Japanese Americans, there was no concerted official violation of the civil liberties of the citizen in World War II. Though the Roosevelt administration and Attorney General Francis Biddle deserved much credit for this record, the improvement could also be explained, at least in part, by the lack of any real opposition to the war. This almost universal acquiescence helped to account for the improved record of the government in the matter of civil liberties as compared with World War I. Assured of general support, the Roosevelt administration could afford to be tolerant of its few academic and intellectual critics. The sensational raids and vindictive prosecutions of World War I were, on the whole, avoided, and the attempt to prosecute a group of American pro-nazi sympathizers resulted in a mistrial. Aside from a few disloyal individuals, the alien population of the United States proved no great problem, and only a few hundred were interned besides the Japanese Americans.[33]

Whatever the reason, liberals could hardly complain over the comparative absence of serious infringements upon civil

liberties. Of more immediate concern to many liberals therefore were some of the trends in the United States which,
however normal and expected in wartime, gave indications
that they would continue far beyond the period of actual
hostilities. This was particularly true in the matter of the
increasing concentration and control of the economic life of
the nation by the joint forces of big business and big government. When the Temporary National Economic Committee, created back in 1938 to investigate just this problem,
submitted its final report in 1941, it was embarrassed to find
on every side fresh evidence of the concentration of economic power. Later, in the midst of the war, a special committee appointed by the Senate to study the status of the
smaller business and industrial plants, reported an alarming
rate of wartime casualties so that there were one-half million
fewer enterprises in 1943 than in 1941. Other figures showed
that a high proportion of government contracts were being
awarded to the largest corporations, which naturally were
thereby placed in a close relationship with the army and
navy. Even allowing for the considerable amount of subsequent subcontracting to smaller firms, an important feature of the war economy seemed to be a strengthening of big
business.[34]

During the war the military did its best to direct the allocation of all industrial output, engaging in a long struggle
over this issue with the civilian War Production Board
headed by Donald Nelson. One of the important matters in
dispute, and a vital factor in the early resumption of a normal peacetime economy, was setting a date for the relaxation
of government controls so that civilian production could be
resumed. In general, this was a problem of greater concern
to smaller businesses without sizable government orders. In
any case, by 1944 Nelson believed that the state of war production was sufficiently healthy to make possible the gradual

reconversion of American industry to postwar peacetime needs. This change-over the army, however, was able to block, thus maintaining for a longer period Federal authority over prices, production, and raw materials.[35]

By the middle of the war the army, in conjunction with those business leaders who favored closer ties between industry and the armed forces, also attempted to secure full control over the nation's manpower through a labor draft. Liberal and labor sentiment, however, regarded such a war service bill as equivalent to slavery. They rejected the time-worn contention that conscription for the army justified a labor draft in industry — an argument that overlooked the fact that the worker in private industry was also making possible profits for his employer. As William Green, president of the American Federation of Labor, was quick to point out, there could be no fair draft of labor without a correspondingly drastic levy on capital.[36] This overambitious effort to regiment all American manpower occasioned much bitterness and resulted further in widespread charges of totalitarianism. In the ensuing reaction against the whole scheme of a labor draft, strong public sentiment also developed against proposals to turn the wartime system of selective service into a permanent peacetime plan for compulsory military training. This question was accordingly postponed until after the war.

Although Congress refused to sanction either peacetime conscription or a labor draft, in almost all other respects the war period was one of tremendous expansion in the powers of government over the individual. Allocation of raw materials and industrial capacity was carried down to the average citizen through a system of rationing and price control of consumers' goods. The long-time trend toward greater concentration and centralization of the political and economic life of the nation had never before been so explicitly institutionalized and brought home to each and every person. Imitative of big business was now big government, full of grave problems and implications for the future of liberalism and democracy.

In the midst of wartime regimentation of the national economy, the argument that centralized economic planning would result in some sort of permanent, totalitarian, collectivist order increased in intensity. This thesis attracted the attention of a wide variety of economists, publicists, and scholars, who depicted the United States as marching toward fascism or returning to serfdom. Of all this wartime literature, the book that had the greatest impact was probably Friedrich Hayek's *The Road to Serfdom,* published in 1944. The work of an Austrian economist teaching in England, Hayek's volume was a far more sensitive and modest book than either its disciples or critics made out. In essence it advanced the contention that the United States and England, though not resembling the Germany of Hitler and World War II, did bear a close analogy to the Germany of World War I and after. The progressive abandonment of freedom in economic affairs, Hayek feared, was leading to a similar destruction of political and personal freedom. Political democracy in itself was no guarantee against arbitrary power, and in the advance of economic collectivism under centralized state planning Hayek saw a new despotism and reversion to a feudal type of social order.[37]

In angry rejoinder to Hayek's book, Herman Finer, one of his former English colleagues who was teaching at Harvard University, hastily published *Road to Reaction,* pointing out some inconsistencies and confusion of purpose in Hayek's writing, but in no sense refuting his major thesis. Instead, Finer resorted to personal invective, berating Hayek as one of the company of men who failed to distinguish between the Fascists and Nazis, and "the pro-popular impulse of the Soviet system." According to Finer, Hayek was also one of a small group of liberals, some of whom had "decided against America's entry into World War II before Pearl Harbor." [38] Undoubtedly, Hayek's book was used by certain reactionary groups to serve a dubious ulterior purpose, out of keeping with the author's own reasonable point of view, but this did not contradict the essentials of his argument that the United States was witnessing a decline of economic freedom that would affect all liberty. Especially interesting, in the light of his own vast influence on New Deal economic thought, was the judgment of John Maynard Keynes, who, without disavowing planning, nevertheless wrote to Hayek that he agreed morally and philosophically with his controversial book.[39]

The Road to Serfdom, published in the middle of World War II, marked a critical break between two eras of national planning. It also illustrated the confusion of individualist liberals caught between the waning New Deal and the waxing war economy of the 1940's. These liberals could not help but feel a growing concern lest modern government degenerate into a species of arbitrary and tyrannical rule administered by a swollen bureaucracy. The emergency powers granted to the New Deal in the crisis of the depression were constantly being expanded in the course of the war. As President Roosevelt told Congress after Pearl Harbor, in announcing his intention to arrogate authority regarding price controls if desired legislation was not passed, "I cannot tell what powers may have to be exercised in order to win this war." [40]

Despite the many precedents for the wartime assumption of authority by the President of the United States, there was the ever-present danger that Congress, as Senator Taft put it, in reply to the President, would be reduced to "a mere shell of a legislative body." Doctrines of presidential power and responsibility, illustrated by Roosevelt's disregard of the third-term tradition in 1940, and again in 1944, and the whole theory of military necessity, as argued in the case of the Japanese Americans, raised the question of whether the government was outrunning both constitutional law and American traditions. The peril was not that of an explicit fascism or a demagoguery of the old Huey Long type but rather, as one writer expressed it, "Our danger is that we are drifting away from the secure anchorage of constitutional government, with little thought as to where the winds of expediency will carry us." Hopeful that trends toward collectivism might be absorbed in the democratic system, various reformers suggested plans for the modernization and reorganization of the Federal government, especially in the field of legislative-executive relationships. At the same time, fearful of the wartime shift of power to the President and the executive bureaucracy, liberals began to take a new interest in preserving the legislative branch of the government as a bulwark of democracy. "The difference between an authoritarian and a democratic state centers on the position of the representative body. If the Legislature is free and strong, authoritarian rule cannot exist." [41]

Liberals' growing concern and criticism, however unwelcome in the midst of a wartime emphasis on undivided national loyalty and unity, nevertheless served the useful and important function of calling attention to problems and trends that transcended even the impact of the war. Looking ahead to the postwar world, American liberals had little basis for an optimistic confidence. A period of total war, characterized by indiscriminate bombing of civilian populations and flagrant violation of neutral rights, was not likely to be the prelude to a coming era of peace and international understanding. Nor was it easy to see how, after a period of severe war destruction and state control of economic life, there could be any quick return to a free economy on either a national or an international scale. Instead, as in the era of World War I, there was every indication that wartime methods and patterns of thinking would continue to hold their own in the years immediately ahead.

17

National Security and the
Garrison State

ON AUGUST 6, 1945, an American plane dropped an atomic
bomb on Hiroshima. Nine days later the Japanese government surrendered. Although the peace settlement with both
Germany and Japan was still to be determined, World War
II had ended. This sudden close, under such fateful circumstances, of the greatest war in modern history gave to the
world a new legacy of mixed hopes and fears, which the
postwar generation seemed unable to resolve or even understand. Only the future could determine whether the scientists, in discovering and applying the principle of atomic
energy, had fashioned "man's masterpiece or his master." [1]

In the United States, which had played a pivotal role in
the war, the return to peace brought no marked change in
the fortunes of a declining liberalism. If every war, as has
often been pointed out, is waged at the cost of a few more
liberties, this was even more true of the periods following
each major war. Americans had only to reread the story of
Civil War and Reconstruction days, and to recall the reaction that swept the country after World War I, to realize the
probable portent of the years ahead. Faced with the prospect
of a renewed challenge to liberal beliefs and values, the liberals themselves entered the postwar period in a state of

extreme confusion. "The lost liberals. Can they find a road map?" was the way one writer expressed it.[2]

Although in the past liberalism had often been endangered by attacks from both the right and the left, it had managed to keep alive a hard core of traditional beliefs and values. Avoiding extremes, liberals, however much they differed on certain matters of politics and economics, had been able to agree on a decent respect for individual integrity and preservation of the rights of minorities and of freedom of opinion. In times of profound historical crisis it was true that liberal tenets were not easily maintained, but until World War I such periods had come at sufficiently long intervals to provide at least a measure of intervening liberal recovery. After 1914, though, the swift succession of two world wars, interspaced with the depression of the thirties, put a strain on liberalism that the new crises of cold war and Korean struggle did nothing to alleviate.

Despite this disheartening background, the postwar collapse of liberalism came as a shock to those who had confused appearance and reality. During the early days of the New Deal, and again in the midst of World War II, too many liberals had allowed themselves to be seduced by the illusion of power. Accepting the necessity of planning at home and war abroad, many lost all sense of proportion. They forgot that crusades are seldom liberal. And at the same time the much-diminished American suspicion of a powerful centralized government all but vanished in response to repeated demands that liberals be practical men of action. Denying most vigorously that they had betrayed classical and traditional liberal values, the new totalitarian liberals argued that such liberalism had become outmoded. "The base we want to build our liberalism on is a democratic collectivism," wrote Max Lerner. More honest than most of his contemporaries, Lerner hastened to add: "It will become apparent to the reader before he has read many pages that I am far more a democrat than I am a liberal." [3] The clash between Lerner's views and those of older schools of thought was illustrated in the comment of an historian of Jefferson's liberalism, who pointed out that "A liberal is a catholic-minded democrat, who often opposed a realistic democracy that would ignore minority rights." [4]

In the stress of the war, a number of those who considered themselves liberals had preached a philosophy of vengeance and hate. The Morgenthau Plan to reduce Germany to a pastoral state, the demand for unconditional surrender, and the war crimes trials at Nuremberg and Tokyo were fruits of this policy which later were to prove embarrassing to the United States. This was especially the case when in the postwar era erstwhile disarmed enemies were suddenly desired as newly rearmed allies. At home the doctrine of guilt by association had been invoked by the administration in a mass sedition trial of Americans who had sympathized with the Nazis or who had been members of German-front organizations. In the instance of the two largest wartime minority groups, the Japanese Americans and the conscientious objectors, self-styled liberals in official position had made little protest over unfair or discriminatory treatment. Silent as long as the ugly type of World War I incident was avoided, the war liberals, as Norman Thomas later noted, had been content to let a conservative like Senator Robert Taft assume the onerous task of speaking out most openly in regard to certain aspects of conscription or of the forced evacuation of Americans of Japanese descent.[5]

Thus the thirties and early forties, when liberals under Franklin Roosevelt seemed most strongly entrenched, was actually a period of grave potential peril for traditional liberal values. This, however, was only fully realized after the close of the war, when the liberal retreat was beginning to turn into a rout. Preoccupied by the struggle to gain first economic and then military security, American liberals set the pattern in the 1930's and 1940's for the sacrifice of the very individual freedoms on which all personal, and ultimately national, security is necessarily based. In one of his early messages to Congress before the war, President Roosevelt had indicated the liberals' possible future dilemma in regard to the new instruments of public power that he was helping to fashion. "In the hands of a people's Government," he asserted, "this power is wholesome and proper. But in the hands of political puppets of an economic autocracy such power would provide shackles for the liberties of the people." [6]

As New Deal regulatory powers fell more and more into antiliberal hands, postwar liberals of various shades of opinion were placed on the defensive. Although they could not afford to ignore the popular and official shibboleth of security, it seemed clear that in their concentration on so-called realistic political and economic ends liberals had yielded the less tangible but more important values associated with individual freedom and dissent. The preservation of the Federal bureaucracy had become an end in itself. Accustomed to power and office, New Deal liberals had lost the capacity of self-criticism and vigorous opposition, qualities that might have served them in good stead in the postwar years of hysteria and reaction. [7]

In spite of the undoubted pressures upon American liberals during World War II, it soon became evident that the hardships of the postwar period would prove infinitely more trying. Before the American people could translate the joy of victory into the hope of an enduring peace they were faced with a rapid deterioration in relations between Russia and the West and with the sordid realities of the cold war. Overshadowing the concept of the United Nations and the ideals of the Atlantic Charter was the specter of a third world war and the new means of destruction indicated by the atomic and hydrogen bombs. Meanwhile, permanent world peace, even if remote, seemed all the more necessary as a matter of sheer biological survival. Yet, despite the popular wartime slogan of "One World" and the ready assumption that internationalism had replaced isolationism, it was apparent that the postwar world would still be dominated by considerations of military power, and by a narrow nationalism.

During the war Carl Becker, a respected historian, had asked the question "How new will the better world be?" And he went on to show that the postwar world would continue to be an evolution based on the historical past, and not nearly so new as customarily imagined. For example, war and unemployment, which he saw as the two chief faults of modern civilization, were not likely to be eliminated by World War II. And the world would also find it difficult to lessen nationalism, imperialism, and power politics. Becker, a close student of the eighteenth century, pointed out in his essay that many of the modern goals of internationalism and cosmopolitanism, highly prized in liberal circles, had actually been better realized in the Age of the Enlightenment. But just as the French Revolution and ensuing general European war had turned peoples from internationalism to nationalism, so in recent times the Russian Revolution and two world wars were having the same effect.[8]

However one looked at the postwar picture, filled with new and frightening uncertainties, there was ample basis for a reappraisal of American policies in connection with the late war. This seemed especially true if one accepted in any way the verdict of a prominent American wartime diplomat that "A government's foreign policy must be judged far more by its results than by its intentions." [9] Unfortunately, much of the revisionist treatment of American foreign policy was as biased as the policies it criticized. While revisionist historians spent considerable time exploring the alleged ulterior motives and conspiratorial character of President Roosevelt's diplomacy, their more orthodox colleagues contented themselves with defending the President's ends, if not always his means. Meanwhile, the real issues received little attention. For example, less important than whether Hitler intended to attack the United States was the question of whether he could have done so successfully. Even more fundamental was the challenge in the revisionists' argument that World War II did not serve American interests but paved the way for Russian dominance in Europe and Asia. With Germany's attack on Russia, and Britain not invaded, would the war have ended, as some asserted, in a stalemate? Should the United States therefore have tried harder to stay out of the struggle, making the necessary concessions to Japan in China and the Pacific? [10]

Such problems unfortunately were obscured in the war and postwar emphasis on a bipartisan foreign policy. Revisionists were all too easily dismissed as neo-isolationists or doctrinaire pacifists, while their writings were bypassed in favor of the stream of official and quasi-official accounts prepared by those with ready access to confidential government records.[11]

One of the ironies of the postwar period was that anti-revisionist liberals, in their anxiety lest the United States return to a post-World War I intellectual pattern of isolationist pacifism, came to condone and even to abet a resort to the opposite extreme of a militant, interventionist nationalism, masquerading as idealistic internationalism. At the same time, talk of bipartisanship often concealed the essentially conservative nature of American postwar foreign policy. In what was really a turn to the right in American diplomacy, war liberals, who had formerly shared in many a leftist cause or program, now vied with conservatives for leadership in the crusade against communism. Although most liberals, unlike most conservatives, were anxious to keep the fight against communism from spreading to a campaign against the noncommunist left, they were slow to recognize that any crusade, foreign or domestic, was susceptible of strongly illiberal influences.

It was not the least of the ironies of these years therefore that, in the struggle against communism and Russian expansion, the noncommunist forces were often reduced to copying illiberal Soviet methods. Liberals or progressives, committed to a philosophy of a democratic collectivism, were reluctant to see in their program any similarities to the collectivism of fascism or communism. Yet, in attacking the Soviets, as E. H. Carr pointed out, the Western world was often denouncing what already, in an advanced stage, existed in their own countries.[12] Others noted the paradox of Soviet communism, with its ostensible commitment to materialism, generating a body of ideas with a terrifying power to spread, while the United States, with its heritage of values and ideals, tried to throw up against it a barricade of money.[13]

Although much of Russian foreign policy could be explained in terms of a traditional expansionism that went back to the days of the early czarist rulers, it was more popular to stress the new danger of Soviet communism, rather than historic Russian nationalism or imperialism. "Conservative passions in the United States are aroused," as Archibald MacLeish remarked, "not by Russia as a nation but by Russia as the Communist party. Communism is not feared because it serves the purposes of Russian aggression; Russian aggression is feared because it serves to spread Communism. To strike at Communism directly, therefore, was to establish a policy which, it was hoped, would be effective abroad and popular at home." In their fear of Russian communism, Americans were even ready to accept the Marxist notion of an inevitable war between capitalism and communism. "We hate war and we desire peace but we no longer assume that the choice of war or peace is ours." [14]

Thus in the development of an American policy seeking to contain Russian expansion and the communist threat, there was the danger that the United States would succumb to a purely negative diplomacy. By assuming an automatic anti-Soviet position, the United States could fall prey to the very Russian ideological conquest that American diplomacy sought to avoid. "Stalin has really conquered the United States," Oswald Garrison Villard noted, "in that he has completed its militarization and has frightened it to death." [15] Moreover, it seemed likely that a war with Russia, coming on top of two world wars, would only sacrifice the rest of the personal freedom and capitalism that the United States wanted to protect, which had also been the basis of traditional American liberalism and democracy. Seeing the danger therefore in an American policy that attempted to explain every decision on the basis of strategical calculations about a possible war with Russia, Walter Lippmann concluded: "This damnable obsession has gotten to the point where we can hardly send milk to babies abroad without explaining that this is an important action in our cold war with Russian communism." [16] The results of such a policy could be seen in the evolution of the foreign aid program from one of relief and rehabilitation to full-scale military assistance.

The Soviet impact, in which the United States sought to mirror in reverse the policies of the Kremlin, even to the point of discussing a possible preventive war, had as one of its important results an unprecedented peacetime militarization of the American government and economy. As a part of the struggle against communism, the American people were won over to the necessity of military preparedness on a virtual wartime basis. In America as well as in Europe, the individual citizen accordingly continued to live in a near-war atmosphere, in which his own aspirations were subordinated to the demands of the state. Tremendous expenditures, largely for military needs, mounting national debts, military conscription, a vast bureaucracy of civil servants, and the growing official nature of thought and culture were some of the evidences of the growth of statism and the decline of individualism. For most of the world the cold war meant the indefinite postponement of a return to normal standards of living. Much heard was the cynical comment that war had become the norm and peace the exception in modern civilization.

For the first time in its peacetime history the United States took on many of the features of what Harold Lasswell has called "the garrison state." [17] Never before had wartime militarism been carried over with so little change into the postwar period. The world's failure to achieve a real peace and demobilization intensified the postwar threat to all liberal ideas and values. The United States, it was true, disbanded most of its mass army, but in all other respects demobilization was so curtailed that the war and postwar periods, in terms of military policy and practice, became practically indistinguishable. The growing importance of the military, unprecedented in peacetime, was evidence of a new and dangerous national psychology. According to Hanson Baldwin, military analyst for the *New York Times* and author of "The Military Move In":

There is no doubt that since the war the military influence in American government has been increasing, no doubt but that the trend toward greater centralization of federal power has been increasing, no doubt but that our nationalism is, if not rampant, at least feverish. Our unilateral Pacific-islands policy, the lone-hand MacArthur administration in Japan, our occasional by-passing of the United Nations, the increasing "crisis psychology" of the nation and the prevalence of war talk — above all, the growing American tendency to find solutions for complex problems in physical strength or military force — are perhaps natural consequences of our psychological attitudes.[18]

Even before relations with Russia descended to the point of an avowed cold war, the armed forces began to exert their influence upon American foreign policy. Somewhat paradoxically, this influence became greater in peace than it had been in war, when President Roosevelt and his civilian advisers had exercised a large measure of control over military strategy as well as over general foreign and domestic policy. In contrast to his predecessor, President Truman seemed peculiarly susceptible to military influence and advice. "No President since Grant," as Sumner Welles later wrote with some malice, "has had such childlike faith in the omniscience of the high brass as the present occupant of the White House." [19] "The truth is," Oswald Garrison Villard wrote to Charles Beard, "we have a highly militaristic, lower middle class, back-slapping American legionnaire in the White House who has given free rein to the militarists, and we are being made over under our own eyes into a tremendous military imperialistic Power — exactly what we went to war with Germany to prevent their becoming!" [20]

The establishment of the National Security Council, which President Truman recommended to Congress in June 1946 as part of a measure for unification of the army and navy, gave to the Secretary of Defense not only vast military powers but also virtual coordinate authority with the President and the Secretary of State in the formulation of foreign policy. Moreover, the whole theory of containment and of peace through force naturally strengthened the voice of the military in American postwar diplomacy. This trend was made explicit in 1947 with the unprecedented appointment of a professional soldier, General George C. Marshall, as secretary of state. Even when the top authority remained in the hands of a civilian, the experts who determined policy and procedure were likely to be military men. Although they were often thrust unwillingly into jobs for which civilians were not available, there was nevertheless the grave danger that military men, by reason of their training and background, would tend to regard every problem within the framework of war and every individual as subject to the regimentation of military discipline.

A basic factor helping to enhance military influence was the sheer size of the armed forces, paralleling an ever-expanding civilian bureaucracy. The large postwar military establishment, never under a million men, and by the 1950's at three times that number, with half as many civilian employees, naturally kept in positions of authority a large number of high-ranking officers. At the same time the presence of United States occupation forces in Germany and Japan gave the army important political and economic, as well as diplomatic, duties. In all branches of the government, an increasing range of civilian jobs were taken over by military personnel. Despite a traditional dislike of the military as an institution, Americans showed singularly little fear of entrusting important positions, including even the presidency, to high-ranking officers. Generals Marshall, MacArthur, and Eisenhower were all talked of as possible nominees for the nation's highest office. Other ranking military men became top executives in corporations having important defense contracts. And after the Korean War, Congress passed a special law to permit General Marshall to become secretary of defense, making an exception to the rule that a civilian secretary should be over the armed services.

Much of the military's influence, of course, went beyond that of personnel and was a product of the large proportion of the Federal budget that was devoted to preparedness. The argument of political scientists that a society may be judged by an analysis of the proportion of expenditures that are devoted to peace or war left little room for liberal optimism. Throughout the postwar years, the direct sums appropriated for the armed services were never less than one-third the entire Federal budget. If the agencies related to the military, such as the Atomic Energy Commission, the Veterans Administration, and the Foreign Aid Program, were included, the amount of the budget embracing noncivilian expenditures approached two-thirds of the entire total. And if interest on the war debt was added, practically the entire Federal budget could be said to relate directly to wars, past, present, or future. Although these proportions did not vary greatly, the outbreak of the Korean War drastically increased all Federal expenditures and heightened the military's influence over the national economy.

Protest against the increasing postwar militarization of American life, though it was widely attacked as without precedent and as a threat to freedom, was blunted by the menacing international situation. It was not difficult for Congress and the country, faced with the cold war and then the struggle in Korea, to be convinced that the high level of military spending must be kept up. Also, few Americans probably realized the extent to which military influence and control had penetrated what would normally have been regarded as exclusively civilian responsibilities and institutions. Underlying the specific instances of the extension of military power into civilian fields, and an even greater threat to civil supremacy, was the growing ability of the military to influence both public and Congressional opinion. Flourishing in the atmosphere of perpetual crises and war hysteria pervading Washington, the military expert with his argument of military necessity usually took first rank at Congressional hearings. Utilizing their new-found prestige, the armed services also conducted effective lobbying campaigns and spent large sums on public relations.[21]

Much of the military's propaganda had as its object the enactment of some system for the compulsory peacetime training of all American youths. Such a measure, whether in the form of military training or of a universal service law, was calculated to give the army virtual control of American manpower. President Truman, an enthusiastic advocate of conscription, cooperated with the drive for a permanent law by appointing in December 1946 a Presidential Advisory Commission on Universal Training. Sometimes mistakenly considered by the public as an impartial scientific committee to study the merits of UMT, the Commission was rather a body whose members were already wholly convinced of the desirability of such training. In his informal introductory remarks to the newly formed Commission, President Truman stressed the importance of UMT as a disciplinary and educational measure, valuable for instilling a spirit of patriotism in American youth. "I don't like to think of it as a universal military training program," the President declared. "I want it to be a universal training program." [22]

In broadening the scope of the training to include non-military as well as military service, the President argued that in modern total war security no longer depended solely on the armed forces. But the idea of universal service to the state, which the President urged his Advisory Commission to recommend, was also a totalitarian concept that had been much used by fascist and communist regimes. The Advisory Commission in its report denied this charge of totalitarianism and contended that universal training was no more un-American, militaristic, or compulsory than public education. But the Commission's emphasis upon the responsibility of the individual to the state, though fully in accord with European practice, represented a relatively new idea in the United States. It reflected a philosophy, popular even in some liberal circles, which had come to regard any service, so long as it was to the state, as a democratic privilege. "Greater self-love has no government than this," commented a young war veteran in his bitter article "Conscription ad Infinitum." Whatever the mutual obligations of the citizen and his government, the American liberal tradition had always been one in which the state was considered the servant and not the master of the people. This tradition was contradicted, however, by the report of the Presidential Advisory Commission on Universal Training.[23]

A prominent feature of the militarization of the United States, paralleling the growth of the garrison state, was the rise of what has been termed a permanent war economy. In the half-peace that characterized the cold war, the American economic system was neither the welfare state, as envisaged by New Dealers, nor the free enterprise system, espoused in theory at least by big business. Although all predictions in regard to the probable nature of the American postwar economy appeared to have gone astray when an expected and much-feared depression failed to materialize, the elaborate schemes of public works designed to alleviate such a catastrophe found a ready substitute in the rearmament program. Military expenditures became the answer to economists who had so widely predicted a postwar depression. Businessmen, though they decried "creeping socialism," nevertheless welcomed defense contracts. And to all the important economic interest groups in the country, a paternalistic preparedness economy seemed preferable to the uncertainties of an exclu-

sively civilian peacetime market. Charges that the preparedness program unduly favored big business were shrugged off
in the midst of the prosperity generated by government
spending. Thus there was little diminution of the wartime
tempo of concentration in American industry, with its attendant decline of small business.[24]

According to a summary report of the Federal Trade
Commission, it required no great imagination to foresee the
possibility of giant corporations taking over the economy of
the country or of their being subjected to direct government
regulation to avert such an outcome. "In either event," it
concluded, "collectivism will have triumphed over free enterprise, and the theory of competition will have been relegated to the limbo of well-intentioned but ineffective
ideals." [25] Meanwhile, some government agencies, created
originally to preserve competition, actually encouraged
monopolies by the protection that they extended to established business and property interests. In all the postwar
emphasis on security and bigness, in an economic as well as
in a military sense, there was little enthusiasm for the
tougher philosophy of the antitrust laws, which, as Thurman Arnold pointed out, were "designed to give security to
nobody. They recognize that competition means someone
may go bankrupt. They do not contemplate the game in
which everyone who plays can win." [26]

The significance, and also the confusion, attendant on the
marriage of big business and big government in a war economy was illustrated by the case of a large company which was
asked by the government to take over some of the details of
producing atomic bombs on an industrial basis at the same
time that it was being subjected to a Federal antitrust action.
As David Lilienthal observed in his book *Big Business,* the
very bigness that was to be prosecuted by the government

was desired by the government in connection with helping to turn out atomic bombs. Lilienthal, formerly chairman of TVA and later first head of the Atomic Energy Commission, was typical of the new liberals who had come to feel that bigness on the part of business, labor unions, and government was inevitable. Big business, he maintained, was responsible for many of the positive gains of American civilization and it was now more than ever necessary for national security.[27]

The most dramatic example of the subordination of traditional capitalistic free enterprise to the interests of the state, and at the same time an important illustration of the way in which science, technology, and industry were related to modern war, occurred in the field of atomic energy. In passing the legislation that established the Atomic Energy Commission, Congress provided for a complete government monopoly of nuclear power. Although tentative plans were made for eventual dissemination of the knowledge of atomic energy to other countries and to private users, present considerations of national security dictated that the military retain a large measure of control over all developments in the field of nuclear fission. Thus the Commission guarded carefully its work, and the only tangible result of the greatest discovery of modern science was the constant production of hitherto unimagined and almost inconceivable weapons of destruction. Commenting editorially on the Commission's twelfth annual report, the *Washington Post* observed:

All of this is doubtless necessary. Things being as they are, the AEC must spend its four billion dollars largely on weapons of destruction. And it must shroud all that it does in such secrecy as to make judgment of its wisdom and efficiency altogether impossible. But if it is necessary, it is also immensely dangerous to the maintenance of government by the consent of the governed. We shall do well to beware of this Leviathan.[28]

The whole idea of a permanent war economy, exemplified in the way in which atomic energy was being developed, had frightening implications for a liberal democratic society. As the government entered more and more into the realm of private business and industry, often with the enthusiastic encouragement of business interests themselves, it was involved also in practices incompatible with free and responsible self-government. Government became a partner and accomplice in some of the illegal, unethical, and monopolistic techniques of big business. Morality in American politics was subject to a new kind of institutionalized graft dependent on securing government contracts. Although individual standards of government employees were often high, the maze of government-business relations encouraged the rise of a new profession of high-powered lobbyists bent on securing a division of government spoils for their clients. Shutting the door on fraudulent dealing by Wall Street, the government opened the Treasury portals to another generation of financial buccaneers. In the words of Blair Bolles, the New Dealers' welfare state had become "the rich man's welfare state, aiding those who don't need help or don't deserve it — at public expense." A concept of government that had a measure of justification in the depression became less than liberal in a period of postwar inflationary prosperity. "The agencies created to end privilege have become bulwarks of privilege," Bolles concluded.[29]

Because so many individuals and practically all the major economic interest groups in the country were enjoying prosperity, criticism of the illiberal nature of the government's war economy could make little headway. In the United States, as production soared to new high levels, it became possible to have guns and butter — or at least oleomargarine — and the traditional liberal objection to war spending seemed to have less force. Nevertheless, according to some of the government's own economists, the average citizen's standard of living would have been improved with less government spending. Although the disparity in incomes between the higher and lower levels had undergone an amazing revolution since the early thirties, there was evidence that, despite the incidence of taxes, a new wealthy class and a corresponding disparity of income were developing again in the period of postwar inflation. Also in the world at large, though the effect of the international arms race was not as much as expected, the consumption of food according to United Nations figures had not yet climbed back to prewar levels.[30] President Truman, in his valedictory message to the nation, was inclined to credit the domestic policies of his administration for the remarkable postwar prosperity of the United States. "Realism would acknowledge, however," Marquis Childs pointed out, "that the present prosperity owes a great deal to war, the rehabilitation of war-stricken nations, and the spending of huge sums for defense since the end of World War II." [31]

However, even if a war economy could be maintained without serious impairment of the American standard of living, it created other problems of no less importance in a liberal democratic society. Likely to be a characteristic feature of the economics of war mobilization was a callous disregard of the individual and the consumer, except as their interests served those of the state. Thus, in pressing its preparedness program, the Truman administration fell into the inconsistency of urging discipline and savings upon the citizen, while at the same time the government's own spending policies encouraged the very inflation it was supposedly trying to avert. Moreover, the official disposition to denounce the enjoyment of material pleasures on the part of the people was evidence of a dangerous authoritarian tendency to assume that renunciation and self-sacrifice were somehow good in themselves. Such policies recalled the old fascist plea that constantly intoned the citizen's duty to the nation. Thus in the modern totalitarian state, anxious to secure soldiers, even an individual's health became a matter of public concern. "You owe it to the government to keep well, so that you can do your duty in the work army or in the armed forces," was the bitter comment of a believer in laissez faire.[32]

The decline of liberalism in the domestic economy, which was one result of the postwar preparedness program, was paralleled by similar developments in the field of international trade and commerce. As considerations of national security and military strength continued to dominate the thinking of the United States and the other major powers, international trade degenerated into a species of economic warfare between rival blocs of nations. State economic policies were governed by issues in the cold war between East and West, and there was little opportunity to return to even the limited degree of free international trade that had existed before the depression and World War II. State-controlled foreign trade accordingly became one of the important facts of the new economic nationalism under which the world was beating a steady retreat from liberalism to the mercantilist theories that had characterized Europe up until the end of the eighteenth century.[33]

In the United States, the Truman Doctrine and the Marshall Plan were promulgated as means of bolstering up the economies of the noncommunist nations, and so fortifying their powers of military resistance. In some of the less developed areas of the world, the United States also sought to counter the appeal of communism by offering American industrial products and techniques. Thus the foreign aid program of the United States, often mistakenly defended as an example of altruistic internationalism, was actually part of a new conception of national interest.

Nationalism in the guise of internationalism was most attractive to the postwar group of business, political, and military leaders whom C. Wright Mills dubbed "the sophisticated conservatives." These conservatives actually were neither conservative nor liberal in a traditional sense. On labor, for example, they departed from old-fashioned reactionary techniques in favor of a policy of political manipulation designed to secure labor's support in the crusade against Soviet communism. By interjecting the communist issue into labor controversies, labor could be forced to cooperate with the conservatives' views on foreign policy in order to prove its innocence of communist connections.

Meanwhile the foreign aid program, with its stimulus to American industry, became "the spinal nerve" of the sophisticated conservatives' postwar plans for the expansion of American export markets. In the words of *Fortune* magazine, "We are asking the U.S. businessman to think of Wendell Willkie's *One World* not in fancy geopolitical terms, but merely in market terms." Admirably suited to the conservatives' purposes were the solid ties forged among industry, armed forces, and State Department — ties that were constantly being strengthened under the duress of the cold war and the policy of a permanent war economy. Aided by the widespread propaganda in behalf of a bipartisan foreign policy, these new-type conservatives were able to assume a dominant position in both major political parties. "If the sophisticated conservatives have their way," Mills predicted in 1948, "the next New Deal will be a war economy rather than a welfare economy, although the conservative's liberal rhetoric might put the first in the guise of the second." [34]

The danger to the individual and the threat to liberalism in the postwar economy therefore came not so much from the growth of big government or big business as in the merging of the two under the concept of a permanent war econ-

omy or garrison state. The argument that there was a coun-
tervailing power between different types of big business, and
between big business and big labor or big government, was
plausible except when the interests of all such groups were
joined in the drive for military preparedness and national
security. As Senator Paul H. Douglas pointed out in a popular article on the causes and cure of big government, if it
were not for war the government colossus could be trimmed
to almost pygmy stature. "All in all, nearly nine-tenths of the
financial outlays of the government and six-sevenths of its
personnel are caused by the institution of war. It is, therefore, the warfare world and not the welfare state which is
primarily responsible for the growth of big government." [35]
It was also this problem that caused Senator Douglas's colleague, Robert A. Taft, to sound a warning that "we could
destroy our liberty by a military and foreign expenditure in
time of peace so great that a free economic system cannot
survive." Contending that the very liberty the United States
sought to protect might be lost by a philosophy of perpetual
war, he added that it could also be destroyed "by expenditures so great as to turn this country into a garrison state in
time of peace." [36]

Despite the apparent economic gains derived from the inflated prosperity of the cold war economy, the costs of rearmament and the growing militarization of life and thought
exacted a heavy tribute from the American people. "No nation is more force-minded today than our own," declared
Supreme Court Justice Robert H. Jackson in a public address in 1953. "The people are burdened and unhappy under
it, but they do not know how to withdraw because the stakes
seem so high that the dreadful game must be played on to
fortune or ruin." [37]

In the curious blend of welfare state and war economy,
following the close of World War II, liberals could see only a

further threat to traditional economic and human values, with the accompanying destruction of individual freedom. The continual identification of the purpose and program of governments with the possibility of war, and the knowledge that such a war would, in all likelihood, be fought with atomic weapons, plunging the world into still unplumbed depths of barbarism, naturally heightened public anxiety. The new sources of power inherent in the utilization of atomic energy, instead of freeing man from many of the limitations of his environment, had seemed only to make him more subject than ever to the laws of physics and the vagaries of politics. In the sense of enhancing individual freedom and encouraging a more liberal society, the possibilities of atomic energy remained unfulfilled. For the present, discoveries in nuclear physics continued to be most important as an adjunct of American military preparedness. Meanwhile, under the impact of the series of recurring crises that troubled the postwar years, there was the danger that people might become apathetic toward important and fundamental political questions. Thus the cold war effected its own disillusionment. Insistence on complete loyalty and conformity enhanced this disillusionment and added to the dismay of liberals as they contemplated the state of civil liberties and the prospects facing the free individual. To the danger of the garrison state there was added the new threat of a police state, with its grim portent for American liberalism.

18

National Loyalty and the Police State

THE UNCERTAIN future of liberalism in a world embracing many of the features of a garrison-police state was driven home to the American people by the new cult of national loyalty that came into prominence after World War II. On the eve of American entrance into that global conflict, a distinguished American liberal had sounded a warning that was even more apposite to the postwar years. "Let us not," he urged, "in our anxiety to protect ourselves from foreign tyrants imitate some of their worst acts, and sacrifice in the process of national defense the very liberties which we are defending." [1]

In the United States by mid-century, the tensions generated by the cold war and the accompanying militarization of the American economy were bringing a new series of attacks upon traditional civil liberties. With the outbreak of an actual shooting war against the Red armies in Korea, public hysteria in the United States over the danger of communism and the accompanying fear of disloyal or subversive activities reached a new high point. The American temper seemed dangerously close to the type of fanaticism from which totalitarian movements derived their chief strength. An official campaign of organized hatred toward an unpopular minority group could also be interpreted as a sign of loss of faith in American institutions. Meanwhile, on all sides there was evidence, as Supreme Court Justice Robert H. Jackson pointed out, that "Of late years the Government is using its power as never before to pry into . . . lives and thoughts upon the slightest suspicion of less than complete trustworthiness. It demands not only probity, but unquestioning ideological loyalty." [2]

Underlying the whole structure of postwar American concern with security and loyalty was the fact of atomic energy. After the explosion of the first atomic bombs over Japan, the awestruck popular expectation of a new world era gave way to widespread horror over the destructive nature of the new weapon, and an even more pressing fear lest an atomic war be unleashed against mankind. In the rapid deterioration of the wartime spirit of Interallied cooperation, this latter concern was directed mainly against the possibility of war between Russia and the United States. For its part Russia feared further American use of the bomb, while the United States sought to keep Russia from gaining an understanding of the technique of its production.

The decision of the Truman administration to keep atomic energy as a "sacred trust" had fateful international and domestic implications. Signifying distrust of Russia, it also quite naturally intensified Soviet fears of American power. The decision likewise largely ignored the counter-recommendation of Secretary of War Stimson, that the United States enter at once into direct negotiation with Russia for the purpose of working out some method for the international control of atomic energy. Stimson, who had played an important role in encouraging the research that had led to the bomb and who had also advocated its use against Japan, was, without regretting those decisions, nevertheless most anxious that the United States try every possible means to reach an agreement with Russia in the whole area of nuclear energy.[3] Stimson knew that reputable scientists discounted the possibility that America's exclusive knowledge of the bomb could long be kept secret. However, even temporary sole possession of the bomb greatly increased American fears of espionage. The exposure of a Russian spy ring operating in Canada, followed by revelations of similar espionage activity in the United States, naturally reinforced the public's anxiety.

While spying, or intelligence and counterintelligence work, was an obvious corollary of the pursuit of power politics, American concern over atomic secrets plus the presence of an active communist group in the United States intensified the problem. Not all American Communists were potential espionage agents of the Soviet, but their essential loyalty to the United States was certainly open to question, and it was in no sense desirable that they should work in sensitive or important positions in the government. The dilemma facing the American people, and a matter of vital concern to liberals, was how to handle the communist problem without destroying fundamental American liberties. The general solution that was worked out — involving the Federal loyalty program, the prosecution of Communist party leaders, and the McCarran Internal Security Act virtually outlawing the party — was, however, neither liberal nor legally defensible from the standpoint of traditional American values and constitutional law.

The actual number of Communists in the United States after World War II was small. According to testimony offered in 1950 by J. Edgar Hoover, director of the Federal Bureau of Investigation, the numerical strength of the party was somewhat over fifty thousand persons, while the circulation of the *Daily Worker* was only half this figure. Although Hoover contended that "for every party member there are ten others . . . ready, willing, and able to do the party's work," thus making up "a potential fifth column of 540,000 people," this seemed an exaggeration. Hoover evidently accepted as doing the party's work anyone whose interest may have happened to coincide with some cause also advocated by the Communists, such as the abolition of the poll tax in the South, for example. Also, he confused ex-Communists and Communists at a time when the party was suffering heavy losses in membership and influence. Moreover, the possibility that the communist movement could attract any number of Americans to its ranks through the mere advocacy of its doctrines was practically nonexistent. Radical doctrines had never been successful in winning converts in the United States, and it seemed apparent that communism represented no threat to the American way of life that could not be met in the free market place of ideas. Thus in appraising the real strength of the Communist party and its fellow travelers or hidden supporters it was essential, as Alan Barth has pointed out, "to distinguish between their aims and potentialities. Their capacity for evil is not necessarily commensurate with their evil design. It is a fundamental misapprehension to suppose that they are powerful simply because they are abhorrent." [4]

In contrast to their lack of importance on the basis of numbers or influence, there were undoubtedly among American Communists some who stood ready to work in conjunction with Soviet agents to do damage to the United States. But this damage would be of a criminal sort that could be detected by the American police and intelligence systems and prosecuted under the laws forbidding such conduct. In any case, it could hardly be seriously maintained that communist activities were a revolutionary threat to American institutions and government. The evident American intention to go beyond a rational approach to the communist problem indicated a desire not only to punish crimi-

nal and seditious acts on the part of Communists but also
to suppress all communist or radical speech and thought.
This determination, shared even by some liberals, rested
on the assumption that communism was a conspiracy and
an ideological threat that could not be governed by traditional American conceptions of due process and clear and
present danger. Militant liberals of the New Deal and
World War II period, who had revised these historic concepts and had also added the doctrine of guilt by association
as a means of combating American Nazis and of finding some
advance point for security, now saw the same technique invoked against left-wing and communist elements. Underlin-
ing this dramatic shift, Arthur M. Schlesinger, Jr., concluded:

> The immediate result, of course, has been to transfer attention
> from *acts* to *thoughts*. Unpopular ideas and organizations become
> the quarry. People who hounded the intellectual fellow trav-
> ellers of fascism must not be surprised to find other people in-
> voking the same principles in order to hound the intellectual
> fellow travellers of Communism.[5]

The question of communism as a conspiracy came before
the Federal court in New York in 1949 in the trial of eleven
leading American Communists on charges of violating the
Smith Act by organizing to teach or advocate the overthrow
of the government of the United States by force and violence. Their conviction on grounds of what might be called
intellectual conspiracy, without any overt revolutionary act
on their part, seemed to many American liberals to reverse
the standard for free speech offered by Justice Holmes after
World War I — "whether the words used are used in such
circumstances and are of such a nature as to create a clear
and present danger that they will bring about the substan-
tive evils that Congress has a right to prevent." [6] Although

the Supreme Court in 1951 upheld the Communists' conviction, Justices Black and Douglas in their dissenting opinions reaffirmed Holmes's argument for free speech and denied that there was any evidence of the defendants' urging
a specific overt act of terror or violence. Uneasy over a
conviction that hinted at thought control, some liberals
also pointed to the additional practical difficulty that now
the Communists would be driven underground and would
thus be less subject to either prosecution or persuasion. On
the other hand, many liberals accepted the contention that
communism was a conspiracy of such magnitude that, even
without overt action on its part, it represented the clear and
present danger referred to by Justice Holmes.[7]

The definition of sedition in terms of a person's words
instead of his deeds still did not go far enough to satisfy
those who demanded complete national unity and unswerving loyalty, in thought as well as in speech and action, on
the part of all Americans. This illiberal pressure for one
hundred per cent conformity gained extraordinary success
in the postwar era through the use of what has been called
"the simple stratagem of charging a man with disloyalty,
instead of with treason or espionage or sabotage." This
device evaded all the constitutional safeguards and requirements surrounding a charge of treason and confronted an
individual with accusations often difficult to disprove if
only because of their vague and secret nature.[8]

Since it was not easy to read a man's mind or to probe
the depths of his innermost thoughts, the enforcement of so
unprecise a value as loyalty came to depend largely on the
use of the doctrine of guilt or innocence by association. The
organizations a man belonged to, his friends, what he read,
or how he spent his leisure time, all became indices of his
loyalty or disloyalty. For this there was, of course, a certain
logic that was at once both primitive and highly sophisti-

cated. Obviously almost everyone was likely to draw con-
clusions about people on the basis of their associations; and
relevant associations, not torn from their proper context,
had always been a stock in trade of historical writing and
criticism. The danger was not in drawing inferences from
associations — an often necessary feature of exercising judgment and making decisions — but it was rather the growing
practice of determining guilt by association that was out of
harmony with the American tradition that crime must be
personal and proved before an individual stand condemned.
In the forthright opinion of Henry Steele Commager, which
admirably stated a liberal position, the doctrine of guilt by
association was unsound in logic and law, impractical and
unhistorical, and wrong morally. The whole concept, Commager asserted, rested on "what may be called the rotten
apple theory of society — the theory that one wicked man
corrupts all virtuous men, and that one mistaken idea sub-
verts all sound ideas. . . . Why," he asked, "is there no
doctrine of innocence by association? Why is it that our
present-day witch-hunters pay this frightened tribute to the
power of communism, that they think its doctrines irresist-
ible?" [9]

With Congress and the country apparently convinced that
communism was a conspiracy that automatically involved
its disciples in crime, and with their growing acceptance of
the doctrine of guilt by association, the only remaining task
was to formalize the procedures for uncovering persons suspected of disloyalty or subversion. This exercise in thought
control, which reflected too the growing nationalism and
centralization of all values, was achieved through such devices as Congressional investigations, loyalty-security pro-
grams, and the official registration or listing of organizations
deemed subversive. These steps were reinforced by state

laws governing criminal syndicalism and excluding Communist party candidates from a place on the ballot.[10] The argument of some liberals that political purges or tests of this type were justified if confined to Communists overlooked the problem of how Communists could be discovered without also probing the views and associations of those suspected of being Communists, or fellow travelers, or individuals who secretly sympathized with the party. It was simple logic in looking for "Reds" to direct a passing glance at some of the other colors in the left-wing political spectrum. Thus even socialists and certain varieties of liberals could be, and were, placed under attack.

What many anticommunist liberals overlooked, in the zeal of their often new-found faith, was that a society could create a class of political untouchables only at the peril of being itself affected by the very virus it sought to isolate. The danger in the antiradical and anticommunist crusade after World War II did not stem primarily from the irresponsible tactics of the various Congressional investigating committees or individuals like Senator Joseph McCarthy, reprehensible though their methods were. "McCarthyism," after all, was a result or a symptom, not a cause. The danger rather lay in the assumption that there was a minority class or group of political lepers guilty of so-called wrong thinking. The contention, popular with some liberals, that communism was not heresy but conspiracy, even if true, overlooked the fact that all heresy which went beyond mere academic protest contained the seeds of possible conspiracy and subversion. Expressed in action, by sedition or revolution, such heresy or conspiracy could and undoubtedly would be met by a vigorous and rightful counteraction. But the censorship of ideas was different from resistance to rebellion. No matter how radical or subversive an idea or ideology, the attempt to eradicate it by force or suppression was purely and simply the application of methods of thought control traditionally practiced by totalitarian regimes.

The way in which the campaign against communism could be broadened, under the doctrine of guilt by association, into a general onslaught against all those whose patriotism was questioned was best illustrated by the Federal loyalty-security program. Some of the procedures in this program were not unlike the normal investigation conducted by the Civil Service Commission of all applicants for government jobs. The vital differences, of course, were the damage to the reputation of an individual whose loyalty was questioned, and the program's reliance on a whole web of circumstantial evidence furnished by secret informers. President Truman supported the FBI's contention that its function was investigatory and that it could not reveal its sources of information or attempt to usurp judicial and administrative responsibility by evaluating the materials in its files. Though the FBI position was justifiable, the dismissal of an employee on the basis of the testimony of informers whom he could not cross-examine was obviously susceptible of injustice. A heavy burden was placed on the Loyalty Review Board charged with evaluating the uneven, and often malicious or trivial, materials in a person's file. And the question also arose of how valid or reliable an FBI report actually was.[11]

There was a growing danger that the use of the FBI to investigate loyalty and to uncover evidence of subversive activities would result in the creation of the type of Federal police force long regarded as the badge of a totalitarian state. These functions, which had been taken away from the Bureau after its unsavory role in the antiradical campaign of 1919 and 1920, were restored to it in 1939 by order of President Roosevelt, who requested the Bureau "to take charge of the investigatory work in matters relating to espionage, sabotage, and violations of the neutrality regulations." Increasingly therefore the FBI was being changed from a normal investigatory and law-enforcement agency into an instrument of counterespionage, using the techniques of paid informers, *agents provocateurs,* and wiretapping. These methods, together with the tremendous expansion in the personnel and budget of the Bureau that necessarily accompanied its added tasks, aroused fears on the part of many liberals that the United States was coming under the sway of a Federal police force.[12]

Nevertheless, despite all the problems that the loyalty program gave rise to, certainly no fair-minded citizen could maintain that the government should give employment to individuals disloyal to the United States. Criticism of the loyalty program therefore rested chiefly on the question of whether government workers received sufficient guarantees against improper accusations, and of whether jeopardizing the reputations of a large number of individuals was worth the tremendous cost, direct and indirect, of exposing a small minority of subversive or disloyal persons. By March 1952, out of four million individuals whose loyalty was checked, only one out of two hundred required a thorough field investigation and one out of two thousand needed to be removed from government service.[13] These removals, it had to be remembered, were for alleged disloyalty and presumably not for any misdeeds that could be prosecuted by the courts. Indeed, the whole intent of the loyalty program was to dismiss those individuals whose activities, though suspect, were not such as to subject them to normal legal and judicial procedures.

Many liberals, on the assumption that some sort of governmental machinery was necessary to stamp out disloyalty, devoted their major efforts to setting up additional administrative safeguards to help prevent the unjust dismissal of government workers innocent of any disloyalty. What these liberals failed to perceive, however, was that the more numerous the safeguards the greater the potential damage to the reputation of anyone finally adjudged disloyal in a secret hearing before an administrative tribunal. No program, no matter how circumspect, could expect to achieve perfection in measuring such intangibles as loyalty and disloyalty. Basically the question to be decided was not factual or legal, but motivational, with all the subjectivity which that implied. Accordingly, there was reason to believe that the whole problem of disloyalty among government employees would have been far better handled by an extension of the practice of allowing supervisors to dismiss, without prejudice and without record, those individuals whose conduct, or even whose views, they had reason to suspect. This right of summary dismissal had already been granted by Congress to the Secretary of State and the heads of certain other sensitive agencies. Those guilty of wrongdoing as distinct from alleged wrong thinking would, of course, still be subject to indictment and action by the courts.

Under such procedure, dismissal from the government would not have carried the invidious distinction that was the unfortunate lot of those whose loyalty had come under a cloud. And the loss of Federal employment would not have had the effect of virtually placing an individual on a blacklist for any kind of responsible position. Moreover, the need for continuity and efficiency in government operations would interpose a check on any disposition toward wholesale firings. Unfortunately, most liberals, wedded to the historic fetish of civil service reform, failed to perceive that their preoccupation with job security had led them into the most monstrous insecurity of all — the plight of the individual denied a position, not through the workings of the business cycle or the whims of an employer but through the systematic tyranny of an official administrative body. "Men might as well be imprisoned," John Stuart Mill observed, "as excluded from the means of earning their bread." Disloyalty, to be sure, was not a crime, but the findings indelibly recorded on an individual's civil service personnel file were tantamount to conviction by a court.[14]

Liberals, though often suspicious of the loyalty program to the point of desiring to see it abolished entirely, were reluctant to yield the civil service rights of government employees. Thus, in bitter practice, they were reduced to chasing the will-o'-the-wisp of reforms in the management of the program. If liberalism was to remain viable, however, liberals had to face the unpleasant fact that liberty and security were not always compatible, either for the individual or for society. The danger in the modern liberal's tendency to rely for his freedom on the solicitude of his government was nowhere better illustrated than in the growing contradiction between the concepts of civil rights and civil liberties. It was not entirely a coincidence therefore that government's increasing concern over civil rights was in direct proportion to its mounting tendency to violate civil liberties.

The postwar disposition to substitute new rights for old liberties was an important measure of the decline of traditional liberalism in the United States. Many of the rights now boldly asserted, though bearing a relation to historic liberalism, could also exist in a totalitarian society completely lacking in liberal values. Thus equality and freedom from want, for example, were also important goals of the communist utopia. And laudable though these aims were in the context of their American support, it was questionable how well they were served by certain American policies such as the loyalty program, which deprived individuals not only of their equal rights but also frequently of the means of a livelihood.

Whatever its practice, the theory behind Federal protection of civil rights was based on the belief that positive aggressive legislation was needed to safeguard the liberties of the citizen. It was thus in conflict with the older juridical concept of liberty, which stressed the preservation of the rights of the individual from violation by the government. The classic example of the latter type of liberty was that embraced in the Bill of Rights, while the former received its first important Federal support in the civil rights legislation following the Civil War. A noteworthy feature of this and other Federal legislation in respect to civil rights was that it was almost always related to some antecedent invasion by government of the civil liberties of its citizens. Thus over two centuries of legal protection for the enslavement of the Negro was the reason why legislation was necessary to accord the freedman his equal civil rights. What the state had done it had to undo. Other prominent fields where protection of civil rights became a concern of the Federal government, such as police brutality, lynching cases, and election law violations, also were directly related to a failure on the part of some branch of the government to respect the civil liberties of the individual.[15]

In the 1940's the decline in civil liberties, beginning with the ordeal of the Japanese Americans and culminating in the postwar loyalty crusade, was curiously paralleled by the government's growing interest in the protection of certain areas of civil rights. In 1939, a few months before President Roosevelt enlisted the aid of the FBI in searching out radical activities, Attorney General Frank Murphy established a Civil Rights Section within the Criminal Division of the Department of Justice. This step was followed two years later by President Roosevelt's executive order creating a

Federal Committee on Fair Employment Practice to help eliminate "discrimination in the employment of workers in defense industries or government because of race, creed, color, or national origin." Negroes, greatly underrepresented in defense industries in the months before Pearl Harbor, had threatened a protest march on Washington under the leadership of A. Philip Randolph, president of the Brotherhood of Sleeping Car Porters. This possibility, together with growing labor shortages and the desire to counter the nazi racist propaganda, forced the administration's hand.[16]

Aided by the full employment of the war years, by the partial breakdown of segregation in the armed forces, and by the insertion of antidiscrimination clauses in government defense contracts, the wartime FEPC was able in large part to reach its goal. But there was strong opposition to any Federal legislation for a permanent, compulsory fair employment practice law. This issue, which divided liberals, recalled similar struggles over proposals for a Federal election law or an antilynching statute. Although no national FEPC law was enacted, a number of states and municipalities led by New York approved legislation that seemed effective in lessening discriminatory hiring practices in many lines of business and industry. In 1947 the whole problem of Federal protection of civil rights received additional examination with the appointment by President Truman of a Committee on Civil Rights. Although optimistic over the achievements already made, the President's committee found the record still short of the goal. Accordingly, it recommended continued government interest in the problem, the creation of a new civil rights section in the Department of Justice, and the establishment of a permanent national commission on civil rights.[17]

The movement for government enforcement of civil

rights won its most striking success in helping to break down racial discrimination against the Negro. Gains were made in reducing, or even eliminating, patterns of segregation and discrimination in such important public matters as education, transportation, housing, and employment. Even here, however, the government was only redressing an ancient wrong, and there was always the danger that unwise legislation would destroy the progress toward equality that was already coming about irrespective of government action. Thus the Negroes' own efforts and achievements, and especially their economic progress, were important factors in helping to destroy old prejudices. But as the Negro was accepted more and more into the mainstream of American life, following the similar process of assimilation that had taken place earlier in respect to immigrant groups, he began to lose his significance as a standing test of American liberalism. Moreover, in the garrison state, requiring the productive energies of the whole population, the government could not afford to lose the labor skills of any minority group because of racial discrimination. Although much remained to be accomplished, it was beginning to be true, at least outside the South, that the advocacy of equality for the Negro had become a respectable and, consequently, no longer a radical liberal cause.

In striking contrast with the government's efforts to abate discrimination against the Negro were its actions to increase discriminatory treatment of aliens and immigrants. The McCarran-Walter Act of 1952 re-enacted previous legislation barring the entry into the United States of anyone likely to engage in so-called subversive activities. Under the new tightened procedures, visitors' permits were denied to an increasing number of distinguished foreign liberals who represented no conceivable threat to American institutions. At the same time the United States continued the policy of deporting allegedly subversive aliens. Also in the case of immigrants, although an outright racial discrimination in fixing quotas was largely abandoned, discrimination on the basis of nationality and religion remained.[18]

One of the important problems that arose from the attempt to enforce equality by statute in civil rights legislation was the danger of what might be termed the intolerance of intolerance, or the persecution of people because of their prejudices. When those prejudices were reflected in law or in active discrimination in public matters, then the civil rights of other individuals were violated and in need of protection. Otherwise, there was merit in the plea that people be allowed to think what they pleased. On this basis a number of liberals including Oswald Garrison Villard, one of the founders of the National Association for the Advancement of Colored People, objected to the New York state antidiscrimination law, which interfered, they felt, with a private employer's right to his own prejudices in the subjective matter of hiring his employees. Also, the passing of laws could not eradicate many of the racial and religious prejudices that continued to exist beneath a surface liberalism. In point of fact, individuals who boasted most loudly of their lack of prejudice were often the least tolerant in practice. Thus, where the matter was outside the province of the government or the general public interest, some liberals preferred to deal with discrimination and intolerance without official intervention.[19]

A further paradox that developed out of the increasing official and popular emphasis on tolerance was the attention that it directed to differences of race and religion, matters that formerly had been taken largely for granted and regarded as the individual's private business. Even in America, the nazi crimes against the Jews, however much they were denounced, had the effect of heightening race consciousness.

Partly as a defense mechanism, Catholics, Jews, and Negroes in the United States developed their own particular kinds of nationalism or exclusiveness and sometimes used their influence to thwart majority opinion. From fear of offending powerful minority groups, politicians and businessmen catered to their particular interest or demands. This same tendency was apparent in many of the agencies of public information, where the press, radio, and movies went along with minority group pressures in censoring material deemed offensive. The sheer size and variety of the audience on which the different mass media depended often meant that, in the anxiety to offend no group, all controversial issues were automatically barred. Thus tolerance could run the danger of stultification by conforming to the vague mass prejudices drawn from the selfish interests of different powerful minority groups.[20]

Allied with the modern fear of popular debasement through the tyranny of mass media in the hands of centralized societies and governments went the apprehension of neo-Malthusians lest the world's growing population outrun its sources of food and raw materials. Also, in the disparity of population growth between nations and areas and in the differential birth rate within class and racial groups, eugenicists saw a possible danger that superior individuals might not perpetuate themselves. But at the same time that some regarded the general level of intelligence of the population as declining, even in the United States, others raised the question of how the ever-increasing stream of college graduates were to find jobs commensurate with their training and background.[21]

All these anxieties, and sometimes conflicting possibilities, reinforced intolerance and pessimism, and at the same time opened up new avenues and approaches for government's somewhat contradictory efforts to preserve human rights and welfare. Meanwhile, those who argued strongly that the sword of government protection was a needed instrument for the preservation of civil rights, which liberals should not hesitate to use, often overlooked the fact that this sword could cut two ways. What government could grant it could also take away, and the opposition of civil rights and civil liberties was not the paradox that it at first seemed. By mid-century therefore Americans were finding to their dismay that the Federal government's protection of civil rights was not proof against its invasion of civil liberties.

While the requirements of the cold war, with its militarization of large areas of American life and thought, explained much of the expanded scope of the government's invasive activity, Americans were also being persuaded to accept as never before government intervention in matters that were not a part of its official concern. This was particularly true in the field of education, where, despite a long tradition of public support in the United States, there had not been any direct control exercised by the Federal government. But in the battle for men's minds, which was one of the more important features of modern integral nationalism, the educational system was a natural object of increasing official attention and interference.

Even before the rise of the ideological conflict between democracy and communism, close ties were developing in the United States between educational institutions and the Federal government. The first important steps were taken during World War II, when government aid in a variety of forms kept many private institutions alive, especially those in the field of higher education. After the war the GI Bill of Rights, Federal scholarships, and large government appropriations for research in the scientific field perpetuated the bond between the campus and Washington. At the same time, the growing postwar pressure for expanded opportunities in education, encouraged by both educators and government officials, looked to the day when schooling, right on through the college and the university, would become a matter of public concern and support. The main obstacle to such expansion, the lack of funds from private or local sources, strengthened the demand for a program of direct Federal subsidies to general education. In the past all such legislation had been defeated, and in 1949 the most important of the postwar measures, the Barden bill, was rejected. The defeat of this bill, however, was occasioned more by racial and religious issues than by liberal fears over the intrusion of the Federal government into public education.

The church and state question as it related to education was extremely complex. The long-standing American opposition to any tendency to break down the barriers between church and state carried over into the fight to prevent public funds from being used in any way by church schools, or for purposes of religious education in the public schools. While most liberals were in general agreement with this position, they were perhaps too little aware of some of the illiberal forces on both sides of the struggle in regard to church and state problems in education. Thus liberals could hardly agree with the demand that everyone be forced to attend the public elementary schools, nor with the way in which many Protestant groups voiced their own demands for religious education as a substitute for the Catholics' parochial schools. At the same time, the Catholic opposition to Federal aid to education came to be limited to the objection that the proposals with any chance of success in Congress failed to include the parochial schools or otherwise aid the Catholic pupils.[22]

Much of the conflict over religious education reflected more than anything else the rise of a new orthodoxy in both religious thinking and educational philosophy. In the South all these influences were at work, and in addition the dominant white leadership feared that Federal aid to education would serve as a wedge to break down the pattern of Negro segregation in the public schools. Even without direct Federal aid, however, the amount of Federal support for education and research grew tremendously in the later 1940's. In the first full academic year after the war, one-half of the total income of American colleges and universities came from the Federal government.[23]

The most important effect of the close connection between government and education was the way in which the latter became more and more identified with the government's outlook and purpose. In place of education as a private or local interest, the school and the college became an adjunct of the nation. Especially in the field of higher education it became true that the university served the nation rather than pure scholarship. Stated baldly in terms of teaching state propaganda, such a concept was repulsive to most Americans and recalled unpleasantly the surrender of German intellectuals to the nazi regime. But as a past president of the American Association of University Professors pointed out:

Stated subtly — that higher education should exalt the American way of life and should mention communism with a lack of enthusiasm — the idea is more ingratiating, at least to the commonalty and to some college presidents, if not to the scholar whose search for truth must be unimpeded and free.[24]

The affiliation of interest between nation and schools, or "the confusion of state with university," meant, of course, that fear of disloyalty or subversion in the school system was second only to the fear of its existence in the government. Seth W. Richardson, formerly a member of the President's

Loyalty Review Board, in his initial speech after being named head of the new Subversive Activities Control Board established under the McCarran Act, told an audience at the University of Virginia that "the first padlock" in the control of disloyalty in speech should "go on the mouths of teachers and scientists." Asked whether his views would not tend to "control a person's thinking," Richardson replied that "the man who fears that his thinking will be curbed by a check of loyalty may be thinking things that tend to be disloyal to his country." [25]

On all sides there was a demand that the schools conform to the postwar pattern of national loyalty. In the resulting effort to expose alleged communist influences and teachers, pressures, both official and private, were brought to bear on American education that were out of harmony with traditional concepts of liberalism and academic freedom. Teachers, instead of being liberal intellectuals, alert to new ideas, became as a matter of professional survival conservative and careful in their thinking, and above all in their associations. The stimulus to the minds of the young from contact with a daring and unconventional rebel was jettisoned because of its possible tendency to "wrong thinking." Out of such a concern with safety could come unfortunately an even more dangerous general mental sterility.[26]

Interference with freedom of teaching had always existed to some extent in American history, but the specific campaign against radicalism in the schools and colleges was particularly an outgrowth of the period of World Wars I and II. In New York State, for example, the spirit of the notorious Lusk laws, requiring teacher loyalty oaths and state licensing of educational institutions, revived again in the 1930's. Irving Ives, the same state legislator who later lent his name to New York's antidiscrimination law, rather ironically perhaps, assumed leadership in securing the passage in 1934 of a law requiring a loyalty oath of all teachers as a defense against "isms." This was followed by extensive legislative investigations of communist influences in the New York City schools and colleges. Finally, in 1949, New York passed the Feinberg bill, providing for the dismissal of teachers found guilty of advocating the overthrow of the government.[27]

By 1952 a total of thirty states had enacted some sort of loyalty oath for teachers, with the special noncommunist oath at the University of California stirring up the most notable controversy until it was declared unconstitutional by the California Supreme Court. The attack on allegedly communist teachers, usually undertaken with much public excitement by state or Congressional investigating committees, had the effect of throttling liberals together with an extremely small minority of Communists. The ostensible purpose of all such investigations and loyalty oaths was to force communist teachers to resign or be exposed to charges of perjury. Thus the insistence on teacher loyalty, which in practice was often a demand for complete conformity, carried to a climax the various institutionalized pressures that had gradually enveloped much of the educational system. Seldom had private intervention on the part of special interest groups or the naturally conservative influences of many local communities been able to achieve anything like the atmosphere that hung over American education by the middle of the twentieth century.

The question of whether the rights of the communist teacher were included within the principle of academic freedom was a problem that divided teachers as well as laymen. In 1949 the National Education Association affirmed that Communists should not continue to be employed as teachers, while the American Federation of Teachers felt that this should not necessarily be grounds for dismissal. Three

years later the Federation had come over to the position of
the NEA, which was also the stand taken overwhelmingly
by college and university presidents. Only the American
Association of University Professors and the American Civil
Liberties Union adhered to the traditional liberal position
that the individual's competence alone should decide the
question of his employment. Both the NEA and the American Federation of Teachers, however, opposed the Feinberg law in New York State, which was so drawn up that
teachers who had been members of radical organizations
could be considered guilty of fomenting revolution and
thus subject to automatic dismissal.[28] It was this reliance on
guilt by association, and the inevitable spy system it provoked, that Justice William O. Douglas attacked in his
opinion dissenting from the Supreme Court's ruling that
the Feinberg law was constitutional. "What happens under
this law," Douglas asserted, "is typical of what happens in a
police state. Teachers are under constant surveillance; their
pasts are combed for signs of disloyalty; their utterances are
watched for clues to dangerous thoughts. A pall is cast over
the classrooms. There can be no real academic freedom in
that environment." [29]

Among the dwindling minority of forthright individuals
who opposed the automatic removal of communist teachers
was Senator Robert A. Taft. Although he defended the right
of Congress to investigate reports of alleged communist in-
filtration in the field of education, Taft drew a distinction
between the government and a university continuing to
employ Communists. Himself a fellow of the corporation of
Yale University, Taft did not agree that Communists should
be allowed to teach their political beliefs, but he added: "I
must say as a member of the Board of Trustees of a university, I would not favor firing any one for being a Communist unless I was certain that he was teaching communism

and having some effect on the development of the thought of his students." [30]

Taft's liberal philosophy was adhered to by only a minority of educational institutions, of which Harvard University and the University of Chicago were the most illustrious examples. Liberals could not well question Congressional power to conduct investigations even when such investigations seemed to accomplish little in the way of a constructive public purpose. It was not, however, so much the investigations, damaging though they were to liberalism, as the attitude of college administrators toward their findings that should have been the prime object of liberal attack. Although it was true, as conservatives delighted in pointing out, that financiers and business leaders had been haled before Congressional investigating committees dominated by liberals and progressives, still these individuals, no matter how sordid some of their dealings, were not likely to be dismissed by their employers or stockholders. Unlike the corporations, which often did their best to hamper Congressional inquiries, the colleges avowed a willingness and, in some cases, an eager desire to cooperate. Presumably such investigations made it easier for college heads to rid their institutions of certain unwanted professors. Even more shocking, however, was the proposal of a group of educators that the colleges set up their own investigation service to deal with teachers suspected of subversive activities.[31] Although there was some liberal protest against the witch hunt in the schools and colleges, it was more often true, as Arthur M. Schlesinger, Jr., pointed out, that teachers too impotent to secure a living wage would also be helpless against assaults on academic freedom.[32]

In practice the problem of the communist teacher seldom arose in clear-cut fashion. Most of the individuals under attack had already given up the party, and many of those exposed begged the issue by pleading immunity under the Fifth Amendment, which permitted a person to refuse to testify against himself in a criminal proceeding. Although this was accepted by most institutions and administrators as an admission of guilt, it was not necessarily true that the suspect individual was a Communist. But controversy over the ethics of taking refuge in the Constitution avoided the main issue, which was whether a Communist should be permitted to teach.

Ample testimony that admitted Communists had not attempted to foist their doctrines upon their students, and the absurdity of supposing that communist teachers were the spearhead of a coming revolution, resulted in a retreat from this line of attack on their right to teach. Instead, it was contended by many liberals, as well as by most college and school administrators, that the communist teacher had a closed mind and was therefore unsuited to teaching and unfit for objective scholarship. Only an increasingly small minority of liberals was willing to argue the point of whether individuals subject to other disciplines than communism might not have at least partially closed minds on certain matters. Also there was the unproved assumption that all Communists were completely and at all times controlled by, and loyal to, the party line. Finally, as some liberals pointed out, there remained the practical question of how much actual damage or indoctrination even the most dedicated and clever Communists could accomplish in view of their infinitesimally small numbers, and in the face of the overwhelming opposition to communism, and indeed to any sort of radicalism, on the part of their students. As one professor observed, "what the profession needs is indoctrination in the technique of indoctrination — life would be simpler if teachers were more successful in getting their goods across the counter." [33]

The question was not whether Communists were desirable teachers, which liberals would agree they were not. But many liberals, in a minority among their fellow citizens, to be sure, felt that academic freedom was placed in greater jeopardy by violating the tenure of a communist teacher than by allowing him to keep his position. In the long run there would be less damage to American ideals of freedom and liberty from permitting an occasional Communist to air his views than from trying to enforce a rigid intellectual conformity upon American higher education. "In a university, if nowhere else, Jefferson's ideal ought to be respected; for the toleration of error is an inescapable condition of the pursuit of truth." [34]

As Jeffersonian ideals came increasingly under attack in both school and nation, liberals could not fail to protest the general assault on the civil liberties of the individual, of which hysteria over communism was merely one phase. Supreme Court Justice William O. Douglas complained of "the black silence of fear" descending over the American people, while his colleague Justice Robert H. Jackson warned that "Traditional freedoms are less in danger of any sudden overthrow than of being bartered or traded for something else on which the people place a higher current value." The governing body of the Presbyterian Church charged that "loyalty to truth" was being sacrificed for propaganda by demagogic assaults upon basic human rights. Liberals could well wonder therefore whether the price of security on such terms was not too dear.[35]

Security, which was the modern dream of individuals and nations, could in the long run be self-defeating. Once again the temper of America was dangerously like that of the antebellum South, where Jefferson's liberalism had been rejected in the vain effort to perpetuate slavery. Moreover, there was especial irony in the way in which a new

fixation of beliefs and emphasis on truths deemed universal
was being used to demonstrate to liberals that many of the
rights that they had long considered as natural could be
qualified or even taken away in time of stress. Thus, as the
United States left the decade of the 1940's and entered the
second half of the twentieth century, there was no conceal-
ing the sources or extent of liberal dismay.

Public excitement over the communist issue could not be
maintained indefinitely, but in the meantime civil liberties
might be seriously and permanently weakened by being deprived of effective popular support. Moreover, the overriding demands of the militant national state were constantly
reinforcing the economic and scientific pressures working
toward a greater centralization, standardization, and collectivism, in which individual and human values were in
danger of being dwarfed. A war economy, under state capitalism or socialism, offered a version of economic and national security that was being increasingly accepted as a
way out of the world crisis, but it was not the way toward
greater individual and social freedom. And it was a solution that denied all the major values of the American liberal
tradition. On all sides, therefore, the American people were
confronted with mounting evidence of the decline of liberalism. An important tendency and feature of over a century of
American history, this decline had, however, never before
been so clearly outlined against the future's darkening
horizon.

Whatever the shape of things to come, it was not likely
that the forces of centralization, of growing complexity, and
of an increasing concentration of authority would be arrested or subjected to significant modification. Even if dire
predictions of new Caesars and more wars proved false,
there were other illiberal pressures derived from modern
technology, mass psychology, and collectivist economics.

Perhaps America and the Western world of which it was a part were facing the end of an era — the close of the several centuries of expansion and freedom that Walter Prescott Webb has called the period of the Great Frontier. Or, again, modern civilization might already be in the midst of the decline that had overtaken all previous civilizations and cultures. Certainly there were disturbing parallels between the history of the Graeco-Roman world and the state of Western civilization. Especially instructive for the United States was the story of the subversion of the ideals of the Republic of Rome in the new concepts of the Empire. "The perfect democracy of the Roman Empire was in a sense the abdication of the ideal before the material; the saddening fact is that people were almost universally ready to accept this state of affairs and at most only tried to camouflage to their own hearts the full nature of their autocracy." [36]

Without attempting to pierce the heavy haze of the uncertain future, the historian still has ample basis for believing that the decline of liberalism has already proved one of the important facets of American history. Such decline is also impressive evidence that the severe crisis that confronts the world today has its roots in the past. Seen in this light, much of United States history takes on a new form and character. Calamitous though this may be for American liberals, it is nevertheless well to remember that authentic tragedy is of heroic proportions and a part of the epic of life itself. Only positivists seek absolutes, while the true liberal can take heart in the thought that the very idea of decline supports the notion that "the world is process not system, movement not finality. . . . Those who rode with flying wheel along the Flaminian Road could not foresee Frederick Barbarossa or Andrew Carnegie." [37]

Oswald Spengler may have been correct in his assertions that "Only dreamers believe that there is a way out. Optimism is *cowardice*. . . . Our eye for history, our faculty of writing history, is a revealing sign that our path lies downward." [38] But decline need not blot out the great achievements already recorded. So long as honest history is written — a by no means certain circumstance in a totalitarian world — liberals will at least be able to look back with some satisfaction into the distant past, while they do their best to challenge the fate held out by an increasingly illiberal future.

Notes

Foreword

[1] See my article "Parrington and the Decline of American Liberalism," *American Quarterly*, III (Winter 1951), 295–308.

[2] David Lawrence, "What 'Liberalism' Really Means," Washington *Evening Star*, Jan. 2, 1953.

[3] F. W. Coker, "Some Present-Day Critics of Liberalism," *American Political Science Review*, XLVII (March 1953), 3.

Chapter 1

[1] On the history of European liberalism see: Guido de Ruggiero, *The History of European Liberalism* (London: Oxford, 1927); L. T. Hobhouse, *Liberalism* (New York: Holt, 1930); Carl Becker, *The Heavenly City of the Eighteenth-Century Philosophers* (New Haven: Yale U. Press, 1932); H. J. Laski, *The Rise of European Liberalism* (London: Allen and Unwin, 1936); F. G. Bratton, *The Legacy of the Liberal Spirit* (New York: Scribner, 1943); J. S. Schapiro, *Liberalism and the Challenge of Fascism* (New York: McGraw-Hill, 1949); H. K. Girvetz, *From Wealth to Welfare* (Stanford: Stanford U. Press, 1950); J. R. Pennock, *Liberal Democracy* (New York: Rinehart, 1950); T. P. Neill, *The Rise and Decline of Liberalism* (Milwaukee: Bruce, 1953).

[2] See the comments of: J. S. Mill, *On Liberty* (New York: Holt, 1898), chap. 1; W. E. H. Lecky, *Democracy and Liberty* (New York: Longmans, Green, 1896).

[3] Laski, *Rise of European Liberalism,* 15ff.

[4] Ruggiero, *History of European Liberalism,* 82. See also C. B. Rogers, *The Spirit of Revolution in 1789* (Princeton: Princeton U. Press, 1949); John A. Scott, *Republican Ideas and the Liberal Tradition in France* (New York: Columbia U. Press, 1951).

[5] F. B. Artz, *Reaction and Revolution* (New York: Harper, 1934), chaps. 3–4.

[6] C. J. H. Hayes, *A Generation of Materialism* (New York: Harper, 1941), chaps. 2, 6–7.

[7] Ludwig von Mises, *Omnipotent Government* (New Haven: Yale U. Press, 1944), 18ff.; J. H. Hallowell, *The Decline of Liberalism as an Ideology* (Berkeley: U. California Press, 1943).

[8] J. D. Kingsley, *Representative Bureaucracy* (Yellow Springs: Antioch Press, 1944), 4–6, 92; B. E. Lippincott, *Victorian Critics of Democracy* (Minneapolis: U. Minnesota Press, 1938).

[9] H. M. Lynd, *England in the Eighteen-Eighties* (New York: Oxford, 1945), 109ff., 226; Carlton Hayes, *British Social Politics* (Boston: Ginn, 1913), 347.

[10] W. L. Langer, *The Diplomacy of Imperialism* (New York: Knopf, 1935), II, 790.

[11] S. J. Hurwitz, *State Intervention in Great Britain* (New York: Columbia U. Press, 1949), 43–57.

Chapter 2

[1] *An Inquiry into the Nature and Causes of the Wealth of Nations*, ed. Edwin Cannan (London: Methuen, 1904), II, 73.

[2] D. R. Fox in Editor's Foreword to C. P. Nettels, *The Roots of American Civilization* (New York: Crofts, 1938), viii.

[3] J. E. Gillespie, *The Influence of Oversea Expansion on England* (New York: Columbia U. Press, 1920); W. P. Webb, *The Great Frontier* (Boston: Houghton Mifflin, 1952).

[4] E. B. Greene, *The Revolutionary Generation* (New York: Macmillan, 1943), 98.

[5] T. J. Wertenbaker, *The Planters of Colonial Virginia* (Princeton: Princeton U. Press, 1922), 59, 126ff., 151.

[6] Albert Keiser, *The Indian in American Literature* (New York: Oxford, 1933), chaps. 1–2; R. H. Pearce, *The Savages of America* (Baltimore: Johns Hopkins Press, 1953).

[7] W. S. Carpenter, *The Development of American Political Thought* (Princeton: Princeton U. Press, 1930), 44; C. S. Sydnor, *Gentlemen Freeholders* (Chapel Hill: U. North Carolina Press, 1952), 132–134.

[8] J. Hector St. John Crèvecœur, *Letters from an American Farmer* (reprinted from the original 1782 edition; New York, 1904), Letter III.

[9] See the comprehensive and critical Introduction in F. L. Mott and C. E. Jorgenson, *Benjamin Franklin Representative Selections* (New York: American Book Co., 1936).

Chapter 3

[1] Charles and Mary Beard, *The Rise of American Civilization* (New York: Macmillan, 1927), I, 296.

[2] *Main Currents in American Thought* (New York: Harcourt, Brace, 1927–1930), I, 193.

[3] *Ibid.*, I, 235–236.

[4] *Letters*, Letter XII. See also R. H. Gabriel, "Crèvecœur and His Times," *Sketches of Eighteenth Century America* (New Haven: Yale U. Press, 1925), 8.

[5] *The Writings of Thomas Paine*, ed. M. C. Conway (New York: Putnam, 1894–1896), I, 69, 91, 99, 101.

[6] *The Papers of Thomas Jefferson*, ed. J. P. Boyd (Princeton: Princeton U. Press, 1950–   ), I, 429ff.

[7] J. B. McMaster, *The Acquisition of Political, Social and Industrial Rights of Man in America* (Cleveland, 1903), 16–17.

[8] T. V. Smith, *The American Philosophy of Equality* (Chicago: U. Chicago Press, 1927), 38.

[9] S. E. Morison and H. S. Commager, *The Growth of the American Republic* (New York: Oxford, 1942), I, 235.

[10] Greene, *Revolutionary Generation*, chap. 11.

[11] Michael Kraus, *The Atlantic Civilization* (Ithaca: Cornell U. Press, 1949), 161, 193, 302.

[12] *Ibid.*, chaps. 9–10. Gouverneur Morris complained of this penchant of the founding fathers for referring to themselves as citizens of the world. S. E. Morison, *Sources and Documents Illustrating the American Revolution* (Oxford: Clarendon, 1923), 281–282.

[13] H. B. Parkes, *The American Experience* (New York: Knopf, 1947), 104–105.

Chapter 4

[1] Parkes, *American Experience*, 112. This and the following chapter have benefited considerably from the discussion of agrarianism in Parkes, chaps. 6–7.

[2] R. A. East, *Business Enterprise in the American Revolutionary Era* (New York: Columbia U. Press, 1938), *passim*.

[3] C. A. Beard, *An Economic Interpretation of the Constitution* (New York: Macmillan, 1935), 59.

[4] *The Records of the Federal Convention of 1787*, ed. Max Farrand (New Haven: Yale U. Press, 1911), I, 431.

[5] Beard, *Economic Interpretation*, 154–155.

[6] Jefferson to Dupont de Nemours, Jan. 18, 1802, *The Works of Thomas Jefferson*, ed. P. L. Ford (New York: Putnam, 1904–1905), IX, 342–344 footnote.

[7] East, *Business Enterprise*, chaps. 13–14.

[8] L. D. Baldwin, *Whiskey Rebels* (Pittsburgh: U. Pittsburgh Press, 1939), chap. 3, and *passim*.

[9] Howard White, *Executive Influence in Determining Military Policy in the United States* (Urbana: U. Illinois, 1925), 98ff., 128ff.

[10] Madison to Jefferson, May 13, 1798, *Letters and Other Writings of James Madison* (Philadelphia, 1865), II, 141.

[11] *U.S. Statutes at Large*, I, 596.

[12] Adrienne Koch, *Jefferson and Madison* (New York: Knopf, 1950), chap. 7.

Chapter 5

[1] Joseph Dorfman, *The Economic Mind in American Civilization* (New York: Viking, 1946), I, 440.

[2] Quoted in Richard Hofstadter, *The American Political Tradition* (New York: Knopf, 1948), 33.

[3] *The Writings of Thomas Jefferson*, Memorial Edition, ed. A. A. Lipscomb and A. E. Bergh (Washington: Thomas Jefferson Memorial Association, 1903), VI, 391. See also *The Works of John C. Calhoun*, ed. R. K. Crallé (New York, 1851–1856), I, 360ff.; L. D. White, *The Jeffersonians* (New York: Macmillan, 1951), chap. 1.

[4] Parrington, *Main Currents*, I, 356.

[5] Clement Eaton, "The Jeffersonian Tradition of Liberalism in America," *South Atlantic Quarterly*, XLIII (January, 1944), 2–5.

[6] A. J. Nock, *Jefferson* (New York: Harcourt, Brace, 1926), 101–104.

[7] "Notes on Virginia," *Writings*, Mem. Ed., II, 230; Jefferson to Madison, Dec. 20, 1787, *ibid.*, VI, 392–393.

[8] *Ibid.*, I, 121–122. See also Carpenter, *Development of American*

Political Thought, 108; C. M. Wiltse, *The Jeffersonian Tradition in American Democracy* (Chapel Hill: U. North Carolina Press, 1935), 127ff.

⁹ Jefferson to Joseph C. Cabell, Feb. 2, 1816, *Writings*, Mem. Ed., XIV, 423.

¹⁰ J. D. Richardson, *A Compilation of the Messages and Papers of the Presidents* (Washington, 1896–1899), I, 321–324.

¹¹ Jefferson to Gideon Granger, Aug. 13, 1800, *Writings*, Mem. Ed., X, 166–170.

¹² White, *Jeffersonians*, 552–553.

¹³ *Rise of American Civilization*, I, 402.

¹⁴ Russell Kirk, *Randolph of Roanoke* (Chicago: U. Chicago Press, 1951), 20–21, 26, 32, 45, 50.

¹⁵ Dec. 10, 1811, *Annals of Congress*, 12 Cong., 1 Sess., 455.

¹⁶ Kirk, *Randolph*, 125, 136.

¹⁷ *Ibid.*, 67.

¹⁸ *Rise of American Civilization*, I, 392–393.

¹⁹ *Works*, I, 361.

²⁰ Gallatin to Matthew Lyon, May 7, 1816, *The Writings of Albert Gallatin*, ed. Henry Adams (Philadelphia, 1879), I, 700.

²¹ Jefferson to Thomas Ritchie, Dec. 25, 1820, *Writings*, Mem. Ed., XV, 297; "Autobiography," *ibid.*, I, 121–122.

²² George Dangerfield, *The Era of Good Feelings* (New York: Harcourt, Brace, 1952), 348ff.

²³ Adams to Rev. Charles W. Upham, Feb. 2, 1837, *The Selected Writings of John and John Quincy Adams*, ed. Adrienne Koch and William Peden (New York: Knopf, 1946), 389.

Chapter 6

¹ A. M. Schlesinger, Jr., *The Age of Jackson* (Boston: Little, Brown, 1945), 312.

² F. J. Turner, *The United States 1830–1850* (New York: Holt, 1935), 20; Hofstadter, *American Political Tradition*, 65–66; Louis Hartz, "The Whig Tradition in America and Europe," *American Political Science Review*, XLVI (December 1952), 989–1002; Marvin Meyers, "The Jacksonian Persuasion," *American Quarterly*, V (Spring 1953), 3–15.

³ *United States 1830–1850*, 407–408.

[4] Parkes, *American Experience*, 154.

[5] T. C. Cochran and William Miller, *The Age of Enterprise* (New York: Macmillan, 1942), 42, 69.

[6] Carter Goodrich, "The Revulsion Against Internal Improvements," *Journal of Economic History*, X (November 1950), 145–169.

[7] Oscar and Mary Handlin, *Commonwealth* (New York: New York U. Press, 1947), 52, 92, 113ff., 172–173.

[8] *Ibid.*, 205, 242, 261–262.

[9] Louis Hartz, *Economic Policy and Democratic Thought* (Cambridge: Harvard U. Press, 1948), 69ff., 195ff., 292–293.

[10] Leon Whipple, *The Story of Civil Liberty in the United States* (New York: Vanguard, 1927), condemns this disposition of Jacksonian democracy to mob rule; while Edwin Mims, Jr., *The Majority of the People* (New York: Modern Age, 1941), attacks liberals for their concern over minority rights.

[11] Marquis James, *The Life of Andrew Jackson* (Indianapolis: Bobbs-Merrill, 1938), 262.

[12] C. G. Bowers, *Party Battles of the Jackson Period* (Boston: Houghton Mifflin, 1922), chap. 14.

[13] Bertrand Russell, *Freedom and Organization* (London: Allen and Unwin, 1934), 305.

[14] Parrington, *Main Currents*, II, 394ff., 413; Daniel Aaron, *Men of Good Hope* (New York: Oxford, 1951), chap. 1.

[15] Aaron, *Men of Good Hope*, 4.

[16] *Democracy in America*, ed. Phillips Bradley (New York: Knopf, 1945), I, 14, 70, 86.

[17] *Ibid.*, I, 171, 196ff., II, 268.

[18] *Ibid.*, I, 259, II, 95, 114, 290.

[19] A. K. Weinberg, *Manifest Destiny* (Baltimore: Johns Hopkins Press, 1935), 107, 111.

[20] Richardson, *Messages and Papers of the Presidents*, II, 520–521.

[21] Thoreau to Harrison Blake, Feb. 27, 1853, *The Writings of Henry David Thoreau*, ed. F. B. Sanborn (Boston: Houghton Mifflin, 1906), VI, 210.

[22] *Mardi and a Voyage Thither* (London: Constable, 1922), II, 240–241.

Chapter 7

[1] Clement Eaton, *Freedom of Thought in the Old South* (Durham: Duke U. Press, 1940), Preface and chap. 1.

[2] *Ibid.*, 19–21.

[3] John H. Franklin, *From Slavery to Freedom* (New York: Knopf, 1947), 141–143, summarizes the Convention's action on slavery.

[4] *Ibid.*, 143.

[5] Merle Curti, *The Growth of American Thought* (New York: Harper, 1951), 197–198; H. K. Beale, *A History of Freedom of Teaching in American Schools* (New York: Scribner, 1941), 127–132; R. B. Nye, *Fettered Freedom* (East Lansing: Michigan State College Press, 1949), 82–85.

[6] *Writings,* Mem. Ed., XV, 249.

[7] Glover Moore, *The Missouri Controversy* (Lexington: U. Kentucky Press, 1953), chap. 7; Dumas Malone, *The Public Life of Thomas Cooper* (New Haven: Yale U. Press, 1926), 290.

[8] Eaton, *Freedom of Thought,* 29.

[9] Clement Eaton, *A History of the Old South* (New York: Macmillan, 1949), 390ff.

[10] Eaton, *Freedom of Thought,* chaps. 2–4.

[11] Nye, *Fettered Freedom,* chap. 2.

[12] *Ibid.,* 69.

[13] Eaton, *Freedom of Thought,* 127.

[14] Nye, *Fettered Freedom,* 119.

[15] *Ibid.,* 121. See also Hazel Wolf, *On Freedom's Altar* (Madison: U. Wisconsin Press, 1952).

[16] Speech in the Senate on the Kansas Lecompton Constitution, March 4, 1858, *Congressional Globe,* 35 Cong., 1 Sess., Appendix, 68.

[17] Henry Hughes, *Treatise on Sociology* (Philadelphia, 1854), 291, and *passim.*

[18] Hofstadter, *American Political Tradition,* chap. 4; R. H. Gabriel, *The Course of American Democratic Thought* (New York: Ronald, 1940), 110; Parrington, *Main Currents,* II, 69–82.

[19] C. M. Wiltse, *John C. Calhoun Sectionalist* (Indianapolis: Bobbs-Merrill, 1951), 334.

[20] *Ordeal of the Union* (New York: Scribner, 1947), I, 518. See also A. C. Cole, *The Irrepressible Conflict* (New York: Macmillan, 1934), 262–268.

[21] Frederick Grimké, *Considerations upon the Nature and Tendency of Free Institutions* (Cincinnati and New York, 1848), 53.

Chapter 8

[1] Parkes, *American Experience,* 206.

[2] Sumner to Richard Cobden, Sept. 4, 1863, in E. L. Pierce, *Memoir and Letters of Charles Sumner* (Boston, 1877–1893), IV, 144. See also L. A. White, "Charles Sumner and the Crisis of 1860–61," *Essays in Honor of William E. Dodd,* ed. Avery Craven (Chicago: U. Chicago Press, 1935), 187ff.

[3] *Speeches, Lectures and Letters* (Boston, 1863), 421.

[4] *Ibid.,* 422–423.

[5] *Reverses Needed* (Hartford, 1861), 24. See also C. F. Dunham, *The Attitude of the Northern Clergy toward the South* (Toledo: Gray, 1942), chap. 4.

[6] "Chiefly About War-Matters by a Peaceable Man," *Atlantic Monthly,* X (July 1862), 43–61.

[7] R. L. Rusk, *The Life of Ralph Waldo Emerson* (New York: Scribner, 1949), 428, and chap. 22.

[8] J. G. Randall, *Constitutional Problems under Lincoln* (New York: Appleton, 1926), 152; John A. Marshall, *American Bastile* (Philadelphia, 1872), *passim.*

[9] *Speeches* (New York, 1864), 494.

[10] 4 Wallace 127.

[11] T. F. Carroll, "Freedom of Speech and of the Press during the Civil War," *Virginia Law Review,* IX (May 1923), 516–551; Cole, *Irrepressible Conflict,* 368.

[12] *A Constitutional View of the Late War Between the States* (Philadelphia, 1868–1870), II, 571–573.

[13] Greeley to Stanton, June 12, 1863, quoted in J. G. Randall, *The Civil War and Reconstruction* (Boston: Heath, 1937), 607. See also Emory Upton, *The Military Policy of the United States* (Washington, 1904), 443; J. F. Rhodes, *History of the United States from the Compromise of 1850* (New York, 1893–1906), IV, 320ff.

[14] J. P. Grossman, *William Sylvis* (New York: Columbia U. Press, 1945), 50–53.

[15] Parkes, *American Experience,* 207.

[16] Parrington, *Main Currents,* II, 473–474.

Chapter 9

[1] W. E. Barton, *The Life of Abraham Lincoln* (Indianapolis: Bobbs-Merrill, 1925), II, 339.

[2] Parrington, *Main Currents*, II, 360–361.

[3] *Political Essays* (Boston, 1888), 191, 195.

[4] *Considerations upon the Nature and Tendency of Free Institutions,* 320, and Book III, chap. 6.

[5] May 27, 1867, in Pierce, *Memoir and Letters of Charles Sumner,* IV, 319. See also A. P. Grimes, *The Political Liberalism of the New York Nation* (Chapel Hill: U. North Carolina Press, 1953), 7ff.

[6] *The Rise and Fall of the Confederate Government* (New York, 1881), II, 764.

[7] See especially I, chaps. 10–11.

[8] *Texas* v. *White* (1869), 7 Wallace 725.

[9] E. R. Lewis, *A History of American Political Thought* (New York: Macmillan, 1937), chap. 5.

[10] *Political Science or the State* (New York, 1878), I, 117–119, and Part I *passim.*

[11] Frank Freidel, *Francis Lieber* (Baton Rouge: Louisiana State U. Press, 1948), 161, 267.

[12] *Ibid.,* 363, and chap. 15. See also Brainerd Dyer, "Francis Lieber and the American Civil War," *Huntington Library Quarterly,* II (July 1939), 449–465.

[13] *On Civil Liberty and Self-Government* (Philadelphia, 1853), I, 101; Freidel, *Francis Lieber,* 374.

[14] *Political Science and Comparative Constitutional Law* (Boston, 1890), I, 38–39; H. S. Commager, *The American Mind* (New Haven: Yale U. Press, 1950), 47.

[15] Paul Buck, *The Road to Reunion 1865–1900* (Boston: Little, Brown, 1937), viii.

[16] C. Vann Woodward, *Origins of the New South 1877–1913* (Baton Rouge: Louisiana State U. Press, 1951), chap. 1; *Reunion and Reaction* (Boston: Little, Brown, 1951), 64, 104.

[17] *Life and Labors of Henry W. Grady, His Speeches, Writings* (Atlanta, 1890), 113.

[18] Woodward, *Origins of the New South,* 61–62; H. L. Swint, *The Northern Teacher in the South 1862–1870* (Nashville: Vanderbilt U. Press, 1941), 141–142; Beale, *A History of Freedom of Teaching,* 175ff.

[19] Vann Woodward and Fletcher Green quoted in Woodward, *Origins of the New South*, 213–215.

[20] *Ibid.*, 211, 216, chaps. 13–14. See also Rayford Logan, *The Negro in American Life and Thought: The Nadir 1877–1901* (New York: Dial, 1954).

[21] Curti, *Growth of American Thought*, chap. 19.

Chapter 10

[1] Merle Curti, *The Roots of American Loyalty* (New York: Columbia U. Press, 1946), 180.

[2] *Rise of American Civilization*, II, 166.

[3] *Main Currents*, III, 9–10, 20–23.

[4] Herbert Croly, *Marcus Alonzo Hanna* (New York: Macmillan, 1919), 344, 466ff.

[5] "A Paternal Government," May 25, 1870, *A Century of Tribune Editorials* (Chicago: Tribune Co., 1947), 37–39.

[6] "The Financial Conduct of the War," 1865, *Gleanings from a Literary Life* (New York, 1880), 97–98.

[7] *Letters and Literary Memorials of Samuel J. Tilden*, ed. John Bigelow (New York: Harper, 1908), I, 321–323. See also Eric Goldman, *Rendezvous with Destiny* (New York: Knopf, 1952), chap. 2.

[8] *Nation*, XVI (Jan. 30, 1873), 68.

[9] *Century*, XXIV (June 1882), 287–292.

[10] Cochran and Miller, *Age of Enterprise*, 107ff.; P. W. Gates, "From Individualism to Collectivism in American Land Policy," *Liberalism as a Force in History*, Henry Wells Lawrence Memorial Lectures No. 3 (New London: Connecticut College, 1953), 14–35.

[11] Cochran and Miller, *Age of Enterprise*, 108; S. B. Clough, *The American Way* (New York: Crowell, 1953), 54, 199–200.

[12] Fred Shannon, *The Farmer's Last Frontier* (New York: Farrar and Rinehart, 1945), 64, and chap. 3.

[13] L. B. Priest, *Uncle Sam's Stepchildren* (New Brunswick: Rutgers U. Press, 1942), chaps. 5–8.

[14] R. M. Robbins, *Our Landed Heritage* (Princeton: Princeton U. Press, 1942), 283.

[15] *Ibid.*, 284.

[16] George Geiger, *The Philosophy of Henry George* (New York: Macmillan, 1933), chaps. 1–2.

[17] *Overland Monthly*, I (October 1868), 297–306.

[18] *Our Land and Land Policy* (New York, 1902), 19ff., 33–34, 89–90.

[19] Geiger, *Philosophy of Henry George,* chap. 3.

[20] *Arena,* III (January 1891), 159.

[21] *The American Commonwealth* (New York: Macmillan, 1937), II, 304.

[22] Commager, *American Mind,* 45; B. R. Twiss, *Lawyers and the Constitution* (Princeton: Princeton U. Press, 1942), 6off., and *passim.* Twiss shows how corporation lawyers helped persuade the courts to subvert traditional individualist doctrines to the ends of big business. The Supreme Court's laissez faire was actually Federal economic intervention, enabling corporations to escape state regulation.

[23] Lewis, *History of American Political Thought,* 425.

[24] *Ibid.,* 420.

[25] Masthead from the Constitution of the Nationalist Club, Boston, *Nationalist* (Boston, 1889), I, cover page.

[26] E. A. Allen, *The Life and Public Services of James Baird Weaver* (People's Party, 1892), 317. See also Howard Quint, *The Forging of American Socialism* (Columbia: U. South Carolina Press, 1953), 210ff.

[27] "Pure Democracy Versus Vicious Governmental Favoritism," *Arena,* VIII (July 1893), 260–272; John Chamberlain, *Farewell to Reform* (New York: Liveright, 1932), 3.

[28] Goldman, *Rendezvous with Destiny,* 39–40.

[29] *What Social Classes Owe to Each Other* (New York, 1883), 9, 16ff., 101, 120, 143; "State Interference," *North American Review,* CXLV (August 1887), 109–119.

[30] *Nation,* XLVIII (June 13, 1889), 478–479; LI (Sept. 11, 1890), 205–206; *Problems of Modern Democracy* (New York, 1896), 39; *Unforeseen Tendencies of Democracy* (Boston, 1898), v, 37ff.

[31] Aug. 4, Nov. 29, 1898, quoted in E. C. Kirkland, *Business in the Gilded Age* (Madison: U. Wisconsin Press, 1952), 40.

[32] Olney to Charles E. Perkins, Dec. 28, 1892, quoted in Matthew Josephson, *The Politicos* (New York: Harcourt, Brace, 1938), 526.

[33] Caro Lloyd, *Henry Demarest Lloyd* (New York: Putnam, 1912), I, 146–147, 291–295.

[34] *Letters of Henry Adams 1892–1918,* ed. W. C. Ford (Boston: Houghton Mifflin, 1938), 123, 178.

[35] *Watson's Jeffersonian Magazine,* V (October 1910), 817.

Chapter 11

[1] Charles McCarthy, *The Wisconsin Idea* (New York: Macmillan, 1912), 10–12, 174–175.

[2] *Prejudices Second Series* (New York: Knopf, 1920), 111–112, 123–125.

[3] Roosevelt to George Otto Trevelyan, March 9, 1905, *The Letters of Theodore Roosevelt*, ed. E. E. Morison (Cambridge: Harvard U. Press, 1951–1954), IV, 1133.

[4] Elmer Ellis, *Mr. Dooley's America* (New York: Knopf, 1941), 170; D. L. Kemmerer, "Trusts," *Dictionary of American History,* ed. J. T. Adams (New York: Scribner, 1940), V, 326.

[5] H. U. Faulkner, *The Decline of Laissez Faire 1897–1917* (New York: Rinehart, 1951), 156–161, 367. See also Fritz Machlup, *The Political Economy of Monopoly* (Baltimore: Johns Hopkins Press, 1952), 182, and chaps. 7–8.

[6] *The Conservation of Natural Resources in the United States* (New York: Macmillan, 1910), 378.

[7] *Concentration and Control* (New York: Macmillan, 1912), 72, 221, 224. See also A. J. Eddy, *The New Competition* (New York: Appleton, 1912).

[8] Franklin Pierce, *Federal Usurpation* (New York: Appleton, 1908), 101.

[9] David Dykstra, "Patent and Proprietary Medicines: Regulation and Control Prior to 1906," *Summaries of Doctoral Dissertations,* XII (Madison: U. Wisconsin Press, 1952), 192–195; Walter Thompson, *Federal Centralization* (New York: Harcourt, Brace, 1923), 123ff.; E. P. Herring, *Public Administration and the Public Interest* (New York: McGraw-Hill, 1936), 226ff.

[10] Goldman, *Rendezvous with Destiny,* 82–83.

[11] Curti, *Growth of American Thought,* 581–585; C. F. Thwing, *The American and the German University* (New York: Macmillan, 1928), 152ff.; Dwight Waldo, *The Administrative State* (New York: Ronald, 1948), 39ff.

[12] E. S. Corwin, "The Impact of the Idea of Evolution on the American Political and Constitutional Tradition," in Stow Persons, *Evolutionary Thought in America* (New Haven: Yale U. Press, 1950), 182–199.

[13] Goldman, *Rendezvous with Destiny,* 200; Jacques Barzun, *Darwin Marx Wagner: Critique of a Heritage* (Boston: Little, Brown,

1941); Morton White, *Social Thought in America* (New York: Viking, 1949).

¹⁴ *The Conflict between Individualism and Collectivism in a Democracy* (New York: Scribner, 1910), 129.

¹⁵ *Publications of the American Economic Association,* I (March 1886), 6. See also Henry C. Adams, "Relation of the State to Industrial Action," *ibid.,* I (January 1887), 471–549.

¹⁶ *The Spirit of American Government* (New York: Macmillan, 1907), chap. 10.

¹⁷ Charles B. Spahr, *An Essay* . . . (New York, 1896), 27.

¹⁸ Eric Goldman, "The Origins of Beard's *Economic Interpretation of the Constitution,*" *Journal of the History of Ideas,* XIII (April 1952), 234–249.

¹⁹ Goldman, *Rendezvous with Destiny,* 190ff.

²⁰ *The Promise of American Life* (New York: Macmillan, 1909), 29, 48–49, 57, 61, 80–81, 88–89.

²¹ *Ibid.,* 22, 190–192.

²² *Ibid.,* 23, 152, 167–169.

²³ *Ibid.,* 333, 341, 125.

²⁴ *Ibid.,* 360–361, 386, 254, 312; Goldman, *Rendezvous with Destiny,* 201–202.

²⁵ W. E. Leuchtenburg, "Progressivism and Imperialism," *Mississippi Valley Historical Review,* XXXIX (December 1952), 483–504.

²⁶ R. E. Osgood, *Ideals and Self-Interest in America's Foreign Relations* (Chicago: U. Chicago Press, 1953), 47.

²⁷ George Mowry, *Theodore Roosevelt and the Progressive Movement* (Madison: U. Wisconsin Press, 1946), 146; Goldman, *Rendezvous with Destiny,* 189.

²⁸ Roosevelt, *The New Nationalism* (New York: Outlook, 1910), 11, 19.

²⁹ Mowry, *Theodore Roosevelt,* 143ff., 191ff., 203, 212–214.

³⁰ *Ibid.,* 269–272, 280, 335, 12.

³¹ Thornton Anderson, *Brooks Adams* (Ithaca: Cornell U. Press, 1951), chaps. 6–7.

³² W. J. Ghent, *Our Benevolent Feudalism* (New York: Macmillan, 1902), 8; Franklin Pierce, *Federal Usurpation,* chap. 1, 337–338; W. H. Taft, *Our Chief Magistrate and His Powers* (New York: Columbia U. Press, 1916), 2, 94, 139ff.; Matthew Josephson, *The President Makers* (New York: Harcourt, Brace, 1940), 246.

³³ *The Curse of Bigness: Miscellaneous Writings of Louis D. Bran-*

deis, ed. O. K. Fraenkel (New York: Viking, 1934), 104–111; A. T. Mason, *Brandeis* (New York: Viking, 1946), 377ff.; Roosevelt to Horace Plunkett, Aug. 3, 1912, *Letters of Theodore Roosevelt,* VII, 592; Mowry, *Theodore Roosevelt,* 277; Arthur Link, *Woodrow Wilson and the Progressive Era* (New York: Harper, 1954), 21.

Chapter 12

[1] "The West and American Ideals," June 17, 1914, *The Frontier in American History* (New York: Holt, 1921), 307.

[2] Link, *Woodrow Wilson,* 93. See also William Diamond, *The Economic Thought of Woodrow Wilson* (Baltimore: Johns Hopkins Press, 1943), 60, 78ff., 130, and chaps. 5–6; Harley Notter, *The Origins of the Foreign Policy of Woodrow Wilson* (Baltimore: Johns Hopkins Press, 1937), 83ff.

[3] *The Public Papers of Woodrow Wilson,* ed. R. S. Baker and W. E. Dodd (New York: Harper, 1925–1927), III, 158, 225.

[4] "The Effect on American Institutions of a Powerful Military and Naval Establishment," *Annals of the American Academy of Political and Social Science,* XVI (July 1916), 157–172.

[5] "On Understanding the Mind of Germany," *Atlantic Monthly,* CXVII (February 1916), 251–262. See also Dewey, *German Philosophy and Politics* (New York: Holt, 1915).

Most of Dewey's wartime essays are reprinted in *Character and Events* (New York: Holt, 1929). In my discussion of Dewey I am much indebted to the excellent analysis by A. John Alexander, "The First World War in American Thought to 1929" (MS. Doctoral Dissertation, American U., June 1951), 324ff. See also White, *Social Thought in America,* chaps. 10–11.

[6] "Force and Coercion," *International Journal of Ethics,* XXVI (April 1916), 364; "Force, Violence and Law," *New Republic,* V (Jan. 22, 1916), 296.

[7] "The Schools and Social Preparedness," *New Republic,* VII (May 6, 1916), 16. See also "Universal Service as Education," *ibid.,* VI (April 22 and 29, 1916), 309, 334.

[8] *Seven Arts,* II (May 1917), 5.

[9] "The Future of Pacifism," *New Republic,* XI (July 28, 1917), 359. See also "Conscience and Compulsion," *ibid.,* XI (July 14, 1917), 297–298.

[10] "What America Will Fight For," *New Republic,* XII (Aug. 18, 1917), 69; "Conscription of Thought," *ibid.,* XII (Sept. 1, 1917), 128–130.

[11] "A War Diary," *Seven Arts,* II (September 1917), 541.

[12] *New Republic,* VII (July 1, 1916), 217–219.

[13] "The War and the Intellectuals," *Seven Arts,* II (June 1917), 138, 141; "Twilight of Idols," *ibid.,* II (October 1917), 690–692. Bourne's *Seven Arts* articles are reprinted in *Untimely Papers* (New York: Huebsch, 1919).

[14] *Seven Arts,* II (June 1917), 133ff.

[15] *Ibid.,* 143ff.

[16] "A War Diary," *Seven Arts,* II (September 1917), 537ff.

[17] *Untimely Papers,* 141ff.

[18] Goldman, *Rendezvous with Destiny,* 237–238.

[19] John L. Heaton, *Cobb of "The World"* (New York: Dutton, 1924), 268–270.

[20] *Public Papers of Woodrow Wilson,* V, 6–16.

[21] *Our Gallant Madness* (New York: Doubleday, Doran, 1937), 111–112, 196.

[22] "On Being 'Practical,' " *Nation,* CIII (Aug. 3, 1916), 102; *Universal Military Service* (Boston, 1917), 7.

[23] Edward Stanwood, *History of the Presidency* (Boston: Houghton Mifflin, 1928), II, 348.

[24] *New Republic,* XI (June 9, 1917), 148–150; Adams to Charles Milnes Gaskell, June 8, 1917, *Letters of Henry Adams 1892–1918,* 643.

[25] *American Socialist,* III (June 16, 1917), 1; Senate Comm. on Military Affairs, "Temporary Increase of the Military Establishment," *Hearings,* 65 Cong., 1 Sess. (Washington, 1917), 3ff.; R. S. Baker, *Woodrow Wilson* (New York: Doubleday, Page, 1927–1939), VII, 45, 289.

[26] Norman Thomas, *The Conscientious Objector in America* (New York: Huebsch, 1923), 14–15, and *passim.*

[27] J. R. Mock and Cedric Larson, *Words That Won the War* (Princeton: Princeton U. Press, 1939), 4.

[28] *Ibid.,* 4.

[29] *Ibid.,* chap. 2; Zechariah Chafee, *Free Speech in the United States* (Cambridge: Harvard U. Press, 1948), 42ff., 298ff.

[30] Chafee, *Free Speech,* 27, 392; Woodrow Wilson, *A History of the American People* (New York: Harper, 1902), III, 153.

[31] Chafee, *Free Speech,* 51ff.; Belle and Fola La Follette, *Robert M. La Follette* (New York: Macmillan, 1953), II, chaps. 48ff.

[32] *Writings and Speeches of Eugene V. Debs* (New York: Hermitage, 1948), 429–430, 436; Ray Ginger, *The Bending Cross: A Biography of Eugene Victor Debs* (New Brunswick: Rutgers U. Press, 1949), chap. 18, and 383.

[33] Merle Curti, *Growth of American Thought,* 684; and his *Peace or War* (New York: Norton, 1936), 256; H. K. Beale, *Are American Teachers Free?* (New York: Scribner, 1936), chap. 3.

[34] F. L. Paxson, *America at War* (Boston: Houghton Mifflin, 1939), chap. 13

[35] *Military Historian and Economist,* III (April 1918), 112–127.

[36] Mock and Larson, *Words That Won the War,* 187.

Chapter 13

[1] *Seven Arts,* II (June 1917), 145–146; Veblen, *An Inquiry into the Nature of Peace and the Terms of Its Perpetuation* (New York: Macmillan, 1917), 6–7, 21–22.

[2] Villard to House, Feb. 14, 1918, O. G. Villard Papers, Houghton Library, Harvard University.

[3] "What Liberalism May Do," *Nation,* CVII (Dec. 7, 1918), 692.

[4] John W. Dickinson, *The Building of an Army* (New York: Century, 1922), 323ff., 367.

[5] Harold and Margaret Sprout, *Toward a New Order of Sea Power* (Princeton: Princeton U. Press, 1940), chaps. 4–5.

[6] "Peace and Naval Policy," *Scientific American,* CXIX (Nov. 30, 1918), 432; see also "America's Military Menace," *Literary Digest,* LXIII (Dec. 6, 1919), 23–24.

[7] Dec. 21, 1918, *Congressional Record,* 65 Cong., 3 Sess., 727.

[8] "The Navy's Future," *Independent,* CI (Jan. 10, 1920), 51–52, 71.

[9] Villard to MacDonald, Sept. 27, 1919, Villard Papers.

[10] Villard to La Follette, Aug. 5, 1919, Villard Papers.

[11] *New Republic,* XIX (May 24, 1919), cover; see also editorials, *ibid.,* 100–110.

[12] *Ibid.,* XX (Oct. 8, 1919), 285.

[13] Harold Stearns, *Liberalism in America* (New York: Boni and Liveright, 1919), vi, chap. 1.

[14] *Ibid.,* 102–103, 110, 124, 143, 168, 213.

[15] Goldman, *Rendezvous with Destiny,* 275.

[16] *Nation,* CXI (Nov. 3, 1920), 489.

[17] "Liberalism vs. War," *New Republic,* XXV (Dec. 8, 1920), 35.

[18] *Ibid.,* 36ff.; George P. West, "Is the War Responsible?" *ibid.,* XXV (Jan. 12, 1921), 199–201.

[19] Ginger, *Bending Cross,* 406ff.; League for Amnesty, *Free Our Political Prisoners* (New York, 1918), 7; Chafee, *Free Speech,* 106.

[20] Chafee, *Free Speech,* chap. 4, 326ff.

[21] *Ibid.,* 269ff., 317, chap. 8.

[22] Jane P. Clark, *Deportation of Aliens from the United States to Europe* (New York: Columbia U. Press, 1931), 216ff.

[23] Chafee, *Free Speech,* 196ff.

[24] *Ibid.,* 204ff.; Max Lowenthal, *The Federal Bureau of Investigation* (New York: William Sloane, 1950), Part II.

[25] *The Deportations Delirium of Nineteen-Twenty* (Chicago: Kerr, 1923), 95.

[26] *Ibid.,* 150–153; Clark, Deportation of Aliens, 225.

[27] Zechariah Chafee, *et al., The Mooney-Billings Report* (New York: Gotham, 1932), *passim;* G. L. Joughin and E. M. Morgan, *The Legacy of Sacco and Vanzetti* (New York: Harcourt, Brace, 1948), *passim.*

[28] Address at Boston, Feb. 24, 1919, *Public Papers of Woodrow Wilson,* V, 439.

Chapter 14

[1] "The Democratic Party and the Liberal Vote," *New Republic,* XXIV (Sept. 22, 1920), 82–83.

[2] "The Defeat of Wilsonism," *Nation,* CXI (Nov. 10, 1920), 520.

[3] Villard to J. Ramsay MacDonald, March 8, 1921, Villard Papers.

[4] See, for example, "One Condition of Effective Disarmament," *New Republic,* XXVI (May 4, 1921), 281–282.

[5] C. L. Hoag, *Preface to Preparedness: The Washington Disarmament Conference and Public Opinion* (Washington: American Council on Public Affairs, 1941), 30ff., 74ff., 89ff.

[6] M. R. Konvitz, *Civil Rights in Immigration* (Ithaca: Cornell U. Press, 1953), 3–4, 9–10, and *passim.*

[7] H. P. Fairchild, *The Melting-Pot Mistake* (Boston: Little, Brown, 1926); E. G. Hartmann, *The Movement to Americanize the Immigrant* (New York: Columbia U. Press, 1948).

[8] Goldman, *Rendezvous with Destiny,* 300.

[9] P. W. Slosson, *The Great Crusade and After* (New York: Macmillan, 1930), 307ff.

[10] Beale, *Are American Teachers Free?* chap. 4; B. L. Pierce, *Public Opinion and the Teaching of History* (New York: Knopf, 1926), Part I, chaps. 4–5; Marcus Duffield, *King Legion* (New York: Cape and Smith, 1931), 250ff.

[11] *Liberalism in America,* 69.

[12] Samuel H. Church, *The Liberal Party in America* (New York: Putnam, 1931).

[13] Lowenthal, *Federal Bureau of Investigation,* chap. 3.

[14] Morris Ploscowe, *Sex and the Law* (New York: Prentice-Hall, 1951), 1, and *passim.*

[15] Thompson, *Federal Centralization,* 61; D. P. Wilson, *My Six Convicts* (New York: Rinehart, 1951), 329ff.

[16] Chafee, *Free Speech,* 543–544.

[17] Ernst Freund, *Standards of American Legislation* (Chicago: U. Chicago Press, 1917), 21.

[18] Thompson, *Federal Centralization,* 320.

[19] *Prejudices Third Series* (New York: Knopf, 1922), 313–314.

[20] *Notes on Democracy* (New York: Knopf, 1926), 22ff., 38, 181ff.

[21] *Prejudices Fifth Series* (New York: Knopf, 1926), 20–21; *Prejudices Sixth Series* (New York: Knopf, 1927), 38ff.

[22] Quoted in Slosson, *Great Crusade and After,* 102.

[23] Frank Tannenbaum, *Wall Shadows: A Study in American Prisons* (New York: Putnam, 1922), chap. 3; E. J. Hopkins, *Our Lawless Police* (New York: Viking, 1931); Walter White, *Rope and Faggot: A Biography of Judge Lynch* (New York: Knopf, 1929); H. E. Barnes, *The Story of Punishment* (Boston: Stratford, 1930), 15ff., 229, 265ff.; Wilson, *My Six Convicts,* 35ff., 180ff.

[24] *Absentee Ownership and Business Enterprise* (New York: Huebsch, 1923), 30–31, chap. 4.

[25] Herring, *Public Administration,* 125ff., 213, and *passim.* See also Lewis Corey, *The Decline of American Capitalism* (New York: Covici-Friede, 1934); 492ff.; A. R. Burns, *The Decline of Competition* (New York: McGraw-Hill, 1936), chap. 1.

[26] Quoted in Charles Beard, "The Constitution and States' Rights," *Virginia Quarterly Review,* XI (October 1935), 493. See also Morison and Commager, *Growth of the American Republic* (1942 ed.), II, 533–536; Goldman, *Rendezvous with Destiny,* 309.

[27] *The Folklore of Capitalism* (New Haven: Yale U. Press, 1937), 211.

[28] Adolph Berle and Gardner Means, *The Modern Corporation and Private Property* (New York: Macmillan, 1933), 345ff.; Stuart Chase, *Government in Business* (New York: Macmillan, 1935), 2–4, 100ff.

[29] Selig Perlman and Philip Taft, *History of Labor in the United States, 1896–1932* (New York: Macmillan, 1935), chap. 38; Karl Polanyi, *The Great Transformation* (New York: Farrar and Rinehart, 1944), 26ff.

[30] Goldman, *Rendezvous with Destiny*, 291ff.

[31] *The Confessions of a Reformer* (New York: Scribner, 1925), 282.

[32] *Ibid.*, 53–54, 135, 176, 255–256.

[33] F. C. Howe, *Revolution and Democracy* (New York: Huebsch, 1921), 142–143.

[34] Alfred Lief, *The Brandeis Guide to the Modern World* (Boston: Little, Brown, 1941), 4, 70; Mason, *Brandeis*, 558; *Baldwin* v. *Missouri* (1930), 281 U. S. 595.

[35] *The Growth and Decadence of Constitutional Government* (New York: Holt, 1930), 51–52, 282, chaps. 7–10.

[36] Parrington to Prof. Ross L. Finney, Jan. 23, 1929, quoted in Eric Goldman, "J. Allen Smith," *Pacific Northwest Quarterly*, XXXV (July 1944), 209.

[37] Babbitt, *Democracy and Leadership* (Boston: Houghton Mifflin, 1924), 267; Krutch, *The Modern Temper* (New York: Harcourt, Brace, 1929), 233ff.

See also J. T. Adams, "Shadow of the Man on Horseback," *Atlantic Monthly*, CXLIX (January 1932), 1–10; David Spitz, *Patterns of Anti-Democratic Thought* (New York: Macmillan, 1949).

[38] *Selections from the Correspondence of Theodore Roosevelt and Henry Cabot Lodge* (New York: Scribner, 1925), I, 487.

See also J. C. Malin, *The United States After the World War* (Boston: Ginn, 1930), 279ff.; Francis Miller and Helen Hill, *The Giant of the Western World* (New York: Morrow, 1930), 19ff., 286.

[39] C. E. M. Joad, *The Babbitt Warren* (London: Paul, Trench, Trübner, 1926); Georges Duhamel, *America the Menace* (Boston: Houghton Mifflin, 1931), xiv.

[40] *America Comes of Age* (New York: Harcourt, Brace, 1927), 55, 227, and *passim*.

Chapter 15

[1] Hofstadter, *American Political Tradition,* 282.

[2] Curti, *Growth of American Thought,* 733.

[3] Quoted in *Social Frontier,* I (October, 1934), 1. This journal gave full expression to collectivist ideals in education. See especially vol. I, nos. 1, 4, 9 (October 1934, January–June 1935).

[4] See, for example, T. S. Eliot, "Modern Education and the Classics," *Essays Ancient and Modern* (New York: Harcourt, Brace, 1936), 169–185; R. M. Hutchins, *The Higher Learning in America* (New Haven: Yale U. Press, 1936), *passim.*

[5] "A Planless World," chap. 2 in the symposium on planning, *America Faces the Future,* ed. Charles Beard (Boston: Houghton Mifflin, 1932), 16.

[6] *A New Deal* (New York: Macmillan, 1932), 252. See also George Soule's books in the thirties, especially his *A Planned Society* (New York: Macmillan, 1932), which was dedicated to Herbert Croly.

[7] *The Method of Freedom* (New York: Macmillan, 1934), 25. See also Hofstadter, *American Political Tradition,* chap. 12.

[8] Raymond Moley, *After Seven Years* (New York: Harper, 1939), 23–24, 184.

[9] *The Public Papers and Addresses of Franklin D. Roosevelt* (New York: Random House, etc., 1938–1950), I, 752.

[10] T. P. Jenkin, *Reactions of Major Groups to Positive Government in the United States, 1930–1940* (Berkeley: U. California Press, 1945), 265. See also Dwight Waldo, *The Administrative State* (New York: Ronald, 1948); A. T. Mason, "Variations of the Liberal Theme," *The Democratic Process,* Henry Wells Lawrence Memorial Lectures No. 2 (New London: Connecticut College, 1948), 32–33.

[11] Goldman, *Rendezvous with Destiny,* 329.

[12] *Public Papers and Addresses,* II, 246.

[13] Charles and Mary Beard, *America in Midpassage* (New York: Macmillan, 1939), I, 234–235.

[14] *Wealth of Nations* (Cannan ed.), I, 130.

[15] Goldman, *Rendezvous with Destiny,* 346–351; Lowell B. Mason, "Darrow vs. Johnson," *North American Review,* CCXXXVIII (December 1934), 524–532.

[16] National Recovery Review Board, "First Report to the President," May 4, 1934, mimeographed by Ward and Paul, Washington,

D.C., pp. 26, 65; National Recovery Administration, "Reports to the President by the Administrator and the General Counsel," May 15, 1934, mimeographed copy in Library of Congress, pp. 3-4.

[17] "A Statement to the President," *Nation*, CXXXVIII (May 30, 1934), 617–619.

[18] The growing commercialization and collectivization of American agricultural thought and practice is admirably analyzed in Grant McConnell, *The Decline of Agrarian Democracy* (Berkeley: U. California Press, 1953).

[19] *T V A Democracy on the March* (New York: Harper, 1944), chap. 14.

[20] Broadus Mitchell, *Depression Decade* (New York: Rinehart, 1947), 357.

[21] Philip Selznick, *T V A and the Grass Roots* (Berkeley: U. California Press, 1949), 92–93, 262ff.; R. G. Tugwell and E. C. Banfield, "Grass Roots Democracy — Myth or Reality," *Public Administration Review*, X (Winter 1950), 47–55.

[22] Seymour Harris, *The Economics of New England* (Cambridge: Harvard U. Press, 1952), 109, 116. On the same date that the Sunday *New York Times* carried a special section given over to an advertisement for "Tennessee Proved in Both Production and Markets," it contained an article by the U.S. Senator from Massachusetts, John F. Kennedy, entitled: "What's the Matter with New England?" Section 10 and *New York Times* Magazine, Nov. 8, 1953. See also Kennedy, "New England and the South," *Atlantic Monthly*, CXCIII (January 1954), 32–36.

[23] *Journal of Forgotten Days* (Hinsdale: Regnery, 1948), 33.

[24] *The Challenge to Liberty* (New York: Scribner, 1934), Introd., and 102, 126ff. See also Ogden Mills, *Liberalism Fights On* (New York: Macmillan, 1936), *passim*.

[25] Walter Johnson, *William Allen White's America* (New York: Holt, 1947), 445–446.

[26] *The Liberal Tradition* (New York: Van Nostrand, 1935), 10–12, 15ff.

[27] (Boston: Little, Brown, 1937), Introd., and 8ff., 47, 87–89, 153–155, 315 fn. 4.

[28] C. H. Pritchett, *The Roosevelt Court* (New York: Macmillan, 1948), 71–72, 82, 92–93, 265ff.

[29] "Investigation of Concentration of Economic Power," *Final Re-*

port and Recommendations of the Temporary National Economic Committee (Washington, 1941), 7. See also David Lynch, *The Concentration of Economic Power* (New York: Columbia U. Press, 1946), 5ff., 362.

Chapter 16

[1] "The Pot and the Kettle," *Nation*, CXXXV (Oct. 26, 1932), 390.

[2] *World Affairs Pamphlets No. 3* (1934), 31.

[3] C. A. Beard and G. H. E. Smith, *The Open Door at Home* (New York: Macmillan, 1934), 44–45, 99, 111, 131, 319.

[4] Dixon Wecter, *The Age of the Great Depression* (New York: Macmillan, 1948), 78; R. E. Sherwood, *Roosevelt and Hopkins* (New York: Harper, 1948), 75–76.

[5] *Where Are We Heading?* (New York: Harper, 1946), 3.

[6] Feb. 1, 1939, quoted in *Congressional Record*, 76 Cong., 1 Sess., Appendix, 402–404.

[7] Oct. 4, 1939, *ibid.*, 76 Cong., 2 Sess., 97.

[8] Broadus Mitchell, *Depression Decade*, chap. 11 "War to the Rescue."

[9] *Our Enemy the State* (New York: Morrow, 1935), 205–206; *Letters from Albert Jay Nock 1924–1945* (Caldwell: Caxton, 1949), 103; *Memoirs of a Superfluous Man* (New York: Harper, 1943), 247–248.

[10] *Man and Society in an Age of Reconstruction* (New York: Harcourt, Brace, 1940), 135. The literature on the impact of fascism is extensive, but especially provocative is Peter Drucker, *The End of Economic Man* (New York: John Day, 1939).

[11] (Washington: American Council on Public Affairs, 1941), 6–7, 66ff. See also Mauritz Hallgren, *Landscape of Freedom* (New York: Howell, Soskin, 1941), 426.

[12] *The Managerial Revolution* (New York: John Day, 1941), 152, 196–197, 257–258.

[13] See Villard's letters to William T. Evjue, Aug. 8, 1937; Frederick H. Allen, Oct. 17, 1937; Frank E. Gannett, Sept. 17, 1938; Franklin D. Roosevelt, Oct. 5, 1938; E. P. Adler, Aug. 2, 1939; Van Wyck Brooks, Sept. 27, 1940, Villard Papers. See also Villard, "Credo of an Old-Fashioned Liberal," *American Mercury*, LV (October 1942), 464–470.

[14] Julien Benda, *The Treason of the Intellectuals* (New York: Morrow, 1928), 104, 158–159.

[15] *The Irresponsibles* (New York: Duell, Sloan and Pearce, 1940),

3, 9, and *passim*. See also Lewis Mumford, *Faith for Living* (New York: Harcourt, Brace, 1940); Herbert Agar, *et al., The City of Man* (New York: Viking, 1940).

[16] Writers' War Board, *Third Annual Report,* January 1945.

[17] Philip Rahv, *Image and Idea* (Norfolk: New Directions, 1949), 161–164.

[18] A. R. Ogden, *The Dies Committee* (Washington: Catholic U. Press, 1950), chap. 1, and 152.

[19] Chafee, *Free Speech,* 441, 443, chap. 12.

[20] "Alien Registration Act," June 28, 1940, Title I, *U.S. Statutes at Large,* LIV, 670–671.

[21] Chafee, *Free Speech,* 470.

[22] *Ibid.,* 467.

[23] *Ibid.,* 465, 484.

[24] See, however, as examples of contemporary concern: "Civil Liberties in Minneapolis," *New Republic,* CV (July 28, 1941), 103–104; "The Issues at Minneapolis," *Nation,* CLIII (Dec. 13, 1941), 602; American Civil Liberties Union, *The Bill of Rights in Wartime* (New York, 1942), 27–28.

[25] Aug. 12, 1940, *Congressional Record,* 76 Cong., 3 Sess.,10114.

[26] *New York Times,* July 9, 1940, p. 4, col. 1.

[27] *Nation,* CLI (Aug. 3, 1940), 81, 85–86; *New Republic,* CIII (July 1, Sept. 2, 1940), 6–7, 294–295.

[28] CL (June 29, 1940), 4027–4029; CLI (Aug. 3, 1940), 591–593.

[29] Mulford Sibley and Philip Jacob, *Conscription of Conscience* (Ithaca: Cornell U. Press, 1952), Part 3.

[30] *Ibid.,* 83ff., 313–319. See also American Civil Liberties Union, *Conscience and the War* (New York, 1943).

[31] Morton Grodzins, *Americans Betrayed* (Chicago: U. Chicago Press, 1949); Caleb Foote, "Have We Forgotten Justice?" *Fellowship,* VIII (May 1942), 79–81; A. C. L. U. *Military Power and Civil Rights* (New York, 1942), 4; and *Freedom in Wartime* (New York, 1943), 29.

[32] *Federal Reporter,* 2d ser., CLXXVI, 953ff.; *New York Times,* Aug. 27, 1949, p. 5, col. 4.

[33] The reports of the American Civil Liberties Union, published under various titles from 1941 to 1944, provide a good summary.

[34] "Economic Concentration and World War II: Report of the Smaller War Plants Corporation," *U. S. Senate Doc. No. 206,* 79 Cong., 2 Sess. (Washington, 1946), vii–viii, and *passim*.

[35] Donald Nelson, *Arsenal of Democracy* (New York: Harcourt,

Brace, 1946), xvii, 363, and chaps. 19–20. See also the excellent summary by Jack W. Peltason, "The Reconversion Controversy," *Public Administration and Policy Development,* ed. Harold Stein (New York: Harcourt, Brace, 1952), 228ff.

[36] Senate Comm. on Military Affairs, "National War Service Bill," *Hearings,* 78 Cong., 2 Sess. (Washington, 1944), 184. *Christian Century,* LX (March 24, 1943), 356–359.

[37] (Chicago: U. Chicago Press, 1944), 2, 13, 71, 206, 215.

[38] (Boston: Little, Brown, 1945), 106.

[39] R. F. Harrod, *The Life of John Maynard Keynes* (New York: Harcourt, Brace, 1951), 436.

[40] Sept. 7, 1942, *Public Papers and Addresses,* XI, 364–365. See also Roosevelt's "Fireside Chat on Cost of Living," Sept. 7, 1942, *ibid.,* 372–373.

[41] Sept. 7, 1942, *Congressional Record,* 77 Cong., 2 Sess., 7046–7047; Merlo Pusey, *Big Government: Can We Control It?* (New York: Harper, 1945), 48ff., 96, 111ff.; T. K. Finletter, *Can Representative Government Do the Job?* (New York: Reynal and Hitchcock, 1945), 13, 18.

Chapter 17

[1] David Bradley, *No Place to Hide* (Boston: Little, Brown, 1948), dedication page.

[2] John Fischer, in *Harper's Magazine,* CXCIV (May 1947), 385–395. See also: W. A. Orton, *The Liberal Tradition* (New Haven: Yale U. Press, 1945); Morris Cohen, *The Faith of a Liberal* (New York: Holt, 1946), chap. 12; Eric Goldman and Mary Paull, "Liberals on Liberalism," *New Republic,* CXV (July 22, 1946), 70–73; Dorothy Thompson, John T. Flynn, "What Liberalism Means to Me," *American Mercury,* LXV, LXVII (September 1947, August 1948), 322–328, 169–176; Louis Filler, "The Dilemma, So-Called, of the American Liberal," *Antioch Review,* VIII (Summer 1948), 131–151; H. S. Hughes, *An Essay for Our Times* (New York: Knopf, 1950); Eric Goldman, "The American Liberal: After the Fair Deal, What?" *Reporter,* VIII (June 23, 1953), 25–28.

[3] *It Is Later Than You Think* (New York: Viking, 1943), ix–x.

[4] Clement Eaton, "The Jeffersonian Tradition of Liberalism in America," *South Atlantic Quarterly,* XLIII (January 1944), 2.

[5] Norman Thomas, "Who Are the Liberals?" *American Mercury,*

LXV (November 1947), 552. See also the prophetic and perceptive letter of Lawrence Dennis, one of the defendants, to Norman Thomas congratulating him for his liberal stand against the sedition trial, Feb. 4, 1944, copy in Villard Papers.

[6] Jan. 3, 1936, *Public Papers and Addresses*, V, 16.

[7] See Irving Howe, "This Age of Conformity," *Partisan Review*, XXI (January–February, 1954), 7–8, 15; Robert Bendiner, "The Liberals Political Road Back," *Commentary*, XV (May 1953), 431–437.

[8] *How New Will the Better World Be?* (New York: Knopf, 1944), chaps. 1–2, and 63ff.

[9] Sumner Welles, *Where Are We Heading?* 334.

[10] John E. Pixton, Jr., "The Ghost of Charles Beard," *Christian Century*, LXIX (Oct. 1, 1952), 1120–1122; Felix Morley, *The Foreign Policy of the United States* (New York: Knopf, 1951), vi–vii, 87ff.

[11] H. E. Barnes, *The Struggle Against the Historical Blackout* (7th rev. ed. n. p. 1951), 11ff.; C. Vann Woodward, "Can We Believe Our Own History?" *Johns Hopkins Magazine*, V (February 1954), 2–6, 16.

[12] *The Soviet Impact on the Western World* (New York: Macmillan, 1947).

[13] R. M. Weaver, *Ideas Have Consequences* (Chicago: U. Chicago Press, 1948), 122; Reinhold Niebuhr, *The Irony of American History* (New York: Scribner, 1952), 7–8, 116, 134, 146ff.

[14] *Freedom Is the Right to Choose* (Boston: Beacon, 1951), 68, 73, 79ff.

[15] Villard to Dorothy Detzer, Aug. 31, 1948, Villard Papers.

[16] "Today and Tomorrow," Washington *Post*, June 1, 1950.

[17] For a recent synthesis of Lasswell's thoughts on this subject, see his *National Security and Individual Freedom* (New York: McGraw-Hill, 1950), chap. 2.

[18] Quoted in Baldwin, *The Price of Power* (New York: Harper, 1947), 136. See also "The Military Move In," *Harper's Magazine*, CXCV (December 1947), 481–489; "When the Big Guns Speak," in Lester Markel, *et al.*, *Public Opinion and Foreign Policy* (New York: Harper, 1949), 97–120.

[19] "Military Emphasis," Washington *Post*, Sept. 28, 1948. The literature concerning military influence on foreign policy is extensive, but see as an early example Blair Bolles, "Influence of Armed Forces on United States Foreign Policy," *Foreign Policy Reports*, XXII (Oct. 1, 1946), 170–179.

[20] Villard to Beard, Feb. 6, 1946, Villard Papers. Beard felt that the Truman policies were reminiscent of the Reconstruction and Harding eras. Letters to Villard, Feb. 9, 1946, Jan. 17, 1948, Villard Papers.

[21] This is elaborately documented in John Swomley, *Press Agents of the Pentagon* (Washington: National Council Against Conscription, 1953).

[22] *New York Times,* Dec. 21, 1946, p. 5, col. 3.

[23] Karl T. Compton, *et al., A Program for National Security,* Report of the President's Advisory Commission on Universal Training, May 29, 1947 (Washington, 1947), 37–40; Russell Kirk, "Conscription ad Infinitum," *South Atlantic Quarterly,* XLV (July 1946), 313–319.

[24] Joseph Rosenfarb, *Freedom and the Administrative State* (New York: Harper, 1948), 48, 55; W. A. Orton, *The Economic Role of the State* (Chicago: U. Chicago Press, 1950), 12, 191–192; Jules Abels, *The Welfare State* (New York: Duell, Sloan and Pearce, 1951), 32ff.; Sheldon Glueck, ed., *The Welfare State and the National Welfare* (Cambridge: Addison-Wesley, 1952).

[25] *Report of the Federal Trade Commission on the Merger Movement. A Summary Report* (Washington, 1948), 68.

[26] "The Sherman Act on Trial," *Atlantic Monthly,* CXCII (July 1953), 38.

[27] *Big Business: A New Era* (New York: Harper, 1953), 102–104, chap. 12.

[28] Washington *Post,* Aug. 2, 1952.

[29] *How to Get Rich in Washington* (New York: Norton, 1952), 12. See also George Graham, *Morality in American Politics* (New York: Random House, 1952).

[30] Seymour Harris, *The Economics of Mobilization and Inflation* (New York: Norton, 1951), 29ff., 111; Associated Press interview with top government economists from Commerce Dept. and Federal Reserve System, Washington *Post,* May 26, 1952, p. 2, col. 1; Arthur F. Burns, *Looking Forward,* 31st Annual Report, National Bureau of Economic Research (New York, 1951), 3ff.; *Yearbook of the United Nations 1952* (New York: Columbia U. Press, 1953), 406, 502–503.

[31] Washington *Post,* Jan. 10, 1953.

[32] Lewis Haney, *How You Really Earn Your Living* (New York: Prentice-Hall, 1952), 242–243.

33 M. A. Heilperin, *The Trade of Nations* (New York: Knopf, 1947), Introd., chap. 5. See also Samuel Seabury, *The New Federalism* (New York: Dutton, 1950), 5–8, 248.

34 *The New Men of Power* (New York: Harcourt, Brace, 1948), 25, 187, 242–243, 248–249.

35 "Colossus on the Potomac," *Harper's Magazine*, CCVII (July 1953), 22.

36 *New York Times*, Feb. 22, 1953, p. 29, col. 3.

37 Washington *Post*, Nov. 3, 1953.

Chapter 18

1 Chafee, *Free Speech*, 566.

2 *Frazier* v. *United States* (1948), 335 U.S. 515.

3 Henry Stimson and McGeorge Bundy, *On Active Service in Peace and War* (New York: Harper, 1948), chap. 24.

4 Alan Barth, *The Loyalty of Free Men* (New York: Viking, 1951), 37.

5 *The Vital Center* (Boston: Houghton Mifflin, 1949), 203. See also Robert Carr, *The House Committee on Un-American Activities 1945–1950* (Ithaca: Cornell U. Press, 1952), ix–x.

6 *Schenck* v. *United States* (1919), 249 U.S. 52.

7 *Dennis et al.* v. *United States* (1951), 341 U.S. 579ff.; Morris Ernst and Roger Baldwin, "Liberals and the Communist Trial," *New Republic*, CXX (Jan. 31, 1949), 7–8. See also C. H. Pritchett, *Civil Liberties and the Vinson Court* (Chicago: U. Chicago Press, 1954), 72ff.

8 Barth, *Loyalty of Free Men*, 10.

9 *Freedom Loyalty Dissent* (New York: Oxford, 1954), 98ff., 121–122.

10 Walter Gellhorn, *The States and Subversion* (Ithaca: Cornell U. Press, 1952), chap. 7.

11 Eleanor Bontecou, *The Federal Loyalty-Security Program* (Ithaca: Cornell U. Press, 1953), 22–23, 30ff., 64ff.

12 Barth, *Loyalty of Free Men*, chap. 7.

13 Bontecou, *Federal Loyalty-Security Program*, 145.

14 Barth, *Loyalty of Free Men*, 124.

15 Robert Carr, *Federal Protection of Civil Rights* (Ithaca: Cornell U. Press, 1947), vii, chap. 1, and 210; M. R. Konvitz, *The Constitu-*

tion and Civil Rights (New York: Columbia U. Press, 1947); E. S. Corwin, *Liberty Against Government* (Baton Rouge: Louisiana State U. Press, 1948), 3–7, 182–183.

[16] Louis Ruchames, *Race Jobs & Politics: The Story of FEPC* (New York: Columbia U. Press, 1953).

[17] *To Secure These Rights* (Washington, 1947), 13ff., 151ff.

[18] M. R. Konvitz, *Civil Rights in Immigration,* 9, 16, 28ff.

[19] Villard *et al., Letter to New York Times,* Feb. 13, 1945, p. 22, col. 5; Morroe Berger, *Equality by Statute* (New York: Columbia U. Press, 1952), vii–ix, chaps. 4–5.

[20] R. M. Hutchins, *A Free and Responsible Press* (Chicago: U. Chicago Press, 1947), 1–7; David Riesman, *The Lonely Crowd* (New Haven: Yale U. Press, 1950), 215, 218; Norbert Wiener, *The Human Use of Human Beings* (Boston: Houghton Mifflin, 1950), 146ff.

[21] William Vogt, *Road to Survival* (New York: William Sloane, 1948); Robert Cook, *Human Fertility* (New York: William Sloane, 1951), viii, chap. 13; Seymour Harris, *The Market for College Graduates* (Cambridge: Harvard U. Press, 1949).

[22] Leo Pfeffer, *Church, State and Freedom* (Boston: Beacon, 1953), 480ff.

[23] J. E. Russell, *Federal Activities in Higher Education* (New York: King's Crown, 1951), 68–69.

[24] E. C. Kirkland, "Intellectual Freedom in a Time of Crisis," *Key Reporter,* XV (Spring 1950), 2.

[25] Washington *Post,* Dec. 1, 1950.

[26] R. M. Hutchins, "Are Our Teachers Afraid to Teach?" *Look,* XVIII (March 9, 1954).

[27] L. H. Chamberlain, *Loyalty and Legislative Action* (Ithaca: Cornell U. Press, 1951), 1–8, 53ff., chaps. 3, 5.

[28] R. F. Butts and L. A. Cremin, *A History of Education in American Culture* (New York: Holt, 1953), 551ff.

[29] *Adler et al.* v. *Board of Education of the City of New York* (1952), 342 U.S. 510.

[30] Washington *Evening Star,* Feb. 21, 1953.

[31] *Ibid.,* Oct. 9, 1953; Washington *Post,* Oct. 10, 1953.

[32] *Vital Center,* 205.

[33] Howard Mumford Jones, "How Much Academic Freedom?" *Atlantic Monthly,* CXCI (June 1953), 36–40.

[34] Barth, *Loyalty of Free Men,* 223.

[35] *New York Times Magazine,* Jan. 13, 1952, p. 7; New York *Herald Tribune,* Aug. 25, 1953; Washington *Post,* Nov. 3, 1953.

[36] Chester G. Starr, Jr., "The Perfect Democracy of the Roman Empire," *American Historical Review,* LVIII (October 1952), 16.

[37] Charles Beard, reviewing S. G. Hobson's *National Guilds,* in *New Republic,* XXV (Dec. 8, 1920), 51.

[38] *Man and Technics* (New York: Knopf, 1932), 104, 14.

Index